*THE SONGS OF CHU*

TRANSLATIONS FROM THE ASIAN CLASSICS

# The Songs of Chu

*An Anthology of Ancient Chinese Poetry by*
*Qu Yuan and Others*

Edited and translated by
Gopal Sukhu

*Columbia University Press*   *New York*

COLUMBIA
UNIVERSITY
PRESS

The publisher gratefully acknowledges the generous support to this book provided by Publisher's Circle members John J. S. Balcom and Yingtsih Balcom.

Columbia University Press wishes to express its appreciation for assistance given by the Chiang Ching-kuo Foundation for International Scholarly Exchange and Council for Cultural Affairs in the publication of this book.

Columbia University Press wishes to express its appreciation for assistance given by the Pushkin Fund in the publication of this book.

Columbia University Press
*Publishers Since 1893*
New York    Chichester, West Sussex
cup.columbia.edu

Library of Congress Cataloging-in-Publication Data

Names: Qu, Yuan, approximately 343 B.C.-approximately 277 B.C. |
    Sukhu, Gopal, editor, translator.
Title: The songs of Chu : an ancient anthology of works by Qu Yuan and others / edited and
    translated by Gopal Sukhu. Other titles: Chu ci. English
Description: New York : Columbia University Press, 2017. | Series: Translations
    from the asian classics | Includes bibliographical references and index.
Identifiers: LCCN 2016045048 (print) | LCCN 2017004499 (ebook) |
    ISBN 9780231166065 (cloth : acid-free paper) | ISBN 9780231166072 (pbk.)
    ISBN 9780231544658 (electronic)
Classification: LCC PL2661 .C4613 2017 (print) | LCC PL2661 (ebook) |
    DDC 895.1/11—dc23
LC record available at https://lccn.loc.gov/2016045048

Columbia University Press books are printed on permanent and durable acid-free paper.

Printed in the United States of America

Cover design: Noah Arlow

*To the memory of*
*Seth Bernard Adams*
*Merchant Mariner*
*and jazz aficionado*
*who gave me my first books on Asia*

# Contents

# Acknowledgments

Special thanks to the two anonymous readers for Columbia University Press; its freelance copyeditor Mike Ashby and in-house editor Leslie Kriesel; as well as Mick Stern, Cary Plotkin, John Major, Kim Dramer, Mary Beth Maher, Ammiel Alcalay, Constance A. Cook, Galal Walker, and Li Minru for their valuable comments on the manuscript. I hereby express my appreciation to the Schoff Fund at the University Seminars at Columbia University for their help in publication. Material in this work was presented to the University Seminar on Early China. Thanks to Li Feng, Guo Jue, and the other members of the Early China Seminar at Columbia University for their critiques, encouragement, and support. I am indebted to Robert Hymes, Haruo Shirane, and Shang Wei for giving me the opportunity to test my ideas on Columbia University graduate students; and to Ari Borrell for providing me with unexpected research tools. My heartfelt gratitude also to my wife, Hanna Kim; my daughter, Uma; and my sisters, Radha and Kushelia Sukhu, for helping me stay on course, and to Mr. and Mrs. S. Y. Kim for kindly providing me a peaceful and beautiful place to work.

# Introduction

The first man ever to be known for his poetry in China was Qu Yuan 屈原 (340?–278? B.C.E.). His work is the core of the *Chuci* 楚辭, or *Songs of Chu*, the second-oldest anthology of Chinese verse. He was a high minister in the southern state of Chu, serving both King Huai (r. 328–299 B.C.E.) and his successor, King Qing Xiang (r. 298–263 B.C.E.). So distinctive and influential is his work, which includes some of the most beautiful liturgical poetry in the world, that literary historians think of it as the "second beginning" of Chinese poetry, the first being the ancient and quasi-scriptural *Shijing* 詩經, or *Book of Songs*. Yet the Dragon Boat Festival, held in his honor every year, is less a celebration of his poetry than a commemoration of his suicide.

What drove him to suicide was frustration and despair that began when his feckless king believed the slander of his enemies and demoted him. The king later died a hostage in another state, having been misled by royal officers, among them his own son. The same son, when his brother succeeded his father as king, made sure that Qu Yuan was sent into exile, where in protest and grief he drowned himself. The poem that won him the most fame, "Li sao" 離騷, or "Leaving My Sorrow" (also known as "Encountering Sorrow"), was supposedly written shortly after his demotion. Yet there is much in the poem that was obscure even to those reading it only a century later. Part of the reason for this is that it makes reference to some of the more esoteric aspects of the culture of Chu.

According to the ancient Chinese historical records, the ancestor of the Chu royal family, Yu Xiong 鬻熊, was originally a minister of the Shang dynasty (1600–1046 B.C.E.) who, horrified by the excesses of its last king, fled to the state of Zhou and served King Wen as general. King Wen, with his help, overthrew the evil Shang king and established the Zhou dynasty (1046–256 B.C.E.). King Wen's successor, King Cheng, rewarded Xiong Yi 熊繹, the descendant of the defector Yu Xiong, with the title of viscount and a parcel of land in the south—a barbarian region, in the eyes of the north, known as Chu. It was wild and uncultivated, requiring a great deal of work, often with the forced labor of local tribes, to make it habitable. Eventually Xiong Yi built his capital at Danyang in Hubei. The viscounty gradually expanded, and, by the reign of Xiong Qu 熊渠, in the mid-ninth century, it was strong enough to declare its independence from the Zhou dynasty, which had for a long time treated it as mere wilderness to be raided periodically for metal ore and slaves. Xiong Qu made it a kingdom, but not for long; pressure from King Li (877–841 B.C.E.) of the Zhou brought Xiong Qu back into the fold.

Around the year 771 B.C.E., a combination of internal conflict and barbarian invasion from the north resulted in the flight of the Zhou royal family to the eastern city of Luoyang, the reduction of the king's status to mere figurehead, and the eventual disintegration of the dynasty into powerful independent and contentious states. Thus began what is known as the Spring and Autumn period (772–476 B.C.E.), during which Chu grew both in power and territory, expanded east and north into the Yellow River region, and vied with the larger states. By the Warring States period (475–221 B.C.E.) it was the largest, both in terms of land and population, of the six main states contending for supremacy.

As it rose, Chu not only increased its wealth by absorbing both southern and eastern regions but also created an eclectic culture whose glories rivaled anything in the north. The extent to which that was true was gradually forgotten when Chu fell to Qin, its main rival, in 223 B.C.E. After that, the old clichés about its barbarism gradually replaced the memories of its historical realities.

Cliché has been challenged in recent decades, however, by archaeological discoveries that confirm that Chu, far from being barbaric, enjoyed a highly developed artistic and intellectual culture, especially during the Warring States period, the period of the great Chinese philosophers such as Mencius (or Mengzi 孟子) and Zhuangzi 莊子 (both of the fourth century B.C.E.) and the great poet Qu Yuan. Recently discovered artifacts include truly extraordinary bronze ware, lacquer ware, embroidered silk, and jade ornaments. One of the most spectacular examples is a set of sixty-four bronze bells discovered in 1977 in the tomb of Marquis Yi of Zeng (曾侯乙 Zeng Hou Yi), the ruler of one of the Chu vassal states, in Suizhou, Hubei province. The tomb is dated to about 433 B.C.E., but even after two thousand five hundred years, its contents, including the wooden bell stands, were in a remarkable state of preservation. The bells ranged from the high pitched, weighing a few pounds, to a bass bell, weighing about three hundred pounds. Each of the bells was made to produce two separate tones depending on where it was struck. The largest bell, a gift from another ruler, was inlaid with gold inscriptions, including musical notation. Besides the bells, other instruments, such as stone chimes, and a variety of plucked strings and woodwinds were found. A passage in the *Chuci*, from "Summoning the Soul" (招魂 "Zhao hun"), describes one kind of gathering at which such instruments were played:

> Sixteen women dressed alike
> Rise to dance to the music of Zheng,
> Their overlong sleeves fly up and cross like staves in a fight,
> Then fall together on cue,
> While the *yu* pipes and *se* strings wail,
> And the drums thunder,
> And the palace shakes,
> As the chorus sings, "Rousing Chu,"
> And the Wu songs and the Cai airs,
> And the Great Lü Mode.
> Women and men sitting side by side—
> Now comes the orgy of no distinctions—
> Clothes, sashes, and hat strings fall.

Tombs from the former Chu domains have also yielded material that is beginning to fill in details about Chu conceptions of the sacred, only hinted at in the poems with their gods, goddesses, fabulous creatures, and shamans who travel back and forth between the worlds of spirits and mortals.[1]

Recently discovered texts written on bamboo slips and silk illustrate to what extent those images represented lived beliefs. The most famous example is the diary of a Chu legal officer, whose duties may have been similar to those of Qu Yuan. It emerged from a tomb at Baoshan in Hubei province. Much of it is a record of divinations that he had shamans perform during his tenure, reflecting the nature of his work, his anxieties about his relationship with his king, and his suffering during a long illness. The records show that his shamans enlisted the aid of some of the same deities that figure in the *Nine Songs* (九歌 *Jiuge*) section of the *Songs of Chu*. The Great Unity, for example, was offered a gelded ram when the officer complained about no appetite and distress in his stomach and chest. It was hoped that the deity would help find the source of the illness. The shamans offered a ewe to the Minister of Life Spans (or Controller of Fate) for the same reason. The divination texts also mention many unknown divinities, such as the Two Children of Heaven, Wei Mountain, High Hill, and Low Hill. The divination records also suggest that the officer feared that his illness could have been caused by the spirits of prisoners he might have had executed unjustly in his capacity as magistrate.[2]

The Baoshan texts reveal a highly developed legal system while confirming the Chu reputation for belief in spirits and shamans. Texts from another tomb reveal a rather different side of Chu culture. The Guodian texts were discovered in 1993 in a Chu tomb near the village of Guodian in the vicinity of Jingmen in Hubei. It is one of the only Warring States tombs to yield philosophical manuscripts. These were written on about eight hundred bamboo slips. Their significance in the study of Chinese philosophy has been compared to that of the Dead Sea Scrolls in the study of Western religion. The tomb is dated at approximately 300 B.C.E., possibly within the lifetime of Qu Yuan. The fine artifacts made of bronze, jade, and lacquer found in the tomb suggest its occupant was a member of the nobility, a highly educated one, who died in old age. The texts buried with him include known Confucian and Daoist texts—for example, a chapter of the *Book of Rites* (禮記 *Liji*) and even a version of the *Daodejing* 道德經. They also include previously unknown works such as *The Great Unity Gives Birth to Water* (太一生水 *Taiyi sheng shui*), a cosmogonic text. The presence of such a variety of manuscripts, and a blurred inscription on one of the drinking vessels found with them, has led some scholars to speculate that the tomb occupant must have been a teacher, possibly a tutor to the crown prince, but there is as yet no conclusive proof.[3]

The central theme in the *Chuci* is the hardship encountered by the moral person born in a corrupt age, specifically one who serves a benighted king. The "Li sao," like a number of other Warring States texts, cites counterexamples to illustrate the ideal, kings who had the wisdom to recognize and benefit from talent, even in the socially lowly. For example,

Though Yue labored pounding earth walls at Fuyan,[4]
   Wu Ding made him his minister and had no doubts.

Though Lu Wang swung a butcher's knife at Zhaoge,[5]
   When he met Wen of Zhou he managed to rise high.

A text from Guodian, *Qiongda yi shi* 窮達以時 (Poverty or success is a matter of timing), has a passage with a longer list, mentioning some of the same examples, which concludes with the following statement:

Whether or not [all the aforementioned men] encountered [an appreciative lord] was [a matter controlled by] Heaven. Their actions were not motivated by the prospect of success, and thus, while impoverished, they were not [distressed(?)]; [their learning(?)] was not for the sake of fame, and thus, while no one appreciated them, they had no grudges. [Irises and orchids grow in secluded forests]; they do not fail to be fragrant [just because there is no one there] to smell them . . . Poverty or success is a matter of timing, and whether in obscurity or prominence, one should not act twice [i.e., differently].[6]

The passage is striking because it uses flora as metaphors for virtue that persists despite being unrecognized. Similar floral metaphors occur in other Warring States texts, such as the *Xunzi*, whose author lived for a while in the state of Chu.[7] Whether or not flora in the "Li sao" have a similar metaphorical function has long been disputed in the world of

*Chuci* scholarship. Here, finally, is a Chu text contemporary with "Li sao" that offers support for the claim that they do.

Another text that helps us understand the "Li sao" better is the *Cheng zhi* 成之 (Bringing things to completion), of which the first line is (in my translation based on Cook's reconstruction), "Heaven sends down the great norms, so as to bring order to human relations." The first few words in Chinese are *tian jiang da chang* 天降大常. Now the spirit in "Li sao" descends (*jiang*) from Heaven and his name is Zhengze 正則, which I translate as True Norm. The *ze* 則 in Zhengze is synonymous with *chang* 常 in this case. One can see here how Qu Yuan seems to have taken the idea of Heaven sending down abstract norms and transformed it into the image of a spirit named True Norm descending from the sky. A similar personification or deification occurred in the case of the Daoist concept of Taiyi 太一, or the Great Unity, which in the *Daodejing* is another name for the impersonal Dao and in the *Nine Songs* is the name of a deity to whom sacrifices can be offered.

Another Guodian manuscript, *The Great Unity Gives Birth to Water*, mentioned above, seemingly features the Great Unity in a phase somewhere between abstraction and deity. The Great Unity, Taiyi in the original, instead of giving birth to yin and yang before everything else (as in the *Daodejing*), gives birth first to water and, after a few stages, gives birth to yin and yang: "The Great Unity gives birth to water, and water returns to join with (/assist) the Great Unity, thereby forming Heaven. Heaven returns to join with the Great Unity, thereby forming Earth. Heaven and Earth [further join with each other], thereby forming the spiritual and luminous. The spiritual and luminous further join with each other, thereby joining *yin* and *yang* (345), etc."[8] This seems to be very much an outlier cosmogony, for it does not survive in any other text, not even in "Tian wen" 天問 (usually translated as "Heavenly Questions" but here translated as "Ask the Sky").

"Tian wen" is one of the strangest of the *Chuci* texts in that it is a poem consisting mainly of a long list of questions about subjects such as the origin of the cosmos, the formation of the heavens, ancient myths, and ancient history. No one has as yet offered a convincing explanation as to why such a poem might have been written. It was thought unique in the history of Chinese literature until the recent discovery of a similar text from Warring States Chu, titled *Fan wu liu xing* 凡物流形, or *All*

*Things Are Flowing Forms.* This text is among the Chu bamboo manuscripts of the Warring States period housed in the Shanghai Museum. Those texts, totaling twelve hundred bamboo slips on which were written about a hundred texts, were discovered in 1994 in the antiques markets of Hong Kong. They were purchased by the Shanghai Museum, where they were organized, edited, and studied. The results have been published in a multivolume set. *Fan wu liu xing* is included in volume seven.[9]

A good part of this somewhat shorter text is also a list of questions in verse covering some of the same subjects as in "Tian wen." It is even more of a mystery than "Tian wen" because scholars are unsure not only about the meaning of many of the individual characters and phrases but also about the order of the questions, for the bamboo strips on which it was written fell out of order long ago. I have translated a short excerpt from it in the "Tian wen" section of this book.

The *Qinghua daxue cang zhanguo zhujian* 清華大學藏戰國竹簡 manuscripts also contain examples of Chu verse other than those that appear in the *Songs of Chu*. Of particular interest are texts such as "Zhou gong zhi qin wu" 周公之琴舞, or "The Duke of Zhou's Qin Dance," that feature the *luan* 亂, a moral, or summary appended at the end of a longer poem, often translated as "envoi" or "epilogue," a characteristic feature of "Li sao" and other *Songs of Chu* pieces. The excavated examples promise to clarify the nature of the *luan*, whose exact function, whether musical or poetical, has never been entirely clear.[10]

We are fortunate to be living in a time when so many texts and artifacts are emerging from the tombs, affording us a clearer picture of the literary and cultural background of the *Songs of Chu*. This is especially important because the *Shiji* 史記 (Records of the grand historian) biography of Qu Yuan provides us very little to go on and, as modern research has shown, is a very suspect text. It is nevertheless the unavoidable beginning of all research into the life and career of Qu Yuan.[11]

The biography of Qu Yuan tells the classic story of the virtuous failure, whose advice if taken would have saved his feckless king. Qu Yuan was no outsider. He was from a cadet branch of the royal family. His intellectual skills won him entry into the king's inner circle of policy makers. He was charged with diplomatic duties as well, becoming the main spokesman of the king. His specialty, however, was law.

Being the foremost in ability and the king's favor, Qu Yuan naturally attracted envy. One of his colleagues of equal rank and similar responsibilities, a certain Shangguan Dafu (Hawkes's "Lord High Administrator"), noticing that the king had given Qu Yuan a special legislative assignment, tried to steal some of Qu Yuan's work. When Qu Yuan prevented him from taking it, he went to the king and told him a false story, according to which Qu Yuan bragged whenever he drafted a successful decree for the king, saying that without him the king could never do it. Believing the slander, the king grew angry and soon excluded Qu Yuan from his inner circle and demoted him. Shocked and dismayed by the king's sudden and unjustified hostility, he wrote the "Li sao."

This is where the story becomes controversial in the modern history of *Songs of Chu* scholarship. Clearly Sima Qian believed that the "Li sao" was composed shortly after Qu Yuan lost favor with his king and certainly before the latter's death. According to the earliest extant complete commentary on the *Songs of Chu*, the *Chuci zhangju* 楚辭章句, by Wang Yi 王逸 (d. 158 C.E.), which is as fundamental to the traditional understanding of the "Li sao" as the biography, Qu Yuan composed the poem during his exile.[12] But according to the biography, Qu Yuan was not exiled under King Huai; he was exiled under his successor, King Qing Xiang. King Huai did send him to Qi on a diplomatic mission, but, technically speaking, a diplomatic mission is not exile. Did Wang Yi take it as such? Was he working from a different version of the biography? Complicating matters as well is Wang Yi's claim that in the envoi (*luan*) at the end of the "Li sao," Qu Yuan figuratively declares his resolution to commit suicide, which the biography tells us happened not during the reign of King Huai but during the reign of King Qing Xiang.[13]

In addition, modern scholars by and large do not accept the *Shiji* version of when the "Li sao" was written. Reasoning entirely from their reading of the contents of the poem, especially those passages that express concern about the approach of old age, they claim that Qu Yuan was too young to have written the "Li sao" when the biography said that he did. Modern consensus therefore places its composition either at the end of King Huai's reign or the beginning of King Qing Xiang's reign. This is the main instance where scholars have used their understanding of the poetry to contradict the claims of the biography.

Let us return to the summary of its contents. While Qu Yuan was out of favor, the state of Qin decided to attack the state of Qi but hesitated because Qi was an ally of Chu's. Qin sent an ambassador, Zhang Yi, to promise certain territorial concessions to convince Chu to break its alliance with Qi, which King Huai promptly did. Qin, however, reneged on its promises after it attacked Qi. Chu then attacked Qin but was defeated and lost territory. Chu attacked Qin again, this time with its whole army. Meanwhile, the state of Wei, seeing a rival now vulnerable because its forces were busy elsewhere, attacked Chu. The army of Chu, in alarm, returned empty-handed from Qin to repel Wei.

All these military maneuvers are described elsewhere in the early Chinese historical record. The histories go on to tell how Qin offered to give back the Chu territory it had conquered, and how King Huai rejected the offer, demanding instead that Qin turn over Zhang Yi, the ambassador who had deceived him into breaking the alliance with Qi. The ambassador was sent to Chu presumably to face execution, but by bribing powerful parties at court and influencing the Queen of Chu, he managed to get himself pardoned and returned unscathed to Qin. In the *Shiji* biography, we are told that the demoted Qu Yuan was at this time on a diplomatic mission in Qi, and that he returned to Chu having been informed about Zhang Yi's escape from punishment. In another place in the *Shiji*, "The Hereditary House of Chu," there is no mention of demotion, but Qu Yuan's voluntary return from his diplomatic mission to criticize the king is described in much the same way.[14] In yet another place in the *Shiji*, "The Biography of Zhang Yi," however, neither demotion nor diplomatic mission are mentioned; Qu Yuan simply states that he thought the king had called Zhang Yi back from Qin with the intention of executing him by boiling him to death. He goes on to criticize the king for allowing himself to be duped into letting him escape.[15] In this version of the story the king believes that Zhang Yi will do as he has promised (return land to Chu). In "The Hereditary House of Chu" and the biography, however, the king is convinced by Qu Yuan that he has made an error and orders an ultimately futile attempt to recapture Zhang Yi.

The biography and "The Hereditary House of Chu" both tell us that after the departure of Zhang Yi an alliance of states harried the borders of Chu, defeating it many times, and that King Zhao of Qin managed to persuade King Huai, who was related to him by marriage, to travel to Qin for negotiations. According to the biography, Qu Yuan advised against the trip in the following terms: "Qin is a kingdom of tigers and wolves; they cannot be trusted. It would be best not to go!" "The Hereditary House of Chu," describing the same scene, put the same statement in the mouth of someone else. Both the biography and "The Hereditary House of Chu" tell us that Zilan, one of the king's sons, urged King Huai to go, that the king went, that Qin forces kidnapped him on the way, and that he, after unsuccessful attempts at escape, was detained in Qin. According to the biography, King Huai dies in Qin, his body is sent back to Chu, and then his oldest son becomes King Qing Xiang, while Zilan becomes prime minister. According to "The Hereditary House of Chu," however, the son becomes king *before* the father's death in Qin; neither Qu Yuan nor Zilan are mentioned again. At this point the biography becomes somewhat muddled, for right after describing Qu Yuan's return from Qi, his unsuccessful attempt to dissuade King Huai from going to Qin, the king's kidnapping and death in Qin, and Qu Yuan's consequent hostility toward Zilan, it tells us that Qu Yuan maintained his loyalty even while in exile and never gave up his hope that King Huai would realize his mistake and recall him, but *in the end he was never recalled.*

Up to that point the biography never mentioned that Qu Yuan was sent into exile. Even if we consider the unlikely possibility that Qu Yuan's mission to Qi was a kind of exile, how could Qu Yuan have returned from it without permission—that is, without royal recall—to advise the king not to accept the invitation to travel to Qin? In ancient China one did not return from exile whenever one wished. Moreover, the text clearly states that he was never recalled.

Here is the clearest evidence that the biography, as some scholars have observed, is a patchwork of fragments from other texts. Hawkes, following the lead of He Tianxing and other Chinese scholars who have critically analyzed the text of the biography, believed that this passage—which seems to require the possibility of two Qu Yuans, one in exile and the other at court advising the king—is a fragment from the commentary on the "Li sao" commissioned by Emperor Wu of the Han (r. 140–87 B.C.E.) and written by Liu An 劉安, Prince of Huainan (179–122 B.C.E.).[16]

After a moralizing summary of King Huai's tragedy, the text goes on to say that after Zilan heard something unspecified about Qu Yuan, he plotted with Lord Shangguan to turn the new king, Qing Xiang, against Qu Yuan. The angry king then banished Qu Yuan to the south, where, in frustration and despair, he drowned himself in the Miluo River. After that, Chu rapidly declined and was eventually destroyed by Qin.

I have greatly simplified the narrative that is given in the *Shiji* biography, but the question of when Qu Yuan was sent into exile emerges even on first reading of the original. Other things that strike one on first reading, and which I leave out of my summary, is the fact that a section from the *Chuci*, the story titled "The Fisherman," is inserted into the biography to describe the immediate circumstances of Qu Yuan's suicide, and another *Chuci* piece, the poem "A Bosom Full of Sand" (懷沙 "Huai sha"), is presented therein as Qu Yuan's swan song, or suicide note, composed or recited before he hurls himself into the river. To the modern reader the fictional nature of these sections of the biography is readily apparent, but they were not considered suspect by traditional scholars until the twelfth century.

What is not readily apparent about the biography, except perhaps to the stupendously learned, is what Galal Walker has called "the almost wholly derivative nature of the text." Even during the Han dynasty it was noticed that parts of the biography, especially the parts that appraise "Li sao," are made-up of fragments of a commentary that Emperor Wu ordered the Prince of Huainan to write during the second century B.C.E. Modern scholars, such as Hu Shi 胡適 (1891–1962) and He Tianxing 何天行 (fl. mid-twentieth century), first noticed that the same passage where Qu Yuan refers to Qin as a nation of tigers and wolves occurs almost verbatim elsewhere in the *Shiji*, in the biography of Zhang Yi, but with someone other than Qu Yuan uttering those words.[17] Other parts of the biography seem to have been plagiarized from other parts of the *Shiji* and other sources, such as the *Zhanguo ce* 戰國策 (Intrigues of the warring states). According to Walker's calculations,

> approximately fifty percent of the text (possibly much more) is *verbatim* repetition from other sources still extant. Furthermore, if portions of the biography that repeat information from the source texts in noticeably similar language were to be included in our calculations, then the entire biography could very nearly be constructed to its present condition today. If Qu Yuan's biographer, two thousand years closer to his subject than we, did not demonstrate an access to resources which are significantly greater than

those available to us now, his authority cannot be assumed. We can assume that the Qu Yuan story was as scarce on information for Sima Qian as it is for us today.[18]

In other words, little was known, other than legend, about the life of Qu Yuan even during the Han dynasty, and the *Shiji* biography was a makeshift attempt to fill in the gaps. Willy-nilly it became the first guide to reading the early poetry of the *Chuci*. Yet inadequacies of the biography were recognized early on, which is why the poems themselves became the secondary biographical source. This at best resulted in circular logic.

A third source for biographical information, mostly discounted these days, is the Wang Yi commentary with its clearly fabricated stories and unintended hilarities (such as his claim that the *Nine Songs* hymn "Earl of the Yellow River" simply recounts a fantasy that Qu Yuan had about meeting and befriending that god of the main river in the north while he was exiled in the region of the Yangtze River in the south.) Both Arthur Waley and David Hawkes thought that Wang Yi's absurdly forced interpretations, especially of the *Nine Songs* and "Li sao," had something to do with some peculiar deficiency in his commentarial skills. My own research suggests that was not the case. Wang Yi's exegetical methods were in fact typical of his time. His was the basic method taught in the Imperial Academy, a pseudosystem for decoding (or creating) hidden codes based on such things as correlative cosmology, numerology, and word placement, very similar to late classical allegorical readings of Homer and the biblical hermeneutics of the early Christian fathers and modern evangelical conspiracy theorists.

Wang Yi wrote his commentary while serving as imperial librarian during the reign of Emperor An 安 (r. 106–125 C.E.), but that ruler was not the one who commissioned it. For most of his reign he was emperor in name only, for his aunt, Dowager Empress Deng Sui 鄧綏 (81–121), acted as regent when he inherited the throne as a boy but jealously prevented him from seizing the reins of power even after he came of age. Her reason for this was that he displayed from childhood two tendencies she abhorred. One was boorishness and the other was utter disdain for learning. The latter attitude did not make him unique among young contemporary Han aristocrats. The Imperial Academy had been established many generations previously to put a Confucian face on Emperor Wu's autocratic policies. After the usurpation of Wang Mang 王莽 (ca. 45 B.C.E.–23 C.E.), which had many supporters in the Imperial Academy, that institution and the imperial family were at odds. The friction soon intensified over a new ideology that arose among unorthodox scholars after the restoration of the Liu family to power. Its fundamental theory held that the Liu family were not mere mortals but descendants of the sage-king Yao and therefore had a right to rule no matter the personal qualities of their individual emperors. Accordingly, no one had the right to oppose them in any way. Heredity trumped merit. Loyal dissent was an oxymoron.

The new doctrine had been formulated mainly outside the Imperial Academy by adherents of the *Zuozhuan*, an alternative—which is to say unofficial—interpretation of the quasi-sacred *Spring and Autumn Annals*. Opposing this view were adherents of the orthodox *Gongyang* commentary on the *Spring and Autumn Annals* who dominated the Imperial Academy. They subscribed to the old Confucian view that Yao had manifested his sagehood mainly by choosing to cede his throne to the best man for the job—that is, Shun—rather than his own son, who displayed none of the wherewithal to rule effectively. For the imperial academicians, loyal dissent was not only possible but even necessary to maintain a stable, well-governed empire. The imperial family, in the end, came to prefer the irony of a theory that simultaneously assigned them descent from Yao and affirmed the principle of hereditary, rather than meritocratic, rulership. Accordingly, they shifted their patronage to the *Zuozhuan* scholars and withdrew favor from the Imperial Academy, where *Zuozhuan* scholars were not welcome.[19]

The academy gradually slipped into desuetude, and the education of imperial youth suffered. Dowager Empress Deng Sui, who did not subscribe to newfangled theories, took it upon herself to revive old-fashioned learning by building special schools for young aristocrats and renovating the Imperial Library. Her purpose in undertaking such projects, aside from a real Confucian belief in the transformative power of the classics, was to please those Confucians in the academy who, aside from feeling beleaguered in the generally anti-intellectual atmosphere at court, might otherwise have objected to a woman withholding power from the rightful, though untutored, imperial heir. She took special interest in the *Chuci* because its main author was famous for righteously endeavoring to enlighten his benighted king. By glorifying his project she sought to justify her own.

But there was one problem. The advocates of the genealogy that traced the imperial family's bloodline back to Yao considered Qu Yuan's behavior treasonous. No less a figure than Ban Gu 班固 (32–92 C.E.), son of the author of *The Destiny of Kings* (王命論 *Wang ming lun*), the unorthodox faction's manifesto, had written a critique of "Li sao" accusing Qu Yuan of "denying the validity of government by law and the teachings recorded in the classics and commentaries."[20] By "government by law," he of course did not mean that of the lost state of Chu; he was referring to the government of the Han dynasty. By "teachings recorded in the classics and commentaries," he was not referring to anything studied in Chu, nor even to what was taught in the Han Imperial Academy. He was referring to those interpretations of the ancient literature, such as the *Zuozhuan*, that supported the doctrine of the Liu family's descent from a sage-king and the concomitant authoritarian ideology. He was deploying a very ancient Chinese strategy: using the past to criticize the present. By impugning Qu Yuan's loyalty, he was impugning the loyalty of those who opposed the doctrines of his authoritarian faction.

Deng Sui in choosing Qu Yuan as her model of loyalty was choosing a controversial figure in the debate between those who claimed that loyalty and dissent could coexist in the same person and those who claimed that it could not. The task that she assigned Wang Yi was not only to maintain Qu Yuan as a hero of the supporters of the concept of loyal dissent but also to show that there was nothing in his work that deserved the kind of criticism opponents of that concept, such Ban Gu, had leveled. The riskiness of that undertaking had its analogue in the political project she was defending, but, being a scholar herself, she knew that Wang Yi was well trained in the exegetical methods of the Imperial Academy, which had demonstrated over and over that even the simplest text could be made to reveal unanticipated messages in the hands of the right exegete.[21]

If readers today find little in the "Li sao" that deserves Ban Gu's vehement criticism, it is because Wang Yi removed the offending parts—not by deleting them from the text but by explaining them away. His main method was to read the figurative as historical—not by taking it literally but by deflecting attention away from its logical referents altogether through pseudophilological maneuvers. He thus tore holes in the narrative fabric of "Li sao" allegory, rendering the poem incoherent.

For example, where the poem tells us in the beginning that the main persona of the poem descends from the sky, Wang Yi intervenes to tell us that the verb "descend" means "to be born." Of course the image of someone descending from the sky could be a figurative representation of a birth, a "coming into the world," but even that moribund metaphor had to be neutralized, because in the context of Han political discourse it could be interpreted as Qu Yuan's literally claiming to be a god and thus challenging the quasi-divine authority of the ruler. Neither Deng Sui nor anyone else serving the Han dynasty could afford to claim as moral model a person using such an image, no matter how much the exegete pleaded its figurative or fictional nature.

Accordingly, other signs of supernatural origins, such as the main persona's ascent into the heavens accompanied by an entourage of spirits and his decision to seek out shaman ancestors had to be explained away as mere fantasies of the earthbound Qu Yuan preliminary to his resolution to drown himself in the Miluo River.[22] The "Li sao" was thus transformed from an allegorical story involving spirits and shamans into a rhetorically convoluted and barely comprehensible way of stating what is more plainly, and less dangerously, set forth in Sima Qian's biography of Qu Yuan.

This transformation of the "Li sao" helped canonize Qu Yuan as patron saint of the Chinese intellectual, especially the disgruntled intellectuals, but it was soon institutionalized by the very authoritarianism it was meant to fight. Passed down from teacher to student, incoherent reading engendered ever more incoherent reading, always to achieve the same thematic goal, with few scholars attempting to swim against the current. Some of the few who have, such as He Tianxing, Hu Shi, David Hawkes, Pauline Yu, Galal Walker, and Dong Chuping, have emboldened me to reject the basic exegetical assumptions of Wang Yi, while using his sometimes very useful glosses cautiously, and read the "Li sao" and other poems in the *Chuci* without the filter of Han politics and ideology in order to find out what they tell us about Warring States Chu. This approach is made easier to a certain degree by recent archaeological discoveries, but because the study of that material is still for the most part in the preliminary stages, the references that I make to it in this book will be tantalizingly few.

Wang Yi claimed that the *Chuci* manuscript he found in the Imperial

Library was a compilation by the Han scholar-official Liu Xiang 劉向 (77–76 B.C.E.), who had won fame for his bibliographical work two centuries before. In his catalogue of the books in the Imperial Library, recorded in Ban Gu's *Hanshu* 漢書 (History of the Former Han dynasty), Liu Xiang sets the number of works attributable to Qu Yuan at twenty-five, without listing titles. Wang Yi seems to have followed Liu Xiang, for the number of works he unequivocally attributes to Qu Yuan also amounts to twenty-five. They are "Li sao," *Nine Songs* (eleven pieces), "Ask the Sky," *Nine Cantos* (九章 *Jiu zhang*, nine pieces), "Wandering Far Away" (遠遊 "Yuan you"), "The Diviner" (卜居 "Bu ju"), and "The Fisherman" (漁夫 "Yufu"). (One other work, "The Great Summoning" [大招 "Da zhao"], he was not sure about.) Of these the "The Diviner" and "The Fisherman" and "Wandering Far Away" are now not generally attributed to Qu Yuan— "Wandering Far Away," for being too redolent of Han Daoism and for its similarity to the work of the great Han poet Sima Xiangru, and "The Diviner" and "The Fisherman," for being obvious works of fiction that contribute to the Qu Yuan legend. A somewhat different group emerges when we list all the works of Qu Yuan mentioned by Sima Qian: "Li sao," "Ask the Sky," "Mourning Ying" (哀郢 "Ai Ying"), "A Bosom Full of Sand," and "Summoning the Soul" (招魂 "Zhao hun"). "Mourning Ying" and "A Bosom Full of Sand" are both individual titles in the *Nine Cantos* section, which suggests that the *Nine Cantos* were not originally a set. Many believe it was Liu Xiang who put the nine poems together into a series. "Summoning the Soul" was later ascribed to the Chu poet Song Yu 宋玉 by Wang Yi. Neither the Han scholar-poet Jia Yi 賈誼 (200–169 B.C.E.) in his poems nor the Prince of Huainan in his commentary on the "Li sao" mention any work other than the "Li sao" in connection with Qu Yuan. Clearly more works were added, most of them implausibly, as time went on.

Where did they come from? It is difficult to say, but we should bear in mind that the most important poetic form during the Han dynasty, the *fu* 賦, or "rhapsody," was traceable back to Chu. Chu hymn forms and music were preferred in state ritual. And in the southern princedoms, such as Huainan, which were in the former domains of Chu, poets were still writing in various Chu verse forms. Chu literature did not die with the fall of Chu.

The *Chuci* anthology, despite its name, is mainly a showcase for the work of Qu Yuan, poetry in his style, and poetry about him. It is a Chu anthology only insofar as its core is writing from the last time Chu was still a functioning kingdom. The Chu-derived rhapsody was a kind of court poetry, patronized by emperors and often used as a vehicle for directing praise at the imperial house, especially Emperor Wu, with mostly token gestures of moral instruction or criticism.

The imperial house, in fact, was originally from Chu, a place to be ashamed of in northern eyes. Nevertheless, as Han glory increased, Chu received the reflected light, and Qu Yuan became the symbol of an acceptable, prideworthy, though tragic, Chu. It seems that originally he was known for the "Li sao" only, but the list of his poetical works lengthened with his increasing prestige. Thus many works that had enough "Li sao"–like characteristics, and were not already pinned down to the name of another author, were added to the list of Qu Yuan's works. Imitating the work of Qu Yuan at the same time provided safe cover for those who wished to express dissatisfaction with the vicissitudes of life at the Han court. In this way, the compilers of the *Chuci* were building a small boat of dolorous complaint to sail against the strong current of rhapsodic praise.

Poets used the Chu past in allegorical criticism of the Han present. The Han politician and poet Jia Yi seems to have begun the practice when Emperor Wen exiled him to the same region where Qu Yuan was supposed to have been exiled. In writing "Mourning Qu Yuan" (吊屈原 "Diao Qu Yuan") he was in fact complaining about his own punishment at the hands of Emperor Wen. His poem is the first recorded mention of Qu Yuan, and it is possible that he came to know about the poet for the first time during his exile in the south. If he was the first to bear the lore of Qu Yuan to the north, that might explain why Sima Qian paired his biography with that of Qu Yuan in the *Records of the Grand Historian*. Sima Qian's writings show that after he himself was unjustly punished (with castration) by Emperor Wu for supporting a Han general condemned for having been captured by the Xiongnu tribe, he found his moral analogue and consolation in the figure of Qu Yuan. Liu An, Prince of Huainan, may well also have been using the image of Qu Yuan to justify and defend himself when he wrote his commentary on the "Li sao" at the command of Emperor Wu, who may at the time have suspected him of treasonous activities. We do not have the full text of the Prince of Huainan's commentary. What remains, however, is impassioned praise of a man of integrity who was treated unjustly by his king, a description that might also have fit persons who had been treated unjustly by Emperor Wu, such as the prince himself.

It appears that evoking Qu Yuan for such purposes was a safe practice. The emperor in fact was so interested in Qu Yuan's poetry that aside from commissioning Liu An's commentary on the "Li sao," he invited another expert from the south, one Zhu Maichen 朱買臣, to come to court to chant and explain the songs of Chu. His performance, around 125 B.C.E., marks the first recorded occurrence of the term *Chuci*. We do not know whether he introduced "Ask the Sky," "Mourning Ying," "A Bosom Full of Sand," and "Summoning the Soul," but it is only after his visit that evidence emerges, in the writings of Sima Qian, indicating that those titles had been added to the list of the poet's works.

The Chu craze during the reign of Emperor Wu was replayed not long afterward. Around 70 B.C.E., a Mr. Pi 被 was invited to the court of Emperor Xuan (91–49 B.C.E.) to perform the *Chuci*. Some decades later, as mentioned, Liu Xiang attributes twenty-five works to Qu Yuan. Whether these works were brought to light by Mr. Pi or came from the library of the Prince of Huainan, which Liu Xiang inherited, is hard to say. But by the time the contents of the anthology were finally fixed about two centuries later under the editorship of Wang Yi some twenty-five pieces are ascribed to Qu Yuan. Besides these, a number of poems attributed to Song Yu, Jing Cuo, supposedly disciples of Qu Yuan, and a few Han poets, among them Liu Xiang and Wang Yi himself, were anthologized in the *Chuci*.

During the Song dynasty, Hong Xingzu 洪興祖 (1090–1155 C.E.) added supplementary notes (known as 楚辭補注 *Chuci buzhu*) to Wang Yi's edition, correcting only the more egregious claims of Wang Yi while leaving the biographical interpretation intact, and adding valuable philological information.

The great Song-dynasty philosopher Zhu Xi 朱熹 (1130–1200) also made an edition of the *Chuci*. His approach was only slightly more radical than that of Hong Xingzu. He removed the works of Liu Xiang ("Nine Sighs," 九歎 "Jiu tan"), Wang Yi ("Nine Yearnings," 九思 "Jiu si"), and two other Han sections, "Nine Longings" (九懷 "Jiu huai"), by Wang Bao 王褒, and "Seven Remonstrations" (七諫 "Qi jian"), attributed by some to

Dongfang Shuo 東方朔, replacing them with two works, "Mourning Qu Yuan" (弔屈原 "Diao Qu Yuan") and "The Owl Rhapsody" (服賦 "Fu fu"), by Jia Yi. He also added his "Appendix to the *Chuci*" (楚辭後語 "*Chuci houyu*"), which includes about fifty poems in the Chu style starting in the pre-Qin period and extending into his own time. His edition, minus the appendix, is the basis of most modern Chinese editions of the *Chuci* as well as my translation.

When specialists in Chinese literature these days talk about the influence of the *Chuci* on the development of Chinese literature they usually begin by declaring that Qu Yuan was China's great patriotic poet. Patriotism is of course admirable, but in politics the label often hides a host of sins. This is especially the case when Communist Chinese critics apply the term to Qu Yuan. Qu Yuan for various reasons might be considered a paragon of loyalty, but loyalty to whom? He was a member of the Chu royal clan. Remaining loyal to the King of Chu was at the very least loyalty to his family and at most loyalty to the feudal system the Communists so ardently urge their followers to despise. It was also loyalty to the expansionist ambitions of Chu—in a word, imperialism—to be equally, if not more, despised.

Another modern cliché about Qu Yuan is that he was "the people's poet." This judgment is based on few and far between passages from the various works attributed to him that express a sentiment that has nothing to do with a revolutionary or even a democratic agenda; it is the same noblesse oblige that we find articulated more extensively and eloquently in the works of a number of Warring States philosophers, most notably the great Confucian Mencius.

Many of the same critics also argue that Qu Yuan merits the title "people's poet" because he based the form of his poetical outpourings on the "primitive" songs of the common people. Here again is a hidden paradox. The works in question are the *Nine Songs*, and even if we accept the idea that they are based on hymns sung in rural worship, we must also accept the idea that they are part of religion, which through most of its reign the party has labeled as superstition and has done its utmost to suppress. If Qu Yuan is admirable for improving the style of the people's worship, then he is by the same token guilty of encouraging one of their most reactionary habits.

The party, of course, was not unaware of these "contradictions" in

Qu Yuan's case; these and many more were debated, mostly out of public view, before his image was simplified with the anachronistic label "patriot." The reasons were complex. He had always been the patron saint of intellectuals; and the intellectuals who were day by day refining the revolution by discarding the heroes of the past, like Confucius, were still in the habit of looking to Qu Yuan, even when they, as often happened, lost favor. Another reason was that the process of discarding the heroes of the past was rapidly emptying the cultural display case, leaving the impression that the Chinese had no figures who had contributed to world civilization. This proved embarrassing at large festivals of the international socialist movement, when other countries, like Italy or East Germany, indulged nationalist leanings by wheeling out unshattered their own cultural icons, such as Copernicus or Beethoven.

In rescuing Qu Yuan from the dustbin of history the regime was admitting that the revolution could not dispense with its intellectuals, even its literary intellectuals. And the intellectuals in supporting the regime's image of Qu Yuan as patriot were pledging to make common cause with the party, if not on the basis of ideological purity (whatever that at any moment happened to mean) then, at the very least, on the basis of nationalist pride.

The postrevolutionary period was not the first time Qu Yuan was enlisted to serve both sides of the minister-ruler (or, in this case, party-intellectual) divide. After the Han scholar-poet Jia Yi initiated Han literati into the habit of exploiting *Chuci* imagery in their poetical criticisms of their princes, the Han court poet Sima Xiangru (179–117 B.C.E.) used some of the imagery to praise one of the most dictatorial emperors in Chinese history—Emperor Wu of the Han—in a poem called "Rhapsody on the Great Man" (大人賦 "Da ren fu"), which begins,

世有大人兮，在于中州。
宅彌萬里兮，曾不足以少留。
悲世俗之迫隘兮，朅輕舉而遠游。
乘絳幡之素蜺兮，載雲氣而上浮。

In these times there is a great man
Who lives in the central region,
Who though his residence occupied a thousand square *li*,

It was not enough to keep him there even a short time,
For he lamented being hemmed in by the common run.
Why not, he said to himself,
Lightly rise and wander far away?
So he rode a white rainbow ornamented with a red banner
And carrying nothing but wisps of clouds he floated up.

Then in the manner of the *Nine Songs* the vehicle gathers various adornments, then transforms. Now the Great Man is

駕應龍象輿之蠖略逶麗兮，
驂赤螭青虬之虯幽蟉蜿蜒。

Driving an ivory chariot drawn by flying dragons
Undulating like long inchworms,
And red serpents and hornless green dragons
Slithering like snakes.

Soon he is surrounded by a celestial procession modeled on that in the "Li sao," which he describes, speaking in the first person,

屯余車其萬乘兮，
綷雲蓋而樹華旗。
使勾芒其將行兮，
吾欲往乎南嬉。
歷唐堯于崇山兮，
過虞舜于九疑。
紛湛湛其差錯兮，
雜遝胶葛以方馳。

I mustered my ten thousand chariots,
And gaily colored banners rose above wagon covers of multicolored
    clouds.
I ordered Goumang to lead the retinue,
For I wished to go south for amusement.
We passed by Chong Mountain, Yao's grave,
And saw Nine Doubts Mountain, the tomb of Shun.

We surged forward in a jostling mass,
Galloping side by side in a motley horde.

With his celestial entourage the Great Man travels the universe experiencing many pleasurable adventures until he finds himself face-to-face with the Queen Mother of the West, one of the greatest *xian*, or immortals. Intrigued but unimpressed by her immortal status he then sets forth to find a place or a state that surpasses even her realm. To do this he abandons his entourage and proceeds alone, eventually finding himself in a place very similar to the final destination reached in the "Wandering Far Away" section of the *Chuci*. In fact the words are almost exactly the same:

下崢嶸而無地兮，
上寥廓而無天。
視眩眠而無見兮，
聽惝恍而無聞。
乘虛無而上遐兮，
超無有而獨存。

Below him was a precipitous fall but to no earth,
Above him was endless space, but no sky.
What he saw was a blurry nothing at all,
What he heard was a muffled nothing at all,
And he rode nothingness higher and higher,
Until he passed beyond the Formless to abide alone.

The irony of this piece is that it uses the imagery of transcendent flight derived from *Chuci* poems where such flight is an escape from a world made intolerable by the reign of benighted rulers, in which category many counted Emperor Wu himself. It features the "Li sao"–like flying chariot but with the sad main persona of "Li sao" (taken by many to represent Qu Yuan himself) replaced by the Great Man, who represents Emperor Wu, on his quest to become an immortal.

There were those who no doubt saw the poem as less flattery than satire, but how the emperor read the poem is indicated by the fact that Sima Xiangru remained his quasi-personal poet for the rest of his life.

A countergenre was meanwhile developing on the basis of the same

*Chuci* sources. This was the poetic genre known as *youxian* 游仙, which can mean either wandering as an immortal or wandering among the immortals. The *xian* are people who manage through yogic, dietary, or alchemical practice to become immortal. *Youxian* poetry describes the magical worlds where the immortals live. Those worlds tend to be located on high mountains, in heaven, or on the moon. At the same time the *youxian* genre expresses the poet's desire to become a *xian*. The genre was practiced by devout aspirants to *xian*-hood and by uncommitted littérateurs alike.

Dissatisfaction with the mundane, especially the political, is sometimes expressed in *youxian* poems, but more often than not it remains implicit. Because of the unsubtle quasi-religious subject matter and highly formulaic presentation, most *youxian* poems tend to be boring in translation, but the genre is a very important one in Chinese literary history, for it provided images and tropes that were taken over into other genres, especially landscape poetry and the poetry of secret or unrequited love.

The Six Dynasties period was the golden age of *youxian* poetry, and one of its chief exponents was an occult Daoist practitioner, the scholar-poet Guo Pu 郭璞 (276–324 C.E.). One of his best-known works is a series of poems called *Youxian shi* 游仙詩, of which only fourteen remain. Number three is presented and translated below:

翡翠戲蘭苕，容色更相鮮．綠蘿結高林，蒙籠蓋一山．
中有冥寂士，靜嘯撫清弦．放情凌霄外，嚼藥挹飛泉．
赤松臨上游，駕鴻乘紫煙．左挹浮丘袖，右拍洪崖肩．
借問蜉蝣輩，寧知龜鶴年．

When the kingfisher plays among the flowering thoroughwort,
Its color is even brighter.
When the pine gauze forms in the high forests,
It envelopes the whole mountain.
There the obscure lonely hermit lives
Tranquilly whistling and playing his clear-sounding *qin*,
Sending his heart to dwell beyond the clouds,
Eating medicinal herbs and drinking from flying springs with cupped
    hand.

Red Pine looks down on him from above

As he wanders by driving a giant goose in his chariot of purple mist.

His left hand holds the sleeve of Fu Qiu and his right is on the shoulder of Hong Yan.

Answer this question please, mayfly,

Can you even conceive of a life as long as that of the tortoise or crane?

In this poem Red Pine, Fu Qiu, and Hong Yan are all names of people who became immortal by doing the sorts of the things the herb-eating springwater-sipping hermit is doing. Note that there is also a flying chariot in this poem, but the emperor has been replaced by an immortal. The symbols of immortality are the tortoise and crane, which were traditionally thought to live a very long time. The short-lived mayfly, of course, stands for ordinary mortals who live in the capital wearing themselves out, ever scheming to gain status and wealth.

The immortals are of course airborne, a sign of their transcendence. It is from that vantage point that they can see the vanity and brevity of ordinary human life, which the hermit is attempting to escape. That airborne perspective goes all the way back to "Li sao," where the persona of the poem takes flight at the end of the poem and, hovering over the capital that he once cherished, realizes that in fact there is nothing there worth clinging to. Guo Pu's poem, like most poems in the genre, posits the most generalized dissatisfaction with the world as motivation for those aspirants to *xian*-hood. Such poems invite rulers, ministers, and ordinary people alike to be practitioners. The "Li-sao"–like flight is there, but the moral edge is missing, and that was the case for most *youxian* poetry after "Wandering Far Away," the *Chuci* work considered the main ancestor of the genre.

The moral edge gradually returns as we proceed into the Tang dynasty, especially in the poetry of another of the great *youxian* writers, Li Bai 李白 (701–762). Aside from being one of the great poets in Chinese history, Li Bai, like Guo Pu, was an occult Daoist practitioner, having studied with a number of renowned masters. It was this status along with his genius and unconventionality that inspired the Tang poet He Zhizhang (659–744) to dub him "the banished immortal" (謫仙 *zhe xian*).

The Tang imperial house, which traced its ancestry back to Laozi, considered by many to be the founder of Daoism, was especially interested in occult Daoist practitioners. And Xuanzong, the emperor at the time, loved poets. Li Bai was both. His willingness to use his knowledge and talent to please, if not flatter, can be seen in the following poem "Yu Zhen xianren ci" 玉真仙人詞 (The immortal Jade True), written for Princess Yu Zhen (Jade True), who was the sister of Emperor Xuanzong and who became a Daoist nun:

玉真之仙人，時往太華峰。清晨鳴天鼓，飆欻騰雙龍。
弄電不輟手，行雲本無蹤。幾時入少室，王母應相逢。

The immortal Jade True
Time after time goes to Great Flower Peak,
And in the early morning sounds the celestial drums,
And driving her two dragons on speeding winds,
Casts lightning bolts without dropping the reins.
Like a drifting cloud she appears and disappears without trace.
When will she enter the Chamber of Youth,
Where she will surely meet the Queen Mother of the West?

Great Flower Peak, known as Hua Shan 華山 in Chinese, is one of the five sacred mountains of China, with a long history as a center for occult Daoist practice. The expression "sounds the celestial drums" is probably code for a particular Daoist ritual involving gnashing the teeth together. The loud clicking sound is supposed to drive away evil spiritual forces. There may well be other codes in the poem as well, but the only other things that have been identified so far are the Chamber of Youth (Shao Shi), which is a peak to the west of Mount Song, another sacred mountain, and the Queen Mother of the West, who among other things is the ruler of female immortals. After receiving this poem, Princess Jade True apparently helped Li Bai gain access to the emperor.

Li Bai lost imperial favor as quickly as he won it, and more than once. In the course of his rocky career he wrote a set of poems called *Fifty-Nine Ancient Airs* that offer moral judgments in figurative, and often satirical, form. There is a great deal of flying in these poems. Here the flying becomes a trope, which while still bearing the marks of the *youxian* genre recalls more directly the older parts of the *Chuci* by restoring the spirit of Qu Yuan to the midheavens—that is, making the moral judgments that only a lofty perspective can afford. One of the most famous examples is number nineteen:

西上蓮花山。迢迢見明星。素手把芙蓉。虛步躡太清。
霓裳曳廣帶。飄拂升天行。邀我登云台。高揖衛叔卿。
恍恍與之去。駕鴻凌紫冥。俯視洛陽川。茫茫走胡兵。
流血涂野草。豺狼盡冠纓。

I went west and up Lotus Mountain,
And saw in the distance the mountain spirit Bright Star
Holding a lotus in her hand
As she tiptoed on the air of the highest heaven,
Her broad sashes trailing from her rainbow skirt,
Fluttering as she rose,
She invited me to ascend with her to the cloud tower
To pay our respects to Wei Shuqing.
And away I went with them in a blur
Riding great geese over the purple void.
We looked down on the plain of Luoyang
And saw a vast horde of barbarian soldiers running,
Their spilling blood painting the wild grass red,
And jackals and wolves were there,
All wearing officials' caps.

This is a hybrid *youxian* poem mixing *youxian* elements with the *Chuci*-derived genre of poems that describe erotic encounters between male mortals and female spirits such as "Gaotang fu" (高唐賦, "Rhapsody on Gaotang"), attributed to the late Warring States period poet Song Yu 宋玉, and "Luoshen fu" (洛神賦, "Rhapsody on the Spirit of the River Luo"), by Cao Zhi 曹植 (192–232), which I discuss below. With the exception of "Gaotang fu," such poems give a vision of the beautiful spirit only to describe the erotic frustration of the one who has the vision. In Li Bai's variation, however, the spirit beckons with no erotic intent; she is merely introducing him to another immortal, Wang

Shuqing, a male. He is one of the great immortals, and Li Bai expresses no hint of feeling that "three is a crowd." The goal of the trio is not erotic but moral heights, the same midair perspective from which the main persona of "Li sao" looks down and realizes that there was nothing he should cling to in the state, for there are no men in the state—that is, no one who was not corrupt or useless. When Li Bai and company look down from the celestial heights, they see only war and those who wage it, and they turn out not to be men but beasts dressed up as men.

The intersection of many lines of *Chuci* influence—in this case from the *Nine Songs*, "Li sao," and "Wandering Far Away"—is typical of much of the *Fifty-Nine Ancient Airs* series and a number of Li Bai's poems outside the series. One of the most interesting works in this regard is "Song of the Celestial Grandmother Dream: A Parting Gift" (夢遊天姥吟劉別 "Meng you tian mu yin liubie").

Celestial Grandmother is the name of one of the mountains sacred to Daoism, located in Zhejiang. The poem was a parting gift to a friend Li Bai was visiting. In it Li Bai describes a dream in which he travels to the mysterious and massive mountain, whose image "flickers in and out of view among the clouds at sunset." In ancient China dreams were believed to be a form of spirit travel. The poem accordingly describes Li Bai flying through the air on his own power, the way some of the shamans do in the *Nine Songs* and the disgruntled persona in "Wandering Far Away" does:

一夜飛渡鏡湖月。
湖月照我影，送我至剡溪。

And throughout the night I flew
    over the moon in Mirror Lake,
And the moon shining on my form accompanied me
    all the way to Shan Stream.

Once he reaches the mountain, he marvels at the sights, including the place where one of his favorite poets spent the night, the sun high over the sea, and an expanse of flowers, where he tarries entranced. Suddenly it grows dark and

熊咆龍吟殷巖泉，慄深林兮驚層巔。
雲青青兮欲雨，水澹澹兮生煙。

The roar of bears and the growl of dragons
Thundered through the cliffs and over the streams
Shaking the deep forest, making the craggy ridges tremble.
The clouds grew dark, threatening rain,
And the lakes rippled as they sent up mist.

All the above lines are modeled on lines from the *Nine Songs* both in imagery and meter, including the insertion of a rhythm particle (*xi*) in the middle of the line. But the ancient gods of Chu do not descend at this juncture. Instead the mountain peaks collapse amid thunder and lightning, exposing a massive stone gate that roars open to reveal a "cave heaven" (洞天 *dong tian*)—that is, another dimension, accessed through a cave, entirely inhabited by immortals:

青冥浩蕩不見底，日月照耀金銀臺。
霓爲衣兮風爲馬，雲之君兮紛紛而來下。
虎鼓瑟兮鸞迴車，仙之人兮列如麻。

Inside it was all blue sky vast and endless,
With both sun and moon shining on glistening gold and silver towers,
And, clothed in rainbows, the Lord of the Clouds descended,
With the winds as his horse team, followed by a crowding entourage:
Tigers playing the strings of the *se* as the *luan* phoenixes parked the
    chariots,
And the immortals standing dense as hemp in rows.

The Lord of the Clouds is one of the deities worshipped in the *Nine Songs*. Here we see that for Li Bai at least there was no great distinction between the immortals and the ancient gods of Chu. The vision of the cave heaven ends when Li Bai suddenly wakes up from his dream. The poem thus imitates the structure of the "Li sao," in the midsection of which the persona goes into a trance induced by the spirit of Shun in which he has a vision of his spirit flying through the cosmos in search of a spirit bride. In the end he comes out of the trance and consults a diviner as to the meaning of the vision. On the basis of the diviner's advice the main persona of "Li sao" departs from the kingdom in a flying chariot, free at last, heading in the direction of the Kunlun Mountains, where the spirits of the shaman ancestors live. When Li Bai awakes from his dream vision he is further confirmed in his opinion that mortal life is fleeting and vain, and he asks the friend to whom the poem is dedicated to always have a white deer at the ready to carry Li Bai on his visits to the great mountains in the area upon his return. The white deer is one of the magical animals the immortals prefer to ride, and its first occurrence is, of course, in the *Chuci*—in the section called "Ai shiming." Here, however, Li Bai's aspiration to *xian*-hood is not motivated purely by the devotee's belief in immortality. Here it is really a trope of freedom, expressing his realization that he is out of step with the world of political ambition that is the imperial capital; real fulfillment lies elsewhere. The last lines of the poem are as follows:

安能摧眉折腰事權貴，使我不得開心顏。

How could I lower my brow and bend my waist
to serve the powerful and highborn
and never let my heart or face open?

Li Bai is an example of a poet who obviously learned a great deal from the *Chuci*. Like many Chinese poets who served in the government he saw something of his own career in the experience of Qu Yuan and mined the *Chuci* for appropriate ways of talking about it. This use of Qu Yuan and the *Chuci* is observable in Chinese literature throughout the imperial period and into the Communist era. The influence of the *Chuci* extends beyond poetry of political complaint and the poetry about immortals, a genre that carries a subtle tone of political complaint even at its most mystical. Two other types of poetry deeply influenced by the *Chuci* are love poetry and landscape poetry. They are both very large topics, and I could not do them justice here. However, I offer the following poem as an example of how two lines of *Chuci* influence can intersect in subtle, fascinating, and purely aesthetic ways. The poem is "Mulan zhai" 木蘭柴 (Magnolia enclosure) from the *Wangchuan Collection* (輞川集 *Wangchuan ji*) of the Tang poet Wang Wei 王維 (699–759):

秋山斂餘照，飛鳥逐前侶。
彩翠時分明，夕嵐無處所。

Autumn mountains gather in the last of the sun,
Flying bird pursues its mate.
At times the green peaks stand clear against the golden clouds,
Tonight the mountain mist has no place to stay.

This is a very simple poem until the last phrase, "has no place to stay." The original Chinese is 無處所 *wu chu suo*. For the educated Tang reader this phrase triggered a chain of literary associations going all the way back to the *Chuci*. The phrase comes from "Gaotang fu," a rhapsody supposedly by Song Yu, believed by some to be Qu Yuan's successor, but more likely by a later author. The first part of the poem consists of a dialogue between King Xiang of Chu and Song Yu, who gives an account of an earlier king's dream encounter with the goddess of Shaman Mountain (巫山 Wushan). Song Yu tells the story to explain a strangely behaving cloud that King Xiang has noticed hovering over a distant pavilion.

> Once upon a time King Xiang and Song Yu were enjoying the sights from the lodge at Yunmeng and they saw in the distance the Gaotang pavilion. Hovering over it was a single cloud of mist piled precipitously high, which suddenly changed shape and in a small space of time changed into innumerable shapes. The king asked what sort of mist it was. Song Yu answered, "That is what they call the morning cloud." The king asked, "What manner of thing is this morning cloud?" Song Yu answered, "In the past a previous king was traveling through Gaotang when he grew tired and took a nap. A woman appeared to him in a dream, who said, 'I am the daughter of Shaman Mountain and a guest of Gaotang. When I heard that you, Lord, were sojourning in Gaotang, I desired to offer you my pillow and a sleeping mat.' The king then made love to her, and as she was leaving she said by way of farewell, 'I am on the southern side of Shaman Mountain amid the dangerous rocky heights. At dawn I am a morning cloud, at dusk I am sudden rainfall. Morning after morning, dusk after dusk, I'll be there near the Sunlit Tower.' In the

morning when he went to the place to look, he found that it was just as she had said. He therefore had a temple built on the spot, which he named 'Morning Cloud.'" King Xiang asked, "When the morning cloud comes out at the beginning of the day, what does it look like?" Song Yu replied, "When it first comes out, it is bushy like a pine tree and as straight. As it approaches, it brightens and resembles a beautiful young woman raising her sleeve to shade herself from the sun as she looks in the distance expectantly for the one she yearns for. Then suddenly it changes shape, and it resembles a chariot pulled by four speedy horses with colorful feathered flags raised. Then the air grows chilly as though a storm were about to come. And after the wind calms and the rain stops, the cloud is nowhere to be found."

The poem, which gave the Chinese language the phrase "clouds and rain" (雲雨 *yunyu*) as a euphemism for sexual intercourse, goes on to give a catalogue of the scenic wonders of Gaotang. The phrase that Wang Wei lifted from the text, *wu chu suo*, can mean either "is nowhere to be found" or "has no place to stay." The latter meaning is active in Wang Wei's poem, but the fact that the subject of Wang Wei's sentence is mountain mist recalls the goddess of Shaman Mountain. And the goddess of Shaman Mountain recalls the female divinities in the *Nine Songs*, some of whom are amorous, such as the Mountain Spirit who speaks in the ninth poem of the *Nine Songs*:

"I stand on the mountain exposed and alone,
The clouds a land of shifting shapes beneath my feet.
Vast is the darkness, yes, daylight benighted—
A breeze from the east, the spirits bring rain.
Stay with me, Spirit Adorned, and find such ease you'll forget your
    home.[23]
Once I am late in years, who will make me flower again?
. . .
"Thunder rolls through rain's dark veils,
Hear the gray gibbon weep and the black gibbon's night cry
Against the soughing wind and the whistling trees.
Longing for you, Lord's son, I suffer in vain."

In the *Nine Songs* the landscape is made magical by the presence of the spirit, although the shape-shifting clouds, the threat of rain, thunder, and gibbon call seem there to repel whomever the yearning spirit is beckoning to. In the Song Yu poem the landscape becomes numinous by the immanence of the spirit. Whereas the *Nine Songs* mountain spirit is an elusive presence in cloudy and rainy weather, the Shaman Mountain spirit *becomes* cloudy and rainy weather and announces the fact. The numinousness of the old shamanic spirits, as Chinese literature develops, becomes more and more immanent in the landscapes and weather. We see this happening even in the *youxian* poetry of Guo Pu—for example, number 3, which I quoted above:

> When the kingfisher plays among the flowering thoroughwort,
> Its color is even brighter.
> When the pine gauze forms in the high forests,
> It envelopes the whole mountain.

Here the kingfisher plays amid the plants that are sacred to the various spirits in the *Nine Songs*. The pine gauze in fact is one of the plants out of which the *Nine Songs* Mountain Spirit makes a sash. Here it covers the whole mountain, which is to say that the mountain, by donning the clothes of the spirit, shows that it and the spirit are one. The evocation of numinous immanence becomes more and more subtle in the great Chinese landscape poets, reaching its pinnacle in the poetry of Wang Wei. Even without knowledge of the allusion when we read the phrase that Wang Wei has taken from "Gaotang fu," the mountain mist on Wang Wei's mountain takes on a human aspect, at the very least. Knowledge of the allusion, however, allows us to see in the mist a form of the mountain spirit.

This translation, based on Zhu Xi's Song-dynasty edition, is meant for students, general readers, and scholars, in that order. In China the *Chuci* is considered one of the most difficult texts to read, and few people, even experts in classical Chinese, can read it without constantly consulting explanatory notes. That necessity is only slightly diminished when one is reading it in translation—even into modern Chinese. For most of the poems I have opted to place the notes on separate pages rather than use footnotes. Philological notes are interspersed among the general notes only where I anticipate questions from specialists.

# NOTES

1. For a fine introduction to the study of Chu, see Constance A. Cook, *Death in Ancient China: The Tale of One Man's Journey*, China Studies 8 (Leiden: Brill, 2006).
2. Ibid., 198.
3. Scott Cook, *The Bamboo Texts of Guodian: A Study and Complete Translation* (Ithaca, N.Y.: Cornell University Press, 2012).
4. Yue is Fu Yue 傅說, who was a convict laborer building earthen walls when the Shang king Wuding 武丁 discovered him and made him his minister. Wuding recognized him because he had once had a premonitory dream about him. In the pre-Qin sources the dream part of the story is found in the *Guoyu* 國語, "Chu yu shang," 199–200, and the earthen wall building part is referenced in, e.g., *Mozi*; see *Mozi xiangu*, "Shang xian zhong," 35, and "Shang xian xia," 40–41. In the Guodian text, *Qiongda yi shi* 窮達以時, he is called Shao Yao 邵繇 (see chapter 7). See also Jiang Liangfu, 姜亮夫*Chuci tonggu* 楚辭通故 (Shandong: Qi Lu shushe, 1985), 2:90–110.
5. Lü Wang 呂望worked as a butcher and fisherman just before the rise of the Zhou dynasty. He is also known as Jiang Taigong 姜太公, Taigong Wang太公望, Jiang Shang 姜尚, etc. Legends about him are scattered and varied. According to the *Shiji* (Sima Qian 司馬遷, *Shiji* 史記 [Beijing: Zhonghua shuju, 1992], "Qi Taigong shijia," 32:1477–79), the future King Wen, founder of the Zhou dynasty, divined before going hunting, and the oracle predicted that he would meet someone who would be worthy of becoming his adviser. During the hunt he met Lü Wang (under the name Lü Shang 呂尚) fishing on the banks of the Wei River. The *Shiji* cites an alternative story, according to which Lü Wang once was a learned minister of Djou, the bad last king of the Shang dynasty, whom he left to eventually ally himself with the future King Wen. Wang Yi gives a slightly different account, according to which Lü Wang, after leaving Djou to seek out Wen, found himself in dire straights in Zhaoge 朝歌, where he became a butcher to earn a living, and only after that did he become a fisherman. Later King Wen had a dream in which he was introduced to him by none other than the Lord of Heaven. Having seen his face in the dream, he had no trouble recognizing him on the banks of the Wei River (Hong Xingzu洪興祖, *Chuci buzhu* 楚辭補注 [Beijing: Zhonghua shuju, 1986], 38). The Guodian text *Qiongda yi shi* (Dirk Meyer, *Philosophy on Bamboo: Text and the Production of Meaning in Early China* [Leiden: Brill, 2011], 86–88) refers to a variant of this story (see chapter 7) where Lu Wang was a slave before his rise. See also Jiang Liangfu, *Chuci tonggu*, 2:119–30, and Jin Kaicheng 金開誠, Dong Hongli 董洪利, and Gao Luming 高路明, *Qu Yuan ji jiaozhu* 屈原集校注, 2 vols. (Beijing: Zhonghua shuju, 1996), 1:143–44. See also Sarah Allan, "The Identities of Taigong Wang in Zhou and Han Literature," in

*The Heir and the Sage: Dynastic Legend in Early China*, rev. ed. (Albany: SUNY Press, 2015), 149.

6. Cook, *Bamboo Texts of Guodian*, 463–64.

7. *Xunzi jijie* 荀子集解, vol. 2 of *Zhuzi jicheng* 諸子集成 (Shanghai: Shanghai shudian, 1987), 3–4. See also Burton Watson, trans., *Basic Writings of Mo Tzu, Hsün Tzu, and Han Fei Tzu*, Translations from the Asian Classics, Records of Civilization: Sources and Studies, no. 74 (New York: Columbia University Press, 1963), 17.

8. Cook, *Bamboo Texts of Guodian*, 345.

9. *Shanghai Bowuguan cang Zhanguo zhushu, volume 7* 上海博物館藏戰國竹書 (七), ed. Ma Chengyuan 馬承源 et al. (Shanghai: Shanghai guji chubanshe, 2008).

10. Qinghua daxue chutu wenxian yanjiu yu baohu zhongxin 清華大學出土文獻研究與保護中心, ed., chief ed., Li Xueqin 李學勤, *Qinghua daxue can Zhanguo zhujian (san)* 清華大學藏戰國竹簡 (叁) (Shanghai: Zhongxi shuju. 2010), 53.

11. For a translation of the Sima Qian biography, see David Hawkes, trans., *The Songs of the South: An Ancient Chinese Anthology of Poems by Qu Yuan and Other Poets* (Harmondsworth, U.K.: Penguin 1985), 54–60. For a detailed analysis of the text of the biography, see Galal Walker, "Toward a Formal History of the 'Chuci'" (Ph.D. diss., Cornell University, 1982).

12. Hong, *Chuci buzhu*, 2. Wang Yi seems to have taken *shu* 疏, "estrange," to mean *zhu* 逐, "exiled."

13. Ibid., 47.

14. *Shiji*, 40:1725.

15. *Shiji*, 70:2292

16. Hawkes, *Songs of the South*, 58.

17. He Tianxing 何天行, *Chuci zuo yu Handai kao* 楚辭作於漢代考 (Shanghai: Zhonghua shuju, 1948). Hu Shi 胡適, "Du Chuci" 讀楚辭, in *Hu Shi wencun di er ji* 胡適文存第二集 (Taipei: Yuandong tushu gongsi, 1953), 91–97.

18. Walker, "Toward a Formal History," 77.

19. Gopal Sukhu, "Yao, Shun, and Prefiguration: The Origins and Ideology of the Han Imperial Genealogy," *Early China* 30 (2005–2006): 91–153.

20. Hong, *Chuci buzhu*, 49–50.

21. For an account of Wang Yi's role in Deng Sui's project, see Gopal Sukhu, *The Shaman and the Heresiarch: A New Interpretation of the "Li sao."* Albany: SUNY Press, 2012, 55–71.

22. Hong, *Chuci buzhu*, 47.

23. This is possibly the shaman's cry for the spirit to possess her.

*THE SONGS OF CHU*

# CHAPTER ONE

# Nine Songs

# 九歌

# *Jiuge*

The *Nine Songs* consist of shaman hymns to various divinities, a threnody for fallen soldiers, and a finale. There are in fact eleven pieces in the *Nine Songs*, and no one is entirely sure why this is so. In the opinion of certain scholars, enumeration is the problem. The Ming scholar Wang Fuzhi 王夫之 (1619–1692), for example, thought that the first and last hymns are prelude and finale and therefore do not count. Another example is the Qing scholar Jiang Ji 蔣驥 (ca. 1678–1745), who proposed treating "The Ruler of the Xiang" and "The Lady of the Xiang" as one piece and "The Great Minister of Life Spans" and "The Lesser Minister of Life Spans" as one piece, giving a total of nine. There are several other numbering proposals besides.

Other scholars believe that the title is not to be taken literally. "Nine songs" is a phrase that occurs in more than one Chinese myth. In the "Da Yumo" 大禹謨 section of the *Shujing* 書經, Yu, the first ruler of the Xia dynasty, offers a plan for good government that is divided into nine categories, the successful accomplishment of which he thought should be praised in nine songs to "stimulate" the people.[1] According to the *Zuozhuan* the recommendation to stimulate the people with nine songs is to be found in "one of the Books of Xia."[2]

The "Li sao" and the "Tian wen" (Ask the sky) also mention a series called *Nine Songs*. These *Nine Songs*, however, were stolen from Heaven by Qi, second ruler of the Xia dynasty, brought back to earth, and performed over and over at state-sponsored revels, bringing about the decline of the royal family and Qi's early death. The main source of information on the celestial *Nine Songs* is the *Shanhaijing* 山海經 (The classic of mountains and seas). Qi, traditionally thought to be a historical ruler, is described there as a supernatural man who resides "beyond the southwest sea, south of the Red Waters, west of the Flowing Sands" and who wears green snakes as earrings. Riding in a two-dragon chariot, he went to heaven three times to be the guest of the Sky Lord. On one of his visits he obtained (some say through theft) the *Nine Songs*.[3]

Given its mythological associations, the title *Nine Songs* was chosen for allusive purposes, some scholars believe, rather than as a description of the number of pieces.

Moreover, Galal Walker has offered convincing evidence that the last two pieces, "Those Who Died for the Kingdom" and "Serving the Spirits" were added to the series later. They are not directly addressed to any particular divinity, which leaves nine hymns that are. His findings may finally put the controversy to rest.

The *Chuci Nine Songs* are ascribed to Qu Yuan for the first time in Wang Yi's edition of the anthology. If they were known before that, they were not associated with Qu Yuan, at least according to the extant sources. Wang Yi believed that Qu Yuan composed the *Nine Songs* after he heard the crude hymns sung by southern peoples during his banishment. His purpose in revising them, according to Wang Yi, was to improve the tone of rural worship and offer veiled complaint to the king who had unjustly punished him. There is no trace of this story anywhere before the writings of Wang Yi, yet his explications of the *Nine Songs*, which largely present the hymns as the first-person musings of Qu Yuan, are almost entirely based on it.

Wang Yi's readings of the *Nine Songs* are often laughably forced, and while generations of traditional scholars have tried, no one has managed to find a path through the hymns that satisfactorily leads to their remonstrative content. Most modern scholars have given up trying to find it, but many still see them as folk productions. This is of course a desperate clinging to the last thread of Wang Yi's theory about the *Nine Songs*. Once that thread is let go, one must admit that the elegant classical Chinese in which they are composed and the mention of objects such as bronze bells, associated exclusively with royalty, suggest that the hymns were meant for performance at a royal court.

Wang Yi no doubt recognized this. After all, shamanic performance had been included in Han state cult during the first half of the dynasty. An account from the *Shiji* tells us that sponsorship of shamanic ritual started with the founder of the dynasty, Liu Bang:

> In Chang'an he [Liu Bang] installed officers for invocation and sacrifices. He also introduced female shamans. The shamans from Liang sacrificed to such forces as Heaven, Earth, the Sky Alter, the Celestial Waters, the Bedroom Occupant, and the Upper Hall. The shamans from Jin sacrificed to such forces as the Five Lords, the Lord of the East, the Lord in the Clouds, the Controller of Life, the Shaman Altar, the Shaman Temple, the Members of the Clan, and the First Cook. The shamans of Qin sacrificed to the Master of Altars, the Shaman Guards, and the two gods Zu and Lei. The shamans of Jing [Chu] sacrificed to such powers as the Lower Hall, the Shaman Ancestors, the Controller of Lives, and the Shimi Gruel God. The Nine Skies shamans sacrificed to the Nine Skies. All the above sacrificed in the imperial palace at regular times. The Yellow River shamans sacrificed to the Yellow River and Linjin; the Southern Mountain shamans sacrificed to the Southern Mountain and to the Middle One of Qin. The Middle One of Qin is the second emperor of Qin.[4]

Imperial favor granted such practices reached its apex under Emperor Wu (140–87 B.C.E.). During his reign, however, shamans came to be involved in factional strife, inspiring fear and loathing for their supposed ability to kill or cause illness by casting spells.[5] While interest in shamans never disappeared, by the time of Wang Yi they constituted a reviled class, subject to legal restrictions. His claim that the *Nine Songs* were originally rural productions that were given aristocratic polish and a remonstrative subtext by a scholar banished from the capital reflects the prejudices of his time. What is intentionally missing from his account is the possibility that the *Nine Songs* are products of royally sponsored shamanism, an institution that even historical records available during Wang Yi's time suggest existed in Chu. But to bring to mind such a phenomenon would signal the possibility that Qu Yuan had practiced shamanism, a possibility that was incongruent with the Confucian image of Qu Yuan Wang Yi and his sponsor, Dowager Empress Deng Sui, were attempting to create.

The *Nine Songs* series is one of our only sources of information about the shamanistic practices of Chu. The songs describe the herbs that shamans used to purify themselves, how the sacrificial foods were offered, the musical instruments that accompanied their hymns, their dancing, their clothes, and how they envisioned the spirits. Most importantly, they tell us who some of the deities worshipped were and their relationship to the worshippers.

A fair portion of the meaning of the songs remains mysterious, however. Even during the Han dynasty there was much difference of opinion as to what they actually said. Wang Yi found them so confusing that he wondered whether the bamboo strips on which they were recorded had gotten mixed up. We do not know whether they were simply sung or staged, with different singers acting out different stanzas or lines. Nor do we know enough about the mythology connected with the individual deities to always discern what about them some of the lines allude to. Some of the hymns draw no clear distinction between the mortal and the spirit worlds. Some scholars think that many of the songs are in dialogue form, where different shamans impersonate (or are possessed by) various spirits.[6]

My translation of some of the hymns has been influenced by the "dialogue" theory, but any translation of the *Nine Songs* must remain tentative until anthropologists and archaeologists can teach us more.

What is clear is that some of the pieces are love songs addressed to one or another deity. In those songs the shaman appears to seduce the deity out of the sky for a brief rendezvous only to grieve as the fickle deity ascends again with no promise of return. The jilted shaman sometimes pursues the deity through the sky, riding in a variety of magical vehicles or flying on his or her own power. The only hymn where the love affair leads to marriage describes a courtship on and under water. That hymn, "The Earl of the Yellow River," may well be a remnant of the ancient custom of sacrificing a virgin to the Yellow River.

1

## "AUGUST OF THE EAST, THE GREAT UNITY"

東皇太一

## "DONG HUANG TAIYI"

The Great Unity (Taiyi) as a philosophical concept and alternative name for the Dao is well represented in Warring States period texts.[7] Until relatively recently, however, this hymn was the only evidence that a divinity named Taiyi was worshipped during that era as well. Additional evidence emerged from three ancient tombs, one at Wangshan, one at Baoshan in Hubei, and one at Guodian. The Wangshan tomb, discovered in 1965 and dated circa 332 B.C.E., is famous for yielding in nearly pristine condition one of the swords owned by Gou Jian, king of Yue (ca. 470 B.C.E.). It also contained texts, one of which listed objects considered appropriate to offer as sacrifices to Taiyi. A text offering similar information was discovered at Baoshan during the 1980s.[8] Taiyi was evidently a divinity worshipped in Chu, yet it did not immediately go north with the Chu founders of the Han dynasty, nor is Taiyi mentioned on the list of state cults inherited by the Han from the Qin.

A certain Miu Ji, an expert in ritual and possibly a shaman, convinced the fifth Han ruler, Emperor Wu, to institute state sacrifices to Taiyi in 113 B.C.E. According to Miu Ji, "Taiyi is the most honored of the celestial gods. The assistants of Taiyi are the Five Sovereigns. The Sons of Heaven in ancient times sacrificed a *tailao* 太牢 [an ox, a ram, and a pig] a day for seven days to Taiyi in the southeastern suburban rites. They built an altar for that purpose with spirit paths leading from it in the eight directions."[9]

A number of scholars are of the opinion that the Taiyi cult originated in the state of Qi, the great center of philosophical learning, during late Warring States times. It seems more likely that Taiyi's transformation from philosophical concept to god took place in Chu. *Taiyi sheng shui* (*The Great Unity Gives Birth to Water*), a text representing Taiyi in an intermediate stage between concept and divinity, was discovered in the Chu tomb at Guodian. There Taiyi is a force that acts cosmogonically—first producing water, with the help of which it then produces the sky, with the help of which it then produces the earth; thenceforth come the spirits, yin and yang, the four seasons, cold and hot, wet and dry, and finally the year or harvest.[10]

The title "Dong Huang Taiyi" remains a mystery. Wang Yi, on what basis is unclear, tells us that Taiyi is called August of the East here because he was worshipped in eastern Chu.

### August of the East, the Great Unity

On this auspicious day, this best of times,
Reverently we bring delight to the August on High,
We hold long swords with jade-headed hilts,
Our shining pendant belt gems clatter.[11]
Weights of green jade press mats white as *yao* stone,[12]
Sprigs of precious fragrances we bring in mixed handfuls,
Basil leaves cover the cooked meat offered on beds of thoroughwort,
With the sacrifice of cassia wine and peppered broth.

Lift the mallets, strike the drums,
Slow the rhythm for calming hymns.
But when *yu* reeds and *se* strings play, let the singing swell,[13]
Let the serpent limbs of shamans dance dressed in splendid robes,
Inundating the hall with their fragrances of pollen and herbs
Let every musician sound every note,
May the Lord find joy, pleasure, and peace.


2

## "THE LORD IN THE CLOUDS"

雲中君

## "YUNZHONG JUN"

A bamboo manuscript discovered in a Chu tomb at Tianxingguan in Jiangling, Hubei province, in the early 1980s carried a list of divinities to whom the Chu king offered sacrifices; one of them was Yun Jun 雲君, or Lord of the Clouds.[14] Liu Bang, the first emperor of the Han dynasty, established sacrifices to a divinity called Yunzhong Jun 雲中君, but the shamans who performed the rites were not from Chu but from Jin 晉.[15] If the two names refer to the same divinity, then it would put to rest Hawkes's theory that Yunzhong Jun is the lord of Yunzhong Mountain in Shanxi.[16]

Wang Yi tells us that another name for the Lord in the Clouds is Feng Long 豐隆, the thunder god who appears in "Li sao" (lines 221–22) and in an early text called *The Travels of King Mu* (穆天子傳 *Mu Tianzi zhuan*).[17] Wang Yi also mentions the theory that the Lord in the Clouds is another name for Ping Yi 屏翳, variously identified as a rain god, a cloud god, a thunder god, and so forth.

One of the Chinese words for shaman, *ling* 靈, consists of a graph for cloud at the top, three rain drops below that, and, at the bottom, the more common word for shaman, *wu* 巫. The character may indicate the primary role of the ancient Chinese shaman—rainmaker.

### The Lord in the Clouds

After the thoroughwort bath, her hair washed in fragrant herbs,
In robes of many colors, hung with galangal,[18]
A shaman dances writhing—the god already within her,
His aura spreading in rays clear, unending.
Yes, he will take his ease in the Temple of Longevity,[19]
Paired with sun or moon, his light as bright.

Driving a dragon chariot, dressed in the colors of the Sky Lords,[20]
He soars now, wandering everywhere,
For as soon as the spirit descends in his splendor,
He rushes away, rising into the clouds,
Looking down on us in Jizhou and beyond,[21]
For he goes where he pleases over four seas—what limit has he?
Lord of our yearning, we sigh long sighs,
Our hearts worn out by sorrow after sorrow.

## 3 AND 4

## "THE RULER OF THE XIANG RIVER" AND "THE LADY OF THE XIANG RIVER"

湘君湘夫人

## "XIANG JUN" AND "XIANG FUREN"

Wang Yi believed that "The Lady of the Xiang River" was about the two daughters the sage-king Yao gave in marriage to Shun as a reward for his virtue, a sign that he intended to make him king. He did not identify the Ruler of the Xiang River, which he may have believed referred to one of Yao's daughters. There is a story to support this view.

According to the *Shiji*, the First Emperor of the Qin, on his southern tour of sacred mountains, ran into a storm on the Xiang River near the place where it flows into Lake Dongting. There Mount Xiang stood on an island with a shrine at its foot dedicated to a goddess called Ruler of the Xiang whose mortal body was buried there. The emperor, angry that his progress had been hindered by the storm and assuming that the spirit of the shrine was responsible, asked an adviser to identify it. When the adviser explained that the Ruler of the Xiang was the daughter of Yao and the wife of the sage-king Shun, the emperor flew into a rage and ordered three thousand convicts to cut down all the trees on the mountain and paint the ground ochre to punish the goddess for violation of the law.

It is possible that the term *Xiang jun* (ruler of the Xiang) in the *Shiji* story refers to both women. A passage from "Youyu er fei" 有虞二妃 (The two consorts of Lord Yu) in the *Lienü zhuan* 烈女傳 (Biographies of exemplary women) of Liu Xiang uses the title *Xiang jun* to cover both women, whose names are E Huang 娥皇 and Nü Ying 女英.[22] Because of the differently titled hymns in the *Chuci*, however, some scholars concluded that the titles "Xiang jun" and "Xiang furen" refer to the sister who became the primary wife and the one who became the secondary wife, respectively. Tradition has it that the two sisters followed their husband Shun south. When he died there, they drowned themselves in the Xiang River, becoming river spirits.

Other scholars think that the Ruler of the Xiang River (*jun* 君, in *Xiang jun*, though gender neutral, is usually used for males) is not a woman at all but in fact the title of Shun, and that the two hymns, one where he speaks and the other where his wives speak, are in dialogue or contain dialogues. Who is speaking to whom (or thinking what about whom), however, differs according to the interpreter.[23]

There is a parallel myth, perhaps older, according to which the two women are described as daughters of the Lord of Heaven who reside in the Xiang River region. The *Shanhaijing* (*Zhongci shi'er jing*) has them living on Lake Dongting Mountain, wandering about the riverine landscape accompanied by high winds and storms. According to the fourth century poet and commentator Guo Pu 郭璞, the women in this myth have nothing to do with Yao or Shun.[24] Elements of the various myths may well have merged over time to form new stories.

In my translation, a male speaks in the first hymn, a female in the second. This could mean that a male shaman pursues the spirit princess in the first hymn, whereas a female shaman (impersonating or possessed by the princess?) is pursuing a male (Shun?) in the second hymn. The fact that the speaker of the first poem throws belt ornaments, usually associated with men, into the river, and the fact that the speaker of the second hymn sacrifices a sleeve and inner garments, usually associated with women, seems to support this very tentative interpretation.[25]

### The Ruler of the Xiang River

The princess does not set forth, she lingers,
For whom, alas, is she waiting on the islet midriver?
You of the beautiful form perfectly adorned,
Give my boat of cinnamon bark speed,
Calm the waves of the Rivers Yuan and Xiang,
Let the Long River flow softly.
I watch that princess in the distance coming never,
Playing panpipes, her thoughts on whom?

I am driving flying dragons, my chariot heading north.
I am turning now, taking the path to Lake Dongting,
Creeping fig leaves my banner, with lanyards of basil,
And on flagstaffs of lure leaf, thoroughwort flags.

I see Cenyang in the distance on the far shore,
Crossing the great breadth of the Long River I let my spirit fly,
I let my spirit fly, but it never reaches her.
A bewildered woman sighs long sighs for me,
Tears in torrents cross my face,
I long for you, Princess, in secret agony.

With cassia oars and thoroughwort hull,
I am cutting through ice and piled-up snow.
I am picking creeping fig in the middle of a river,
I am gathering lotuses on the top of a tree,
Hearts out of tune make matchmakers useless.
Love not deep makes it easy to part.

Water over stones, rushing rushing,
Dragons in the air flitting flitting,
If you've been unfaithful, I'll be bitter forever.
You failed to show—"no time," your excuse.

In the morning I gallop the riverbank,
By evening step slow near the northern islet.
Birds inhabit the roof,
Water surrounds the temple.

I throw a cut ring of jade into the Long River,
And drop my belt charms on the shores of the Li.
I gather galangal on the fragrant islet,
To give to the woman who serves you.
Time gone you can never regain
For the moment I wander far and carefree

## The Lady of the Xiang River

The son of a Sky Lord descends on North Islet.
I narrow my eyes to see him—it saddens me.
In light gusts comes the autumn breeze,

Waters of Lake Dongting ripple under leaf fall,
I climb a hill of white sedge to let my gaze run free.

We promised to meet, the splendid one and I,
    to raise a tent for our night time.
But why would a bird perch on floating duckweed?
Why would a fisherman cast his net on a tree?

Fragrant roots grow by the River Yuan, thoroughworts by the Li.
I long for the prince but dare not speak.

I scan the distance. There he is, or is he?
I watch the water flow endless and slow.
What does an elk in an empty courtyard eat?
What does the flood dragon do on the shore?

At dawn I gallop my horses to the high bank
In the evening cross the river to the western strand.
If I hear the splendid one calling me,
I will rush away with him on a leaping chariot.
In the middle of the river we would build a house,
And roof it over with lotus leaves.
Its walls would be of lure leaf, its courtyard of purple cowry,
And we'd sprinkle pepper flowers through all the chambers.
Under cinnamon roof beams and thoroughwort rafters,
And in the angelica bedroom with its magnolia lintels,
We'd hang bed curtains of woven creeping-fig vines.
And spreading apart the entry drapes of basil,
We'd see mat weights of white jade,
Orchids scattered for fragrance,
A ceiling covered with aromatic roots fastened with cords of asarum,
A hundred herbs gathered to fill the garden,
And side rooms built for every fragrance.

But they come for him now,
    the welcome party of Nine Doubts,
A flock of spirits like a cloud.

My outer robe I throw into the Long River,
My inner robe I drop on the banks of the Li,
And gather galangal on the flat islet
To give to the one far away from me.
Time once gone does not come back,
For the moment I wander far and carefree.


5

## "THE GREAT MINISTER OF LIFE SPANS"

大司命

## "DA SIMING"

Warring States–era records of sacrifices to a god called the Minister of Life Spans (司命 Siming, or Minister of Fates) were discovered in Chu tombs at Baoshan, in Hubei province, during the 1980s.[26] None of the records distinguish between great and lesser ministers of life spans. The same holds true for the sacrifices to the god during the Han and later periods.

The *Shiji* lists two sets of shamans—one from Chu, the other from Jin—who were responsible for maintaining regular sacrifices to the Minister of Life Spans, the only god whose name appears twice on the list. Some scholars speculate that the Jin god and the Chu god might have been distinguished by the designations great and lesser. Were that proven so, it would support the case of those who think that the *Nine Songs* were used, or even written, during the Han dynasty.

The Minister of Life Spans later evolved into the Kitchen God, who reports to Heaven about every household on New Year's Day.

Siming, like Taiyi, is also the name of a star.

In the following hymn the Great Minister of Life Spans travels in the entourage of the Lord of the Skies, acting as a kind of forerunner. The female shaman seems for a time to share intimacy with him.


**The Great Minister of Life Spans**

He:
Open wide the Gates of the Sky,

I ride the dark crowding clouds.
Let the whirlwinds charge ahead,
And hailstones sprinkle the dusty ground.[27]

She:
The Lord circles and descends,
Leaping Hollow Mulberry to take me, a woman, for company.[28]
The Nine Regions swarm with mortals.
Whose long life or early death depends on me?

He flies high tracing slow rings,
In a chariot of pure *qi*,
    with yin and yang under his reins.
In reverence and awe I attend on the Lord,
As he guides the Sovereign of the Skies
    to the Nine Mounts,[29]
His spirit robes flowing,
His belt laden with cords of jade.

He:
In all the world of darkness and all the world of light,[30]
Common hearts know not what I do.
I pick the *yao* gem flower of the spirit hemp,[31]
To give to you who dwell beyond.

She:
Age slow as the gnomon's shadow is already here,
We grow in time not closer but farther apart.
In a rumbling chariot he drives his dragons,
Galloping high, ramming into the sky.

Long I stand knotting cassia sprigs.
Yes, the more I think of him the sadder I am.
Sadder, but what can I do?
A day like this I wish would never end,
But fate is always fitting.
Whether we meet or part is not for me to say.

6

## "THE LESSER MINISTER OF LIFE SPANS"

少司命

## "SHAO SIMING"

"Autumn thoroughwort and lovage[32]
Grow in dense rows near the temple,
Green leaves, white flowers,
Their strong fragrance took me by surprise."

Those people all have beautiful children,
Lure Leaf, what brings you such worry and pain?

Autumn thoroughwort dense and dark,
Green leaves with purple stems,
Beautiful women crowd your temple,
Yet your eyes quickly beckon only to me.

You entered with no warning, left with no good-bye,
You rode the spinning wind, cloud banners flying.
No grief greater than to live yet be apart,
No joy greater than love when it is new.

You in the lotus-leaf robe bound with basil sash,
Suddenly came and suddenly went
To spend the night in the suburbs of the God-Lords.
For whom are you waiting on the border of a cloud?

"We could have washed our hair at the Xian Pool,
And dried our hair by the side of the sun.
I looked for you, beautiful one, but you never came.
I sing facing the wind in loud despair."

Under a peacock-feather canopy and halcyon banners,
You ascend the Nine Heavens in a chariot, the Broom Star in your
     hand.

Raise your long sword to protect young and old,
Our fates, Lure Leaf, are yours to decide.

7

## "LORD OF THE EAST"

東君

## "DONG JUN"

Most scholars agree that the Lord of the East (東君 Dong Jun) is the divinized sun. The Han court (employing shamans from the state of Jin) worshipped the sun under the same title. Another term for the sun is Xihe, the name of the solar charioteer, who drives his six-dragon team across the sky. According to some accounts, Xihe is also the mother of the sun, who originally gave birth to nine others. Archer Yi, alarmed that they were overheating the earth, shot those nine out of the sky. The original nesting place of the original ten suns was the *fusang* 扶桑 (meaning "handhold mulberry") tree. After the death of his siblings, the remaining sun took his morning bath in Hot-Water Valley, also known as Daylight Valley (湯谷 Tanggu or 暘谷 Yanggu), and used one or more *fusang* trees as a handhold to climb out of it. Some sources say he continued to live in the *fusang* tree. In this hymn the sun speaks, gratefully addressing the shamans (called *shenbao* 神保, or "spirit guardians" here) who made music and danced for him at his worship service.

**Lord of the East**

I, the sphere of light rising red in the east,
Shine on my fence of handhold mulberries.
Calming my horses I gallop steadily.
Night fades—it will soon be bright.
I ride on thunder as the dragons draw,
Cloud banners open in waves and fly.
Sighing long sighs I will soon be aloft,
With hovering heart, gazing back longing.

Yes, your voices and your beauty delight,
Those who see you find such ease they forget to go home.

Play your high-strung *se* in time with the drums,
Strike the great bronze bells till the bell frames rock,
As the *chi* flutes and the *yu* pipes sing.
I will miss you, spirit guardians, virtuous and beautiful,
Fluttering and soaring on halcyon wings,
Dancing together, unfolding your song,
In tune and in rhythm,
As the onslaught of spirits blocks the light of the sun.

In blue-cloud tunic and white-rainbow robe,
I aim my long arrow and shoot down the Sky Wolf,[33]
And bow in hand I turn and sink out of sight.
Lifting the Big Dipper to take the cassia wine,
And grasping the reins to gallop high and soar
Through vast darkness on my journey east.

8

"THE EARL OF THE YELLOW RIVER"

河伯

"HE BO"

The Yellow River, called He 河 in classical Chinese, was worshipped with sacrifices at least as far back as the Shang dynasty. According to a story from the *Zuozhuan* (Duke Ai, sixth year), Chu had not always offered sacrifices to the river:

> When King Zhao of Chu was ill, a diviner told him that the cause of the disease was the Yellow River [spirit], to whom the king did not offer sacrifices. The grand officers requested permission to offer the river sacrifices in the suburban rites. The king, however, responded as follows: "In the sacrificial offerings of three generations, we have never sacrificed to forces outside our purview. Within the purview of the state of Chu are the Yangtze, the Huai, and the Zhang rivers. Come what may, I will not violate this principle. I may not be a paragon of virtue, but I have never done anything to offend the river."

The king unfortunately died of his illness.

The state of Chu began to offer sacrifices to the Yellow River during the Warring States period after annexing territory through which it flowed. Around that time, too, the name He Bo 河伯, or Earl of the Yellow River, appears as the name of the river god. One of the earliest and most famous appearances of He Bo is in the "Autumn Floods" (秋水 "Qiu shui") section of the *Zhuangzi*.

We do not know whether the state of Chu ever offered human sacrifices to the Yellow River. In the north, however, according to the *Shiji*, young virgins, in at least one locality, were still being offered as "brides" to the river god as late as the end of the fifth century B.C.E.[34] The custom may have continued unofficially into the Han dynasty in certain remote regions. The victim was dressed in the richest bridal finery and then floated on the river on a raft designed to fall apart once it achieved fatal distance from the shore. Few women knew how to swim in those days.

Shamans may have continued to serve the river god after human sacrifice ceased to be practiced. In the same way that dolls buried in the tombs of important people took the place of human sacrificial victims in later funerary rituals, it appears that a female shaman, safely acting the part, took the place of the victim sacrificed to the river, at least in the rites of Chu as reflected in this hymn.

**The Earl of the Yellow River**

With you I will roam the Nine Streams,[35]
Whirlwinds will raise waves across the flow,
We will ride a water chariot with lotus canopy,
Four dragons in harness, the outside bald, the inside horned,
And we'll climb the Kunlun Mountains and gaze in all directions,[36]
And my heart will fly unbound.
Despair will come with sunset, but never a thought of home,
For longing arrives with the thought of far shores
And the fish-scale rooftops and the dragon hall,
And towers of purple cowry shells on palaces of cinnabar.
What do you do, spirit, in the water?
You ride the white tortoise and chase the patterned fish.
With you I will roam the islets of the river,

As ice shards swarm downstream.
Taking my hand you travel eastward,
Squiring your beauty to the southern shores.

Billow on billow waves come to greet me,
And fish are my bridesmaids, shoal after shoal.


9

"MOUNTAIN SPIRIT"

鬼

"SHAN GUI"

In ancient China, important mountains were inhabited by a main spirit
and a number of subsidiary spirits, some of them monstrous and malev-
olent.[37] Shrines, mostly at the foot of the mountains, were dedicated to
them. The beautiful, amorous Mountain Spirit in this particular hymn
has never been conclusively identified, nor has the lover she yearns for.

**Mountain Spirit**

There seems to be someone in the mountain hollow
Draped in creeping fig with pine-gauze sash,
Peering through narrowed eyes, and sweetly smiling too.
"You desire me, for you love my lithe beauty."

Drawn by red panthers, followed by striped wild cats,
Her magnolia wagon flies a flag of woven cinnamon bark.
Cloaked in orchids, asarum sash around her waist,
She picks the sweetest flowers and herbs to give her love.

"I live deep in a bamboo grove and never see the sky.
The road was hard and dangerous—I was the late one.

"I stand on the mountain exposed and alone,
The clouds a land of shifting shapes beneath my feet.
Vast is the darkness, yes, daylight benighted—
A breeze from the east, the spirits bring rain.

Stay with me, Spirit Adorned, and find such ease you'll forget your
    home.[38]
Once I am late in years, who will make me flower again?

"I pick the spirit mushrooms in the mountains
Amid rock piles and spreading kudzu.
I am angry, Lord's son, so hurt I forget *I* have a home.
You long for me, but find no time.

"We in the mountains love the fragrance of galangal,
We find drink in stone springs and shade beneath cypress and pine.
Afraid to act you long for me.

"Thunder rolls through rain's dark veils,
Hear the gray gibbon weep and the black gibbon's night cry
Against the soughing wind and the whistling trees.
Longing for you, Lord's son, I suffer in vain."

10

## "THOSE WHO DIED FOR THE KINGDOM"

國殤

## "GUOSHANG"

This is a hymn dedicated to soldiers who died in battle. The military
equipment mentioned (e.g., Wu halberds, Qin bows) was the best of its
kind. Chu was a wealthy and warlike state. The line "But you trammeled
the horse teams / and planted the cartwheels" refers to a technique men-
tioned in Sunzi's *Art of Warfare*, where a general orders "tying up the legs
of the horses and rendering the chariots inoperable to show his troops
there is no retreat, and to make plain his resolve to fight to the death."[39] I
have melded explanation with translation for the sake of clarity.

**Those Who Died for the Kingdom**

Armor of rhino hide
    swinging halberds of Wu,

Wheel hub scrapes on wheel hub,
    short swords clash.
Banners block sunlight,
    enemy like a cloud,
Warriors pushing to be first
    in the crisscross rain of arrows.
They trampled our positions,
    broke through our ranks,
Horse dead in the left harness
    while another bleeds in the right.
But you trammeled the horse teams,
    and planted the cartwheels
To block your own retreat,
    and when the jade mallets struck the echoing drums,
You charged.
    But even stars fall,
and the daunting gods grow angry.

Brutally slaughtered, all of you,
    abandoned on the wild plain,
You who went out will not come in,
    you who departed will not return,
For the plain is too far
    and the road, too long.
Bows of Qin at your sides,
    long swords on your belts,
Heads severed
    but hearts unshaken,
You are the truly brave—
    the finest warriors,
Steadfast to the last breath
    in your invincible honor.
When your bodies died,
    your spirits found their power.
Your souls are now heroes
    in another world.

# 11

## "SERVING THE SPIRITS"

禮魂

## "LI HUN"

We complete the rite beating all the drums,[40]
Banana leaf passes hand to hand as dancer follows dancer,
And elegant women sing their slow song.
Thoroughwort in spring, chrysanthemum in fall—
May it go on unbroken forever.

## NOTES

1. James Legge, *The Chinese Classics*, 5 vols. (Oxford: Clarendon Press, 1893–1894; repr., Hong Kong: Hong Kong University Press, 1960), 3:55–56.

2. Ibid., 5:249–50.

3. Yuan Ke 袁珂, *Shanhaijing jiaoyi* 山海經校譯 (Shanghai: Shanghai guji chubanshe, 1985), 273.

4. Sima Qian 司馬遷, *Shiji* 史記 (Beijing: Zhonghua shuju, 1992), *juan* 28, 1378.

5. For an interesting study of factional strife during the reign of Emperor Wu, see Liang Cai, *Witchcraft and the Rise of the First Confucian Empire* (Albany: SUNY Press 2015).

6. For a summary of Aoki Masaru's interpretation of the *Nine Songs* as dialogues, see Arthur Waley, *The Nine Songs: A Study of Shamanism in Ancient China* (London: Allen and Unwin, 1955). For evidence that belief in spirit possession was a part of the ancient Chu worldview, see Sarah Allan, "'When Red Pigeons Gathered on Tang's House': A Warring States Period Tale of Shamanic Possession and Building Construction Set at the Turn of the Xia and Shang Dynasties," *Journal of the Royal Asiatic Society* 25, no. 3 (July 2015): 419–38.

7. Taiyi 太一 is also a star name (indicating the deity's celestial residence) in the *Han Feizi*, in a critique of the belief in divination and astrology. See *Han Feizi jijie* 韓非子集解, vol. 5 of *Zhuzi jicheng* 諸子集成 (Shanghai: Shanghai shudian, 1987), 88.

8. See Constance A. Cook, *Death in Ancient China: The Tale of One Man's Journey*, China Studies 8 (Leiden: Brill, 2006), 118, 254, 256, 259, 263 for the Wangshan texts, 65–66 for the Baoshan texts.

9. *Hanshu* 漢書, comp. Ban Gu 班固 (Beijing: Zhonghua shuju, 1962), 25a, 1218. See also Michael Loewe, *Crisis and Conflict in Han China* (London: Allen and Unwin, 1974), 169 and 174.

10. For a discussion of *Taiyi sheng shui*, see Sarah Allan and Crispin Williams, eds., *The Guodian "Laozi": Proceedings of the International Conference, Dartmouth College, May 1998*, Early China Special Monograph Series 5 (Berkeley: Society for the Study of Early China and Institute of East Asian Studies, University of California, 2000), 162–72. For a translation, see Robert G. Henricks, *Lao Tzu's "Tao Te Ching": A Translation of the Startling New Documents Found at Guodian* (New York: Columbia University Press, 2000), 123–29. A good discussion of pre–Wangshan and Guodian scholarship on Taiyi can be found in Li Ling, "An Archaeological Study of Taiyi (Grand One) Worship," trans. Donald Harper, *Early Medieval China* 2 (1995–1996): 1–39.

6. Hong Xingzu believes *linlang* 琳琅 is an abbreviation of *qiulin langgan* 璆琳琅玕. The two gems, he says (quoting the *Erya*), come from the Kunlun Mountains (Hong Xingzu 洪興祖, *Chuci buzhu* 楚辭補注 [Beijing: Zhonghua shuju, 1986], 55–56). The gems are presumably hanging from the belts of the shamans.

7. *Yao* 瑶 I read as a variant of *yaohua* 瑶華 in the "Great Minister of Life Spans" in the *Nine Songs*. There it refers to the color and the texture of the flowers; here it refers to the color and texture of the straw.

8. The *yu* 竽 looks like a cup with thirty-six reed pipes sticking up out of it. It is related to the *sheng* 笙, and its sound is somewhere between that of a harmonica and the high registers of a pipe organ. The *se* 瑟 has twenty-five strings, each with its own movable bridge, strung over a rectangular sound box.

9. See "Jiangling Tianxingguan yihao Chumu" 江陵天星觀一號楚墓, *Kaogu xuebao*, no. 1 (1982): 71–115.

10. Sima Qian, *Shiji, juan* 28, 1378–79.

11. David Hawkes, *Songs of the South: An Ancient Chinese Anthology of Poems by Qu Yuan and Other Poets* (Harmondsworth, U.K.: Penguin, 1985), 103.

12. Rémi Mathieu, trans., *Le Mu tianzi zhuan: Traduction annotée, étude critique*, Mémoires de l'Institut des Hautes Études Chinoises (Paris: Collège de France, 1978), 29.

13. Reading *ruo ying* 若英 as an abbreviation of *duruo ying* 杜若英.

14. Hong, *Chuci buzhu*, 58, reminds us that Emperor Wu of the Han dynasty sacrificed to the Lord of the Temple of Longevity, which was built next to the imperial palace. Shamanist ceremonies were performed there. Perhaps his model was a palace (referred to in this song?) built by the King of Chu.

20. Wang Yi says that the Di, or "Sky Lords," referred to here are the Lords of the Five Directions (Wu Fang Zhi Di 五方之帝). Each wears the color that corresponds to the direction over which he rules.

15. Jizhou 冀州 means the heartland of China, the Yellow River basin. By synecdoche it means all of China.

16. See Anne Behnke Kinney, *Exemplary Women of Early China: The "Lienü zhuan" of Liu Xiang* (New York: Columbia University Press, 2014), chapter 1.

17. For a summary of the theories, see Zhou Xunchu 周勛初, *Jiuge xin kao* 九歌新考 (Shanghai: Shanghai guji chubanshe, 1986), 87–104.

18. See Yuan, *Shanhaijing jiaoyi*, 145. For a discussion of the Guo Pu commentary, see Zhou, *Jiuge xin kao*, 88.

19. See Ma Maoyuan 馬茂元, *Chuci zhushi* 楚辭註釋 (Wuhan: Hubei renmin chubanshe, 1985), 140 and 146–47 for the gender associations of the objects.

20. See Cook, *Death in Ancient China*, 82, 97, 100, 174, 175.

21. Sprinkling the ground with water was a ritual to welcome important personages in ancient China. It reduced flying dust.

22. Hollow Mulberry, or Kong Sang, according to Wang Yi is the name of a mountain. The mountain is thought by some to be legendary and in Lu, or by others to be real and in Chu. There was a place in Kaifeng in Henan called Kongsang Cheng. The "Benwei" section of the *Lüshi chunqiu* claims that Yi Yin, the famous minister of Great Tang, was born in a hollow mulberry tree after his mother was transformed into one. Zhuan Xu and a number of other mythological figures are also associated with hollow mulberry trees. I take *cong* 從 in this line as a causative verb.

23. The Nine Mounts is another way of saying the Nine Regions, which is another way of saying China.

30. Taking *yi* 一 as "all" or "whole" and the yin and yang as the two dimensions, spirit and human.

24. The original is *shuma* 疏麻, or "sparse hemp," which also known as *shenma* 神麻, "spirit hemp," *Cannabis sativa*. Taking it as a medicine is said to bring long life.

25. No one is sure why this god is referred to as "lesser"; the prevalent explanation is that he (or she) is in charge of children's lives, while the Great Master of Fate is in charge of adult lives.

26. The Sky Wolf (Tian Lang 天狼) is the star Sirius, part of Canis Major. It is a star of ill omen.

27. See the story of how a wise official put an end to the practice in Sima Qian, *Shiji*, *juan* 126, 3211–13.

28. A general term for the Yellow River, which myth tells us Yu had divided into nine streams to prevent disastrous flooding.

29. The Yellow River springs from the Kunlun Mountains.

30. No one is sure who the Mountain Spirit is. This hymn is viewed by some as forming a complement to "The Earl of the Yellow River." He is a male (yang) inhabiting the water, a yin element; the Mountain Spirit is female (yin) inhabiting a mountain, a yang aspect of the terrain.

31. The is possibly the shaman's cry for the spirit to possess her.

39. See Roger Ames, *Sun-Tzu: The Art of Warfare* (New York: Ballantine Books, 1993), 159 and note 202. See also Tang Bingzheng 湯炳正, Li Daming 李大明, Li

Cheng 李誠, and Xiong Liangzhi 熊良知, *Chuci jinzhu* 楚辭今注 (Shanghai: Shanghai guji chubanshe, 1997), 76–77.

40. Most scholars take *li* 禮 as a verb, "to serve," as I have translated here. *Li hun* 禮魂 could also mean "the spirit of the rites," perhaps suggesting that this last song is making a statement about preserving the nature or spirit (*hun* 魂) of the rites.

*CHAPTER TWO*

# "Leaving My Troubles"

# 離騷

# "Li sao"

"Li sao" has been called the most innovative and influential work in the history of Chinese poetry. It is the longest of the ancient Chinese poems. It is the first to begin with a genealogical introduction of a first-person poetic persona. It is the first to use extensive dialogue with multiple characters as a poetic device. And, while earlier poetry used herbs and flowers as simple metaphors and symbols, "Li sao" is the first to weave a complex allegory involving a long list of flora.

There are few more difficult poems in the Chinese language, and few more controversial. Complicating its unprecedented use of imagery is an almost perversely playful use of language. It is full of puns and double meanings, most of which are impossible to translate. Even its title, previously translated as "Encountering Sorrow," can be read in at least four different ways. "Li sao" can have two opposite meanings, "leaving trouble" or "encountering trouble." Moreover, the character 騷 *sao* of the title is interchangeable with another character, 臊 *sao*, meaning "stench." Thus, the title can also be understood as meaning "encountering the stench" or "leaving the stench." All these readings are appropriate to the content of the poem and seem to have been intended.

The earliest beneficiary of the "Li sao" was the Han *fu*, or "rhapsody," which utilized many of its innovations. Later, shorter poetry and other forms drew upon it as well. Echoes of the "Li sao" are still audible even in the poetry of the Tang (618–907) and Song (960–1279) dynasties and the musical drama of the Yuan (1271–1368), Ming (1368–1644), and Qing (1644–1911).

The irony of its centrality in the mainstream poetic tradition is the fact that it is the product of what was originally thought of as an alien, if not barbarian, culture. The "Li sao," moreover, represents an esoteric corner of that forgotten culture—the ritual practices of aristocratic Chu. Some of the poem was hopelessly obscure even to the Han royal family, whose commoner founder and his clan came from Chu.

The aristocratic culture of Chu, though partly of northern origin, ran parallel with the northern, Zhou dynasty–centered tradition for over seven hundred years. It was an amalgam of influences from the many places Chu had conquered on its way to becoming a powerful state. The wars out of which the Han dynasty emerged destroyed much of the elite literary heritage of both north and south. The losses in the south were particularly acute, and the Chu commoners who became the Han imperial family were not at first particularly eager to recover them.

The northerners were far more assiduous in reassembling the remaining fragments of their own high literary culture, and they impressed upon the interlopers from Chu that the Han imperial image depended on their assistance in the effort. By the time the Han imperial family was ready to recover the remaining fragments of Chu aristocratic culture, they had already mostly reshaped themselves as aristocrats along northern lines.

The "Li sao" was one of those cultural fragments. When it arrived in the court of the Han emperor Wu, he was struck by its beauty, the glimpse it afforded of a supernatural world, and its air of longing. Many of the gods in the poem were still objects of worship in the Han court—and the emperor was particularly interested in gods, mainly as a means to enhance his power and to prolong his life span. He, like most of the upper class of his day, believed that there existed beings called *xian* 仙, who were once human, but through methods both pharmacological and occult had transformed themselves into immortals. The poem seemed to promise information about them.

Qu Yuan, the author of the poem, was reputed to have been at odds with his king, and this interested the emperor too, for being the ruler of a relatively new dynasty he feared that those who were not convinced of the legitimacy of his family might turn against him. And like all rulers, he was especially suspicious of certain members of the ruling clan itself.

So he called in his uncle, the Prince of Huainan, who was not only an expert in literature, the culture of Chu, and the occult but also suspected of designs on the throne. When the emperor queried him on the meaning of "Li sao," he produced a disquisition with extraordinary alacrity, praising the poem and extolling the virtues of its author, especially his loyalty to his sovereign. Both he and the emperor knew that the operating principle on this occasion was that articulated in the classics: 詩言志 *shi yan zhi*—that is, "poetry verbalizes intention." In other words, what is in a person's heart is appropriately, and sometimes inadvertently, expressed in poetry. During the Han dynasty this was doubly true of commentaries on poetry.

We do not know what the Prince of Huainan had to say about the occult aspects of the "Li sao," for only a fragment of his commentary survives. His literary works were no doubt partially proscribed when he was later accused of treason, for reasons unrelated to his commentary, and preemptively committed suicide.

A certain dynamic between the reader and the "Li sao" was established by the prince's commentary. The reader, like Emperor Wu, is attracted to the poem but does not quite understand it and wants to know more. The commentator promising access appears, armed with a key—to the life of Qu Yuan. Once the commentator gives a tour of that life, he delivers a homily about loyal dissent. The commentator assures the reader that he has provided access to what the poem means, but the reader nevertheless walks away still confused about what the poem says. The commentator will insist that what the poem says and what it means are not separate. And this brings us to the major problem in traditional "Li sao" scholarship: the conflation of the poetic persona with the author, which is also the problem of making no distinction between metaphor and metaphrand, allegory and referent, what is said and what is meant. Traditional scholarship in preventing the poetic persona from speaking as him- or herself blocks the sole mouthpiece in the poem through which the author might speak.

I have already discussed in the introduction and elsewhere how and why Wang Yi interpreted the "Li sao" as he did.[1] Here I discuss the allegorical structure of the poem that removal of Wang's hermeneutical obstacles reveals. The story, in outline, is about a spirit, named True Norm, who descends from the sky attracted by the fragrances of flowers and herbs and desiring to be with the one who cultivates and wears them. That person is a ruler of a shaman kingdom named Spirit Adorned. In order to have a proper relationship with the shaman ruler, the spirit must inhabit the body of a female shaman. As their love affair proceeds, Spirit Adorned's taste in personal adornment changes and he turns to the cultivation of foul-smelling weeds to wear. He also rejects True Norm. The fragrance-loving spirit now merged with the fragrance-loving shaman feels abandoned and hurt but cannot decide whether to leave or not. After much hesitation and consultation with diviners, however, the spirit-shaman decides to leave the shaman kingdom and departs traveling through the sky in a state of triumph mixed with sorrow.

Clearly this is not the story of Qu Yuan that appears in the *Shiji*. It is a far more magical one. Yet it is not an entirely different story. If read as allegory, we might find something of the Qu Yuan story in it. But we must look elsewhere to find a story that might make it comprehensible on its own terms. Take, for example, the following passage:

> In the fifteenth year of King Hui [676–652 B.C.E.] of the Zhou dynasty, a spirit descended in the state of Xin. The king, asking Guo the court historian about it, said, "Why did this happen? Has it ever happened before?" The court historian answered, "It has happened before. When a state is on the rise, its ruler will be of consistent clarity, impartial and just, pure of spirit, benevolent and peace loving. His virtue will be such that it emits a pervasive fragrance, and his compassion will be such as to unify his people. If the spirits enjoy their sacrifices and the people are compliant—that is, if neither people nor spirits have cause for resentment—then a spirit descends to observe the merits of his government and to broadly spread good fortune on his kingdom. On the other hand, when a state is on the decline, its ruler will be greedy, perverted, given to excess, lazy, corrupt, and violent; his government will emit a foul odor, and no good fragrance will rise [to Heaven]. He will pervert the law and punish the innocent, and loyalty will stray away from the hearts of the important families. Then the spirits do not appear, and his subjects wish to be far from him—that is, both the

spirits and the people bear grudges against the ruler—and they have no one to rely on. A spirit will then descend to observe the evil of his government and spread misfortune upon it. Thus spirits appear either when a state is on the rise or when it is in decline. So when Xia was about to rise, [Zhu] Rong [祝融] descended onto Chong Mountain.[2] When it was about to fall, Hui Lu [回祿] resided for days in Qin Sui.[3] When the Shang dynasty was on the rise, Tao Wu [檮杌] appeared on Pi Mountain.[4] When it was in decline, Yi Yang [夷羊] appeared in cattle herds on the grasslands.[5] When the Zhou dynasty was on the rise, the Yuezhuo [鸑鷟] phoenix sang on Qi Mountain. When it grew weak, Du Bo [杜伯] shot the king in Hao.[6] Each of these apparitions is a matter of historical record."

The king asked, "What spirit has descended upon our kingdom?" The historian replied, "In the past King Zhao [of the Zhou dynasty] chose to marry a woman of the state of Fang. She became Queen Fang. She was in fact not a woman of strict virtue, taking very much after her ancestor Dan Zhu [丹朱].[7] Dan Zhu, possessing her body, mated with him [King Zhao] and gave birth to King Mu. Indeed, this spirit oversees the activities of the descendants of the Zhou royal house, sometimes granting good fortune and sometimes sending disaster. Spirits are exclusive and do not move far away. The spirit who has appeared in this case is probably Dan Zhu.[8]

This passage is from the *Guoyu* 國語, a Chinese historical work compiled probably between the fifth and fourth centuries B.C.E. It gives a glimpse of what might be termed pre-Confucian beliefs about the influence of spirits on statecraft and the kind of imagery associated with the beliefs.

The passage is far more useful for understanding the "Li sao" as allegory than anything that appears in the commentarial literature. Here, as in the "Li sao," spirits descend attracted by fragrances. The phrase used in the story is "the fragrance of virtue." (Interestingly, Wang Yi uses the same phrase in his "Li sao" commentary. Could he have been making a veiled reference to the mythology represented in this story?) Conversely, a bad government in the *Guoyu* emits a foul odor—let us call it "the stench of corruption"—that drives away the good spirit, just as in the "Li sao." Moreover, the spirit that King Hui is inquiring about once possessed a woman and through her had sexual relations with a ruler. As we shall see, the main spirit in the "Li sao" appears to do the same thing.

If the "Li sao" is an autobiography, it is an allegorical one where the main character is a male spirit who descends, possesses a female shaman, and through her serves a shaman ruler. The imagery works perfectly in the Chinese cosmological system, where the ruler is classified in the yang category, which includes men, and ministers, generally men, are classified in the yin category, which includes women. The cosmological intergendering of ministers in early China is represented in the poem by the merging of the female shaman with the male spirit, a characteristic of Chu shamanism.

I summarize in the following the allegory of the "Li sao" using the basic structure of the mythology represented in the *Guoyu* passage as a guide.

In the first two stanzas (lines 1–8) the speaker of the poem introduces himself by way of announcing who his ancestors were. His distant ancestor is the divine forebear of a number of royal houses, including the house of Chu. His father is another ancestral spirit of Chu, Zhu Rong, god of fire and the south. That makes the persona of the poem the son of an ancestral spirit, similar to the spirits that descend for good or ill in the cited *Guoyu* passage.

He then gives the month and day when he descended from the sky and his names. The day of his descent and the day when Zhu Rong, the god of fire and the south, according to myth, ceded his position to his younger brother (see the relevant note to the poem) are the same. His first name indicates that he is the spirit of correct principles (正則 *zhengze*). His second name indicates that he is also the spirit of fairness or justice. The strange thing about the second name is that it is a shaman name—its first syllable being *ling* 靈, meaning "spirit" or "shaman." Why the persona is given a characteristically shaman name becomes clear in lines 9–10, where he dresses himself in some of the various fragrant plants that attracted him. This behavior is similar to that of female shamans in the *Nine Songs* who seek thereby to attract male spirits. Given his shaman name, we must therefore be prepared to understand the persona not as a single personality but as a blend of female shaman and male spirit. As the poem proceeds, it becomes clear that fragrant plants represent in the "Li sao" both virtue and those who possess it. Weeds, on the other hand, represent the opposite.

The names that we encounter in the poem suggest that the ruler and the important people at court are all shamans and that the subordinates are the plants that adorn them.

In lines 13–24 the spirit expresses anxiety about the passage of time, evoking the changing seasons with plant imagery. This dovetails with his first complaint: that the ruler is neglecting the fragrant plants and allowing the fields where they grow to be overwhelmed by weeds, the first mention of that corrupting influence in the poem. Here the spirit offers his help, using the image of thoroughbred horses (symbols of good ministers) pulling a chariot (symbol of the state). Next he offers his opinion as to why the fragrant plants should not be neglected. It is an example from history—the variously identified Three Kings, whose "purity" depended on the proximity of various fragrant plants, clearly a metaphor for virtuous ministers. The image thus evoked is of shamans who purify themselves with fragrant flowers and herbs, as in the *Nine Songs*. In the next stanza, the ruler is reminded that there are two paths in statecraft—the good path represented by Yao and Shun, and the bad path, represented by Jie and Djou.[9]

In lines 33–40, the "cabal" is mentioned for the first time. The members of the cabal, it becomes clear, are the same as those represented by the weeds. The chariot metaphor predominates here. The spirit then voices his second complaint—that the ruler has believed slander, presumably concocted by the cabal, about him. The ruler is addressed as Lure Leaf, clearly the main source of the fragrance that attracted the spirit. It should be remembered that Lure Leaf (荃 Quan) is the name of the elusive divinity addressed in "The Lesser Minister of Life Spans," the sixth of the *Nine Songs* hymns. He is later called Spirit Adorned, a shaman name perhaps meaning that the ruler's "fragrance of virtue" is such that it has attracted a good spirit (as well as good officers) who now constitutes his "adornment." The names Lure Leaf and Spirit Adorned (靈修) occur in the sixth and ninth of the *Nine Songs* hymns, respectively. The spirits they name are both elusive and fickle lovers.

In lines 41–48, the spirit tells the shaman ruler that the frank criticism that won him/her his disfavor was offered only out of loyalty. Then the spirit complains that the ruler has been unfaithful. Here the spirit seems to speak in a female voice, confirming that he inhabits the body of a female shaman.

In lines 49–56, the spirit-shaman reports on his/her own herb fields (possibly a metaphor for his/her students or protégés), expressing fear that the weeds may overtake them too.

In lines 57–64, (s)he describes the greed and hypocrisy of the "crowd" (= cabal = weeds). In lines 65–72, (s)he complains that (s)he is not getting enough spirit food (fragrant herbs) to eat, indicating that the "fragrance of virtue" that attracts and maintains beneficent spirits is decreasing. This may be a figurative way of saying not only that the virtuous are losing their positions at the Chu court but also that sacrifices to the spirits, involving fragrant plants, are being neglected. Nevertheless, (s)he does manage to make clothing out of a variety of strong and mild herbs, indicating that this raiment conforms to the ancient style of Peng and Xian, two shaman ancestors. Note that the two names Peng and Xian are usually joined and are traditionally assumed to be one person. There are reasons (given in my notes to the poem) to believe they are two: Wu (Shaman) Peng and Wu (Shaman) Xian.

In lines 77–88, the spirit complains that it is his/her fragrant adornments (worn by the shaman he has merged with) that have gotten him into trouble because they are no longer in fashion. (S)he defiantly vows to continue to make and wear them nevertheless. (S)he again complains about the slander against him/her, again in the feminine voice. In lines 88–104 the spirit rails against the cabal, comparing them to bad craftsmen and buzzards.

In lines 105–28 defiance gives way to regret; here is the first hint that the spirit may decide to abandon this kingdom. (S)he wanders about the wild countryside in indecision near the plants sacred to him/her. Then, in even greater defiance than before, (s)he adorns him-/herself in more and more fragrant plants and scans the horizon considering the possibility of going elsewhere. Next (lines 120–44) a mysterious female, who is probably another shaman, Nü Xu, warns him/her against his/her conspicuous display of lofty integrity, symbolized by the garments made of fragrant plants. She begs him/her to go along with those who wear foul weeds, symbolizing corruption and corrupting influences. (From this point on I use the simple masculine pronoun, for the rest of the poem is primarily the spirit's story.) The spirit is not convinced by her advice and decides to ask the spirit of the sage-king Shun, whose tomb is on Nine Doubts Mountain, what he should do. In lines 145–84 he explains to Shun the predicament the kingdom is in, comparing the fates of corrupt rulers with those of virtuous rulers of the past. His testimony ends in tears, at which point the spirit of Shun sends him a waking dream, or vision, in which he rises into the air on a large bird pulled by dragons. What follows is the spirit's travel through both time and space, impelled by the power of Shun, in search of a bride.

The spirit first tries to enter the gates of the sky but is denied entry, an event that may stand for the loss of his king's favor or Heaven's disapproval of his failing mission to improve the moral tone of the shaman state.

He then goes on a journey back in time to find a bride among famous queens and princesses of the past, most of whom had kings for husbands. All his attempts at wooing them fail. There are many theories about what this section means, but the poem itself provides interpretations, interspersed at intervals in the description of the vision flight. I have put them in italics in the translation.

At line 257, the vision, or waking dream, having ended, the male spirit Zhengze is reunited with the female shaman Spirit Fair Share, and as one entity they seek out Ling Fen. According to Ling Fen's interpretation (lines 259–76), the vision indicates that departure from the kingdom is the appropriate course of action. The spirit, still unsure, seeks the interpretive services of one of the shaman ancestors he admires so much, Shaman Xian herself.

Using examples of outcasts of the past whose virtues and talents were recognized by wise rulers, she encourages the spirit to leave the hopelessly corrupt kingdom (lines 285–312). The rest of the poem is a description of the departure. The last line indicates the ultimate destination of the spirit, the realm of the shaman ancestors Peng and Xian, whom he has just consulted, located, it seems, somewhere west of the Kunlun Mountains. What this and the other references to Peng and Xian seem to imply is that the kingdom the spirit has left has rejected the way of the shaman ancestors.

This, I believe, is the allegory that has been suppressed for over two thousand years under layers of deflecting exegesis. Similar to allegory as it is practiced elsewhere, it is based on metaphor, with one shaman standing for the king and another for his minister, with the beneficent possessing spirit standing for the virtue inborn in the minister (and the favor of heaven embodied in the minister), with fragrant herbs that attract beneficent spirits standing for those whose influence is conducive of rectitude, and rank weeds that repel beneficent spirits standing for those whose influence corrupts. What makes the allegory particularly complex is that its political message depends on the synecdochal relationship of its images to the political realities of Chu. I have referred to the site where the allegorical drama unfolds as a "shaman kingdom." I have implied that it is a separate fictive realm for the sake of simplicity. In all probability, however, the shaman coven was the ritual core of the kingdom, connecting it to those celestial and ancestral powers on which its existence was thought to depend. In such a politico-ritual structure, ministers actually could be shamans, and the king being the chief officiant of the ritual order could in effect be the head shaman. The central complaint of the "Li sao" appears to be that the ritual order based on the traditions of Wu Peng and Wu Xian is being threatened by interlopers who claim other powers but whose influence will ultimately destroy the kingdom.

The irony is that this radically new interpretation of the "Li sao," while not figuratively rendering the story of Qu Yuan's trials as related in the *Shiji* biography in every detail (the goal of much traditional commentary), it is not entirely incongruent with it. If this interpretive road had been taken during the Han dynasty, however, Han Confucian scholars would have had to admit that Qu Yuan wrote the "Li sao" not only out of love for his "shaman kingdom"—that is, Chu—but also to defend shamanism, a practice many of them despised. Moreover, as I have said before, given the importance of the minister in Warring States political theory and practice, it is easy to imagine that the spirit who descends from Heaven to aid a good king in the *Guoyu* story quoted earlier would make a perfect metaphor for the virtuous minister. It is also easy to imagine that a virtuous, but cautious, minister might want to avoid such a metaphor. The spirit in the *Guoyu* passage is an agent sent by Heaven to show its favor. A minister who used such a metaphor to describe himself would appear arrogant, if not seditious—especially during the Han dynasty.

## Leaving My Sorrow

I am latter day kin of the god-lord Gaoyang,[10]
  My late father, august shade, was the Elder Rong.[11]
When the Grip Stars pointed at the first moon of spring,
  On the *gengyin* day, I descended from the sky.[12]

The August Ones, observing and judging my ways at the outset,[13]
  revealed in the tortoise shell cracks their fine names for me:
They named me True Norm,
  Spirit Fair-Share they chose for my cognomen.                    8

This beauty within is not my all,
  I add refinements the eye can see,
I cover myself with lovage and fragrant wild roots,
  And braid the autumn thoroughwort for belt charms.[14]

Rapid waters I'll never outrun, it seems—
  The years, I fear, will not wait for me.
At dawn on terraced hills I gathered magnolias,
  At twilight uprooted slough grass on an islet midriver.          16

Never idle sun and moon hurry,
  Fall goes to spring and spring, to fall.
See the grass and trees fading and shedding,
  Fear the twilight of your beautiful ones.

Never weeding, you offer no comfort as they flower,
  Why not change such ways?[15]
With thoroughbreds under your reins, you could drive at full gallop,[16]
  Come, let me guide your chariot on the road ahead.              24

The sagely purity of the Three Ancient Lords[17]
  Was the clear result of various fragrances crowding near,
They intermingled even prickly ash and cassia bark.
  What cord did they twine of basil and angelica alone?

Yao and Shun with their staunch integrity,
    Found their path by following the Way.
How madly Jie and Djou wandered with their sashes undone,[18]
    into dead ends along the side roads.           32

Consider the fleeting pleasures this cabal enjoys,
    on their dark and dangerously narrow road.
Do I quail at the calamity they've set there for me?
      No. That they will overturn your godly chariot—that I fear.

Around it I would run, eye on the road, front and rear,
    Till it rolled in the tracks of the ancient kings,
But, Lure Leaf, you do not look to see what I harbor within,[19]
      No, trusting slander instead you boil in sudden rage.     40

I know indeed frank talk brings trouble,
    But bear it I will; I can't stop now.
I point to the Nine Skies, let them be my witness.
    Spirit Adorned, all that I do is for you,

(You say: "Let us meet at dusk," yes, but midway you go up another
    road.)[20]

First you give me your promise,
    Later regret changes your mind. You avoid me—you have someone
    else.
It is not being abandoned I take hard,
    It is the ever fickle shifting, Spirit Adorned, that leaves an open
    wound.           48

I grew nine *wan* of boneset,[21]
    I planted one hundred *mu* of basil,
Kept separate the plots of peonies and loosestrife,[22]
    And mixed asarum with the scent roots,

Hoping for tall-standing stems and bristling leaves,
    I was willing to wait for the season to reap them.

Why would I grieve if they nonetheless withered?
  I'd mourn only if all the fragrant ones changed to weeds    56

The crowd wrangles toward you in their greed,
  Seeking and demanding with unslakeable fury.
Yes, each looks within for the rule to measure others
  Finding there nothing save a heart hopping with envy.

At full gallop they chase,
  Yet it doesn't worry me,
Old age is on its sun-slow way,
  That my adornment will never be sung is what I fear.    64

At sunrise I drink the dew magnolia blossoms shed,
  At sunset eat the withered petals of fall chrysanthemums.
As long as beauty is true in my heart and pure at my waist,
  What harm is there in looking sallow and gaunt?

I pick dry tree roots to knot together rootstocks of angelica,
  On which to string the creeping figs' fallen flowers.
With straightened cinnamon bark I twist basil into chains,
  To twine into long, gleaming ropes of garlic stems and snow
  parsley.    72

Yes, I take as my model adornments of the past,
  Not what the vulgar wear now.
Even if they offend the taste of people today,
  Gladly I hold to norms Peng and Xian have passed down.[23]

Deeply I sigh, brushing tears away,
  Lamenting mortal life's many hardships.
Despite my love of adornment, they force on me the bridle and bit,
  Yes, they vilify me by day, and send me away into the night.    80

They send me away because of my horse bellyband of basil,
  Which I lengthened with the angelica roots I gathered
For this is what my heart loves still,
  And I will never regret it, though made to die nine times.

It is your recklessness I resent, Spirit Adorned,
   You who never look to see what they hold in their hearts
They, a crowd of women who envy my moth eyebrows,
   Singing slanderous songs that call me a slut.                      88

Surely they are the vulgar idea of skilled craftsmen these days,
   Who, confronted with compass and try square, place one where
   the other should go.
They turn away from ink string to follow the crooks in the wood,
   And judge others on how well they shift shapes to conform.

Though I am anxious, choked with sorrow, reeling in despair,
   Alone, and at a dead end in these times,
I'd rather drop dead and thereby escape—
   Such postures I could not bear to assume.                          96

The buzzard does not flock,
   It has always been so.
How can round and square congrue?
   With strangers on a strange path what safety have you?

Those who curb the heart and repress the will,
   Who endure the rebukes and take the insults home in a bag,
Yet prostrate themselves before the pure, and die for what is right,
   Surely they were most honored by the sages of old.            104

Regretting I did not watch the road more carefully,
   I stop and stand a long time—but now I am going back,
Turning my chariot around, retracing my tracks,
   Before I find myself too far lost.

I walk my horse slowly through the Thoroughwort Marshes,
   Then gallop to rest in the Pepper Hills.
If I approached they would abuse me, shutting me out,
   So I'll reteat to fashion anew the things I used to wear—    112

I make a jacket of water-chestnut leaves,
   And pick lotus flowers to fashion a robe.

If they think me worthless, let it be,
　　As long as the heart within me is truly fragrant.

My tottering headdress I'll make taller,
　　My motley dragging sashes, longer,
Adding fragrant plants that mix with mire,
　　But never lose their luster.　　　　　　　　　　　　120

Suddenly turning, I let my eyes wander.
　　I will go and look as far as the Four Wilds,
Waist bristling with luxuriant adornments,
　　Their fragrance overpowering, wafting everywhere.

Everyone knows from birth what brings them delight.
　　I, loving adornment alone, make it my constant.
Though they dismembered my body, that would not change.
　　How could that chasten a heart such as mine?　　　128

Sister Nü Xu, bewildered,[24]
　　Chided me again and again,
Saying, "Gun being stubborn was heedless of his own welfare,
　　And wound up dead in the Feather Mountain wilds.[25]

"So how is it that you, lover of adornment, speak the unadorned truth?
　　You alone bear this tangle of beautiful trappings;
The others fill our house with puncture vine, hairy joint grass, and
　　cocklebur.[26]
　　Yet here you stand, conspicuous and lonely, refusing to wear
　　them.　　　　　　　　　　　　　　　　　　　　136

"There are too many, you cannot explain yourself door to door,
　　Who among them cares to look inside our hearts?
They're a generation of side-by-sides on the rise, loving their little
　　gang,
　　How can you be so lofty and aloof that you won't listen even to me?"

"Better to look to the sages of long ago to fairly judge my case,"
　　I thought, sighing with sinking heart that it had come to this.

Crossing the Yuan and Xiang Rivers I journeyed south,
    And when I reached Chonghua, I laid my case before him:[27]  144

"When Lord Qi let them hear the Nine Variations and Nine Songs,
    The House of Xia gave itself to untethered pleasure.
He ignored, as he plotted the future, the oncoming disaster,
    As his five sons waged war within his own house.[28]

"In his zest for the fields, Bowman Yi grew addicted to hunting,
    The giant foxes, his favorite game.[29]
Good endings are rare for the depraved and reckless—
    But Zhuo made it worse when he debauched the bowman's
    wife.[30]                                                     152

"Ao wore the toughest armor on his chest,
    but could not curb his lust once he freed the reins.
In the daily revel he lost himself,
    And then his head fell off and hit the ground.[31]

"King Jie's perversions,
    Ended in catastrophe for the royal house of Xia.[32]
Lord Xin dissected and pickled his ministers in vats of brine,
    And thus cut short the Yin royal line.[33]                    160

"Kings Tang and Yu were majestic and reverent.[34]
    The House of Zhou found their path by choosing the Way.
Elevating the worthy, employing the able,
    They cut along the ink string's line and never strayed.

"The August Heavens have no favorites.
    Where they see someone of virtue there they send their help.
Only the sagely and wise strive to do likewise,
    If they win sway over these lands below.[35]                  168

"Look to the past, turn your eyes to the future,
    Keep in view the ultimate purpose of anyone's plan!
Who can be employed who is unprincipled?
    What can be worn that is not fine?[36]

"Standing close to the cliff's edge I risk death,
    But looking back at how we began I have no regrets.
Cutting the haft before measuring the socket
    Was always why the Adorned of old wound up in brine." 176

Sigh over sob, gagging on grief,
    Lamenting the unfitness of my times,
I raised the soft basil to brush away snivel and tears
    That wave over wave soaked my robe's lapels.

I was kneeling, robe skirts outspread, stating my case,
    When in a blaze of light I received his verdict as follows:
Riding a motley shade bird, hitched to a jade dragon quadriga,[37]
    I'm suddenly journeying upward on a dust-flown wind.[38] 184

I set forth in the morning from Cangwu,[39]
    And by nightfall reach the Hovering Gardens.[40]
And would linger awhile near the Spirit Doors,[41]
    But the sun is on its way down.

So I order Xihe to slow her chariot's pace,[42]
    And keep her eye on Yanzi Mountain, but linger far away,[43]
For on and on the road stretches far,
    where I'll search high and low. 192

I water my horse at the Xian Pool[44]
    Tie its reins to the *fusang* tree,[45]
Break off Ruo-tree branches to brush the sun dry,[46]
    And for a moment wander free and easy.

Ahead I send Wangshu, the moon's charioteer, as my herald,[47]
    Behind, Feilian, the Wind God, to serve as rear guard.[48]
Male simurghs are my forerunners,[49]
    And the Lord of Thunder will warn me of the unforeseen. 200

Then I make my phoenix bird soar higher,[50]
    Without stopping, through day and night.

Now the Whirlwind mustering his entourage,
    Comes to receive me, leading clouds and rainbows.

The clouds, a great confusion of many shapes, some parting, some
    merging—
    The rainbows, above and below, luminous colors in long arching
    bands.
I order the gateman of the Sky Lord to open the Sky Gates,
    But leaning against them he stares at me distantly.[51]        208

Long I wait, as the darkening hours close the day,
    knotting hidden boneset flowers.
*(Chonghua seemed to be saying, People in these times having muddied*
    *the waters make no distinctions,*
*All envy and jealousy, they set barriers in the way of the beautiful.)*

Morning, I am about to cross the White Waters,[52]
    And climb Langfeng Peak to tether my horses.[53]
Not long after looking around, my tears are streaming,
    I am grieving there are no women on this high peak,       216

When suddenly, here I am, wandering in this Palace of Spring.[54]
    I break off branches from the jade tree to add to my belt charms.[55]
Before the blooming flowers fall,
    I will seek to give them to a deserving woman on a lower plane.

I order Fenglong, Lord of Thunder, to ride a cloud,[56]
    To find the place where Consort Fu dwells.[57]
I unknot my ornate belt for an engagement gift,
    And order Bell Stones to be my intermediary.[58]       224

The consort is a great confusion of many shapes, some parting, some
    merging,
    And suddenly perverse and contrary she is difficult to move.
In the evening she goes home to spend the night at Qiongshi;[59]
    But washes her hair at Weipan in the morning.[60]

Let her keep her beauty, arrogance, and pride,
    And amuse herself lewdly in daily revels.
Beautiful indeed she is, but lacks decorum.
        Come, let us leave her and look elsewhere.                    232

I look, examining, observing, as far as the four limits,
    Wandering over all the sky, and then descend.
I see in the distance the involute majesty of the Jade Tower,
    Where I catch sight of the beautiful daughters of Lord Song,[61]

I order the *zhen* bird to be my go-between.
    The *zhen* bird tells me she is no good for such work.[62]
But the male *jiu* bird cries, "I'll go,"[63]
    Yet, since I despise his deviousness,                             240

My heart swithers in doubt;
    I want to go myself, but that is never done.
The phoenix soon accepts my gift for the sisters,
    But fearing Gao Xin has reached them before me,

It tries to perch far away but there was no place to rest.
    So it floats awhile idling adrift.[64]
I might make the two Yao women of Youyu mine
    Before Shao Kang marries them,[65]                               248

But my messengers are timid and my go-betweens inept—
    I fear their introductions would assure me nothing.
*(Chonghua seemed to be saying, People in these times having muddied*
    *the waters envy the worthy,*
    *Setting barriers in the path of the beautiful, their praise goes to the*
    *ugly.)*

His inner chamber is deep underground,
    Nor will the wise king ever rise from his slumber.[66]
Hiding, to air never, the love in my heart,
    How can I go on like this forever?                               256

I searched for the *qiong* straw and slips of bamboo,[67]
    And had Ling Fen cast them to interpret my vision.[68]
The oracle said, "Two beauties will find each other.
    Is mate-finding labor for those of true beauty?[69]

"Think of the vastness of the Nine Regions,
    How could it be there are women here only?"
Ling Fen interpreted: "Force yourself to go far away and have no
    doubts;
    Why would a seeker of beauty reject you?        264

"What place is so unique as to have no fragrant herbs?
    What is there to cherish in your old home?
A generation reared in darkness whose eyes can't bear bright light?
    Who among them can distinguish good from bad in us?

"Could it be that people are *not* all the same in their likes and dislikes?
    Consider the singular oddity of this cabal—
They wear mugwort, filling their sashes with it,
    And deem wild thoroughwort unwearable.        272

"If their eyes cannot tell one plant from another,
    How could they appraise the quality of jade?
They gather dung and soil into scent bags and wear them,
    And call Shen pepper unfragrant."[70]

I wanted to follow Ling Fen's auspicious oracle,
    But my heart swithered in doubt.
Shaman Xian was bound to descend that evening,
    So I welcomed her with crossed lapels stuffed with pepper and
    rice.[71]        280

Her spirit crowd, like a vast canopy, descended over us,
    As the spirits of Nine Doubts thronged to welcome her.
The Majestic One manifesting her power in blazing light,
    Told me why the oracle was auspicious:

She said, "Force yourself to ascend and descend, search high and low,
    Till you find someone whose try square is as true as yours.
Tang and Yu earnestly sought their match in others,
    And with Zhi and Gao Yao they found harmony.[72]            288

"As long as they saw one bent on beautifying the heart,
    What need had they to send the matchmakers?
Though Yue labored pounding earth walls at Fuyan,[73]
    Wu Ding made him his minister and had no doubts.

"Though Lü Wang swung a butcher's knife at Zhaoge,[74]
    When he met Wen of Zhou he managed to rise high.
Ning Qi sang.[75]
    Duke Huan of Qi heard, and brought him back to complete his
    staff.                                                      296

"Avail yourself of your still abundant years;
    Your time is not yet past.
Fear only that the cuckoo might call before then,[76]
    Causing all the herbs to lose their fragrance.

"How intricate and majestic your belt of jade-tree branches,
    The screenlike crowd will block it from view.
Be mindful—members of the cabal are not to be trusted;
    I fear that they in their envy will tear it off you.          304

"The times are in the snarl and snag of change—
    Why delay your departure longer?
The thoroughwort root has turned, fragrant no more.
    Lure leaf and basil have gone to straw.

"Why where fragrant herbs grew yesterday,
    mere sagebrush and mugwort grow today?
What other reason can it be
    Than the treachery of scorners of true adornment."            312

I thought Thoroughwort was one on whom I could rely,
    But she yields no fruit, being mere ornament.

She rejected her own beauty to follow the vulgar;
  She deserves no more to rank among the fragrant.

Pepper, master of flattery, is arrogant and insolent too.
  And Prickly Ash's fondest wish is to stuff herself into someone's scent sachet.
  They seek advancement—they work for favor.
What sort of fragrance can they muster?                                    320

Since it is the nature of the common run to go with the flow,
  Who can last here uncorrupted?
See how Pepper and Thoroughwort are no different from the others?
  How much worse Loosestrife and Lovage must be!

Think how precious this belt of ornaments is—
  When the others rejected its beauty, it suffered as well,
But its far-reaching scent does not easily fade,
  Its fragrance endures even today.                                       328

Adjusting my ways in accord with the oracle, I will find my own joy.
  For the time being, I will wander free seeking a woman,
While my adornments still flourish,
  Traveling everywhere, observing the high and the low.

After pronouncing the auspicious oracle,
  Ling Fen divined an auspicious day for me to set forth,
And broke off a jade-tree branch to make his food offering to me,[77]
  And ground the fallen fragments of jade for my travel grain.  336

And he harnessed flying dragons for me,
  And made a chariot of *yao* stones and ivory.
How can hearts gone separate ways be joined again?
  I will be the stranger now, and journey far away.

Turning my path back toward those Kunlun Mountains,
  Up a long and spiraling road,
I unfurl the shade of clouds and rainbows over my head,
  Jingling raucously my simurgh harness bells of jade,[78]            344

Setting forth from the Celestial Ford in the morning,[79]
    Reaching the Western Limit by evening,[80]
With phoenixes winging in the train of my banners,[81]
    Flapping and gliding aloft in orderly ranks.

Suddenly here I am traveling over Flowing Sands[82]
    Then along Red Waters where I idle free,
Signaling the water dragons to bridge the ford with their forms,[83]
    Summoning the August One of the West to guide me across.[84] 352

Aware that the journey would be long and perilous,
    I order my convoy to clear the way straight to our destination,
To take the road past Imperfect Mountain and turn left,[85]
    And I point to the Western Sea as our place to reassemble.[86]

Then I muster a thousand chariots to come with me,
    Jade axle cap to jade axle cap we gallop abreast,
Driving eight undulating dragons,
    Cloud banners flying in rolling waves.                                    360

Yet I restrain myself and slow down,
    For my spirit speeds high into the vast distance,[87]
Where players play the Nine Songs—and dancers dance the Shao dances,
    My spirit seizing the time to enjoy them.[88]

But as we ascend toward the effulgent festival of the August Ones,[89]
    We suddenly catch sight of our former home below.
My chariot driver seems about to weep, my steeds, looking pensive,
    Crane their necks to look back—they will go no farther.        368

Let us be clear:[90]

It is hopeless! The state has no statesmen![91] And no one sees value in me.[92]
Why remain attached to my old home, the royal city?[93]
Since no one is up to the task of working with me toward beautiful rule,
I will follow Peng and Xian, and go where they dwell.[94]

## NOTES

1. For details, see Gopal Sukhu, *The Shaman and the Heresiarch: A New Interpretation of the "Li Sao"* (Albany: SUNY Press, 2012).

2. Zhu Rong is a fire spirit and lord of the south.

3. Hui Lu is a fire spirit, the younger brother of Zhu Rong, who took his place and bore the same title.

4. Tao Wu is also known as Gun. He was charged by Yao with controlling the Great Flood and failed. Yao consequently killed him on Feather Mountain (羽山 Yu Shan), where his spirit assumed the shape of a golden bear.

5. Yi Yang is a theriomorphic divinity about whom little is known.

6. Du Bo was murdered in cold blood by King Xuan of the Zhou dynasty. Three years later King Xuan assembled his feudal lords for the royal hunt. Suddenly Du Bo appeared wearing red clothes and a red hat, carrying a red bow, and with red arrows he killed the king.

7. Dan Zhu was one of the sons of Yao.

8. *Guoyu* 國語 (Shanghai 1987 reprint of Shangwu 1934 edition of the *Song Mingdao er nian* 宋明道二年 text of 1033), "Zhou yu shang" 周語上, 10–11.

9. The name of the bad last ruler of the Shang dynasty is usually transliterated "Zhou," but here I, following some of my colleagues, have transliterated it as "Djou" to distinguish it from the identical transliteration in, for example, "Zhou dynasty."

10. Wang Yi says that Gaoyang 高陽 was the title of Zhuan Xu 顓頊 when he was "ruler of the world." This accords with the Han idea that Zhuan Xu was the sage-king who ruled (coming after Shao Hao 少昊 and before Di Ku 帝嚳) two dynasties before the sage-king Yao. In the extant indisputably pre-Qin texts, however, Gaoyang is never identified with Zhuan Xu. He is represented as one of the Heavenly Powers 帝, or God-Lords; see Burton Watson, trans., *Basic Writings of Mo Tzu, Hsün Tzu, and Han Fei Tzu*, Translations from the Asian Classics, Records of Civilization: Sources and Studies, no. 74 (New York: Columbia University Press, 1963), 56–57. This may mean that the Han account represents a tradition that was not represented in pre-Qin texts, that we know of.

11. The text has Bo Yong 伯庸, a name that seems to occur nowhere else. I have followed the theory of Rao Zongyi. In *Chuci dili kao* 楚辭地理考 (Shanghai: Shangwu yinshuguan, 1946), 7–10, he notes that in a Southern Song text titled *Lu shi* 路史, the "Yong" of Bo Yong is used to write the "Rong" of Zhu Rong 祝融, and that in a number of pre-Qin texts, such as the Chu Silk Manuscript, "Rong" is frequently written with characters interchangeable with ancient forms of "Yong." Zhu Rong was one of the ancestral spirits of the Chu royal house and a descendant of Zhuan Xu (Gaoyang). According to "Chu shijia" 楚世家; see Sima Qian 司馬遷,

*Shiji* 史記 (Beijing: Zhonghua shuju, 1992), 40:1689, his original name was Chong Li 重黎, who, it should be noted, is two people, Chong and Li, according to some texts. Zhu Rong was a title given him by the legendary King Di Ku 帝嚳 when he employed him as his governor of fire (*huozheng* 火正). When the legendary villain Gonggong 共工 rebelled, Di Ku sent Zhu Rong to punish him, but Zhu Rong did not complete the mission. Di Ku therefore executed Zhu Rong on the *gengyin* 庚寅 day ("the first day" in my translation) and appointed Wuhui 吳回, Zhu Rong's younger brother, in his place. The younger brother thus assumed the title of Zhu Rong. Since the "Bo" in Bo Yong means "elder" and Yong is just another way of writing Rong, it would appear that Bo Yong is Bo Rong, i.e., the elder Zhu Rong.

12. For the ancient Chinese technical terms for marking years, months, and days in this passage, see David Hawkes, *Songs of the South: An Ancient Chinese Anthology of Poems by Qu Yuan and Other Poets* (Harmondsworth, U.K.: Penguin, 1985), 79–82. It should be noted here that *gengyin*, although the twenty-seventh day of the sixty-day cycle, is the first day of spring in this context, where Meng Zou 孟陬 is the first month of spring and the adverb *zhen* 貞 implies that the Sheti 攝提 stars are now indicating its beginning. I was once convinced by Wang Yi's explication of Sheti as an abbreviation of the term Shetige 攝提格, a name for the first month of the ancient Chinese twelve-month cycle, beginning in *yin* 寅, but, like Hawkes, I have come to see the reasonability of Zhu Xi's explanation in the "Chuci bianzheng shang" 楚辭辯證上 section of *Chuci jizhu* 楚辭集注, ed. Jiang Lifu 蔣立甫 (Shanghai: Shanghai guji chubanshe, 2001). *Gengyin* is also the day the younger brother of Zhu Rong, Wuhui, was appointed to his position as governor of fire.

13. The August Ones (皇 Huang) are the ancestral spirits in Heaven.

14. *Jiangli* 江離 is the modern *chuanxiong* 川芎, which was a food, a fragrance that was worn in the clothes, and a remedy for head ailments, among other things. See Pan Fujun 潘富俊, *Chuci zhiwu tujian* 楚辭植物圖鑒 (Shanghai: Shanghai shudian, 2003), 16–17. The English term for this plant is lovage. *Qiulan*, or "autumn thoroughwort," is the late-flowering *Eupatorium japonicum* (or *chinense*), which flowers and fruits from June to November. It is a fragrance, an apotropaic plant, an insect repellent, a soap, and a general purifier. Confucius called it 王者之香 *wangzhe zhi xiang*, "the royal fragrance." See Pan, *Chuci zhiwu tujian*, 20–21.

15. Following the Hong Xingzu text and taking *zhuang* 壯 to refer to the flourishing stage of flora as per elsewhere in the poem; see Hong Xingzu 洪興祖, *Chuci buzhu* 楚辭補注 (Beijing: Zhonghua shuju, 1986), 6–7 and 42.

16. Qi 騏 and Ji 驥 are mythical fine horses capable of traveling a thousand *li* in a day.

17. There are many theories about the Sanhou 三后. I take the term to refer to the three legendary founders of Chu: Zhu Rong 祝融, Yu Yin 粥飲, and Laotong 老童.

18. Jie 桀 is the bad last king of the Xia dynasty and Djou 紂 is the bad last king of the Shang. They are the stock opposites of the sage-kings Yao and Shun.

19. *Quan* 荃 (*Acorus calamus*) has an alternative name, *sun* 蓀. Both terms occur in the *Nine Songs*; "Li sao" has *quan* only. In the *Zhouli* ("Tian guan jiazai"), it is used in sacrifice; wine was poured onto bound bunches of it to convey the wine to the spirits. It grows near water and is fragrant. According to Hong Xingzu, it was used as fish bait. Hong Xingzu quotes a passage from the *Zhuangzi*: "When one catches the fish, one forgets the *quan* [得魚而忘荃]" (*Chuci buzhu*, 9). I therefore call it lure leaf. It is used as a term of endearment here, but if it was meant to be read in the light of the *Zhuangzi* statement, it could have a level of irony if not sarcasm.

20. Hong Xingzu thinks these lines were added later. Many scholars do no include them. I take them as supernumerary lines.

21. There are a number of theories about how large a *wan* 畹 was; it was different at different times. During the Han it was thirty *mu* 畝, but Wang Yi tells us that here it means twelve *mu*, by which he may mean the measure during the Warring States era. In any event, nine *wan* is larger than one hundred *mu*.

22. *Jieju* 揭車 is *Lysimachia clethroides*, or gooseneck loosestrife, which, though fragrant, is highly invasive.

23. No one is entirely sure about the identity of Peng Xian. The earliest occurrence of the name is in "Li sao." Wang Yi writes that he was a grandee of the Shang dynasty who committed suicide by drowning when his king rejected his advice. The idea that Peng Xian was a loyal minister who had drowned seems implied in lines 42–43 (Hawkes's translation) of Liu Xiang's "Li shi" 離世 (Leaving the world) from the "Nine Sighs" (九歎 Jiu tan) section of the *Chuci*; the origin of the idea that he was a grandee of the Shang is unknown. I have followed Gu Jiegang, who followed Liao Ping, in taking Peng Xian as an abbreviation of two names, Wu Peng and Wu Xian; see Gu Jiegang 顧頡剛, *Shilin zashi: Peng Xian* 史林雜識。彭咸 (Beijing: Zhonghua shuju, 1978), 202. Peng and Xian in fact are names of diviners inscribed in the Shang oracle bones; see Guo Moruo 郭沫若, *Buci tongzuan* 卜辭通纂 (Beijing: Kexue chubanshe, 1983), nos. 237, 525, 786, 795.

24. No one is sure about the identity of Nü Xu 女嬃. As I pointed out earlier, shamanesses and supernatural women often have names with Nü as the first element; see chapter 4. Wang Yi, basing himself on a gloss from the now lost commentary of Jia Kui tells us that sisters are called Xu in the state of Chu. He was therefore of the opinion that Nü Xu was Qu Yuan's sister. I think that she is a shaman "sister" in the same coven as Ling Jun. The term *xu* means "secondary wife" in the *Book of Changes*. Such a name makes sense if we think of Ling Jun as the primary wife of Ling Xiu.

25. Gun is the father of Yu, mythical founder of the Xia dynasty. According to the "Yao dian" section of the *Shujing*, Yao gives Gun the task of stopping the Great

Flood—reluctantly because Gun is *fang ming* 方命, "disobedient to orders" (Legge's translation; see James Legge, *The Chinese Classics*, 5 vols. [Oxford: Clarendon Press, 1893–1894; repr., Hong Kong: Hong Kong University Press, 1960], 3:25). In the *Wen xuan* version of "Li sao," *wang* 亡 is written *fang* 方. This has prompted some scholars to believe that the phrase *wang shen* 亡身 is a miscopying of *fang ming* 方命. *Wang* and *fang* are often confused, but not *shen* and *ming*. It seems more likely that *wang*, "disappear," was confused with *wang* 忘, "forget," as Wen Yiduo 聞一多 pointed out (*Li sao jiegu* 離騷解詁 [Shanghai: Shanghai guji chubanshe, 1985], 28). Gun failed in his mission and was consequently executed near Feather Mountain. According to another version of the myth, he was executed for carrying out the mission but inadvertently throwing the five elements out of order (Ruan Yuan 阮元, *Shisanjing zhushu* 十三經注疏 [Beijing: Zhonghua shuju, 1987], 122 and 128). In some versions it is Shun who kills him, and in others it is Yao.

26. Puncture vine (*ci* 薋), *Tribulus terrestris*; hairy joint grass (*lu* 菉), *Arthraxon hispidus*; and cocklebur (*shi* 葹), *Xanthium sibiricum*, are all noxious and highly invasive weeds. See Pan, *Chuci zhiwu tujian*, 52–57.

27. Chonghua is a title of the sage-king Shun. He is buried on a mountain called Jiuyi 九疑 (meaning "Nine Doubts") near the source of the Xiang River in southern Hunan, where he died while attacking the Miao tribes. Shun is also a descendant of Zhuan Xu's and is also sometimes referred to by the title Gaoyang.

28. Hong Xingzu does not follow Wang Yi's attempt to reconcile these lines with Confucian literature, where Qi is a virtuous person. In the *Mencius*, for example, Qi "was good and capable and able to follow in the footsteps of Yu [his father and founder of the Xia dynasty]" (D. C. Lau, trans., *Mencius* [Harmondsworth, U.K.: Penguin, 1970], 145). Hong instead quotes the *Shanhaijing*, according to which, "The Lord of Xia [Qi] was a guest in Heaven three times. He obtained the Nine Variations and the Nine Songs and came down" (Hong, *Chuci buzhu*, 21). The Guo Pu commentary says, "Both are names of the Celestial Lord's music. Qi, ascending to Heaven, stole them, came down, and enjoyed them." There is also a quotation in the *Mozi*, from a lost work titled *Wu Guan* 武觀, which states, "Qi gave himself up to pleasure and music, eating and drinking in the open fields. *Qiang, qiang* the flutes and chimes sounded in unison. He drowned himself in wine and behaved indecently by eating in the fields. Splendid was the Wan dance, but Heaven clearly heard the sound and Heaven did not approve" (Watson, *Basic Writings of Mo Tzu*, 116; *Mozi jiangu* 墨子閒詁, vol. 3 of *Zhuzi jicheng* 諸子集成 [Shanghai: Shanghai shudian, 1987], 161–62). Here we have an image of Qi that is less virtuous than that we see in the classics.

The "five sons" alluded to here are those of Qi, son of the founder of the Xia dynasty, initiator of the practice of hereditary monarchy, and celestial music thief. They are sometimes called Wu Guan 五觀, or the Five Guans, after the place where their princedoms were located. Confusingly, in some texts Wu Guan is the name of the youngest of the sons. His name can be written Wu Guan 五觀 (Five or Fifth Guan) or Wu Guan 武觀 (Martial Guan), giving rise to uncertainty in some texts as to whether Wu Guan is one son or the five. "Li sao" appears to be alluding to elements found in at least two stories about Qi and his sons. The first is that found in the *Zhushu jinian* 竹書紀年 (帝啟十一年 "Di Qi Shiyi nian"), which tells us that after Qi took to dancing the "Nine Zhao" out in the fields, he banished Wu Guan to Xihe. Later Wu Guan rebelled against his father. The other story is from the "Changmai" 嘗麥 section of the *Yi zhoushu* 逸周書, which tells of the "five sons" who forgot the mandate of Yu and rebelled because of the corruption in the royal household (presumably an allusion to their father's revelry). For the best discussion of these and other accounts, see Jin Kaicheng 金開誠, Dong Hongli 董洪利, and Gao Luming 高路明, *Qu Yuan ji jiaozhu* 屈原集校注, 2 vols. (Beijing: Zhonghua shuju, 1996), 1:71–74. Their discussion on this question is based mostly on the commentary of Wang Yingzhi 王引之, quoted in You Guo'en 游國恩, *Li sao zuanyi* 離騷纂義 (Beijing: Zhonghua shudian, 1982), 219.

29. Yi 羿 is usually associated with the story of the ten suns, which one day rose together, threatening the world with hot disaster. The story, in which Yi is the hero who shoots down nine of the suns, seems to have originated during the Han dynasty. In pre-Han sources Yi is something of a villain (see Bernhard Karlgren, "Legends and Cults in Ancient China," *Bulletin of the Museum of Far Eastern Antiquities*, no. 18 [1946]: 267, 272, 294, 311, 323, 326) who has nothing to do with the story of the ten suns. He did, however, shoot at the sun—not to save the world but as an act of hubris. Karlgren believed that the "Tian wen" 天問 (Hong, *Chuci buzhu*, 96) section of the *Chuci*, where it is not clear where Yi is shooting at one or many suns, is the basis of the Han myth of Yi the mighty archer.

The Han myth, as exemplified in such sources as the *Huainanzi*, places Yi in the time of Yao, but the pre-Han sources place him in the Xia dynasty. The pre-Han Yi is a usurper who took advantage of the weakness of the Xia and "relied on his skill in archery, neglected the affairs of the people, and hunted excessively" (*Zuozhuan*, Xianggong, 4th year; see Legge, *The Chinese Classics*, 5:424).

30. Zhuo is also known as Han Zhuo 寒浞. He was the prime minister of Yi. Zhuo took advantage of discontent in Yi's household by inciting the staff to murder him, cook his remains, and serve them to Yi's sons. Refusing to partake, they were killed by Zhuo. He then took Yi's kingdom and Yi's wife, begat two sons, and conquered two other states. A certain Mi united the remains of the two states, overthrew Zhuo, and set Shao Kang (of the original Xia line of Yu) on the throne. See Legge, *The Chinese Classics*, 5:424.

31. Ao 澆 (also pronounced Jiao) is one of the sons of Zhuo. He managed to kill

Xiang, the King of Xia, but Min, the Queen of Xia, escaped and bore Shao Kang, who overthrew Ao and restored the Xia dynasty. See *Zuozhuan*, Xianggong, 4th year; Legge, *The Chinese Classics*, 5:424.

32. Jie 桀 is that bad last king of the Xia dynasty.

33. Lord Xin 后辛 is another way of referring to Djou 紂, the bad last king of the Shang (also known as the Yin) dynasty. He is famous for dismembering dissenting ministers and pickling them in salt.

34. Tang 湯 and Yu 禹 are the founders of the Shang and Xia dynasties, respectively. Xia came before the Shang, and mentioning the two founders out of order is unusual but not unprecedented. To do so makes a pun, for Tang (Great) is also one of the epithets of Yu.

35. This passage—夫維聖哲以茂行兮苟得用此下土—is a source of much dispute among the commentators. Wang Yi glosses it this way: "*Zhe* [哲] means intelligent. *Mao* [茂] means flourishing. *Xia tu* [下土] means all under Heaven. It says that as for those Heaven sets up to be rulers, only those with intelligence of sagely brilliance and with behavior [*xing*] of flourishing virtue therefore obtain power in the world and become lords of the people." Hong Xingzu, Wang Fuzhi, and many other commentators followed his implied reading of *gou* 苟 as *gu* 故 (therefore) or *nai* 乃 (so) (You, *Li sao zuanyi*, 232–33). One of the dissenters was Wang Bangcai, who wrote, "In my humble opinion the sentence should be read in the same way as the ["Li sao"] line, 'If my heart is truly fragrant' [苟余情其信芳], which is to say that it should be taken as an inverted sentence." I have taken his advice, translating *gou* as "if." I have also taken Dai Zhen's and Wu Shishang's advice in taking *mao* 茂 as a borrowing for *mou* 懋, which means "to work hard at" or "make an effort" (勉) (You, *Li sao zuanyi*, 233).

36. Or, who can be served who is not good?

37. The motley shade bird (Yi, 鷖 or 翳) was envisioned by some as a giant particolored gull whose flight blocked the light of the sun. See Hong, *Chuci buzhu*, 25–26.

38. There is no reason to read 埃 as a mistake for *si* 竢, as Wang Fuzhi, Hawkes, and others have done. *Ai feng* 埃風, "dusty wind," is a phrase attested in the "Xiaoyou" section of the *Zhuangzi*. If *ke* 溘 (suddenly) is left untranslated (as in the Hawkes translation), the drama of the passage is lost.

39. Cangwu 蒼梧 is the mountain near or on which Shun (Chonghua) is buried. It is another name for Jiuyi Mountain.

40. Xuan Pu 縣圃 are Hovering Gardens because they are on the summit of the Kunlun Mountains, directly above which the doorway to the sky ("Spirit Doors" in the poem) is located.

41. *Ling suo* 靈瑣 means "spirit chain pattern." The chain pattern was a decoration on palace doors; by metonymy, it means door (Hong, *Chuci buzhu*, 27). The door in

question is the entry to Heaven above the Kunlun Mountains. The Yi bird has within a day taken him from south-central China to the far west.

42. Xihe 羲和 was the female charioteer of the sun, said by some to be his mother.

43. Yanzi 崦嵫 is the mountain in the far west where the sun goes down.

44. Xian Chi 咸池, or Xian Pool, is the place where the sun bathes in the course of rising. Some say it is a star name (see Yuan Ke, *Zhongguo shenhua chuanshuo cidian* 中國神話傳說詞典 [Shanghai: Shanghai cishu, 1985], 265). Here the persona is traveling beyond the west and circling back to the east, sunwise.

45. The *fusang* 扶桑 is the tree the sun uses to dry itself after its bath at the Xian Pool by rubbing against it or beating itself with its branches, Finnish sauna–style (see ibid., 191).

46. There are a number of accounts about the Ruo tree. In the *Shanhaijing*, "Hainei jing," it is situated in the south and is the source of the Ruo River. In the "Dong-huang beijing" of the same work, it is situated in the west. According to the *Shuowen jiezi*, it is the same as the *fusang* (see Yuan, *Zhongguo shenhua chuans-huo cidian*, 228). The *Shuowen* explanation appears to apply here. The persona is poetically referring to the *fusang* tree, where his chariot is tied, by another name. Hong Xingzu, however, has it growing at Kunlun in the west, where it marks the entrance for the setting sun.

   *Fu ri* 拂日 means "to brush or strike the sun"—to dry it after its bath. On the morning routine of the sun, see *Huainanzi*, vol. 7 of *Zhuzi jicheng*, 44.

47. For Wangshu 望舒, see Yuan, *Zhongguo shenhua chuanshuo cidian*, 366.

48. Feilian 飛廉 is the Wind God, according to Wang Yi. Hong Xingzu describes it as a supernatural beast with a deer's body, a magpie's head, and horns. See ibid., 40.

49. Following the *Wen xuan* commentary by Li Zhouhan (one of the Five Ministers), as well as the *Li sao jizhuan* 離騷集傳 of Qian Gaozhi 錢杲之 of the Song, I take *luanhuang* 鸞皇 as the male of the *luan* bird, which Hong Xingzu, quoting the *Shanhaijing*, describes as patterned with all the five colors, having a call like a pheasant's, and a long tail—a bird of extraordinary intelligence whose appearance foreshadows an era of tranquility. See You, *Li sao zuanyi*, 272.

50. The *feng niao* 鳳鳥, phoenix bird or phoenixlike bird, refers to the Yi bird on which he rides.

51. For Changhe 閶闔 (Sky Gates), see Yuan, *Zhongguo shenhua chuanshuo cidian*, 361. It is the main entrance to the palace of the Lord of the Sky (Tian Di 天帝). This is the persona's second visit here; before, the Sky Gates were called Ling Suo 靈瑣.

52. The White Waters (Bai Shui 白水) emerge from the Kunlun Mountains, according to Wang Yi, who tells us, "Drink thereof and never die"; see You, *Li sao zuanyi*, 287. Note that this is the persona's second visit to the Kunlun Mountains in the far west after following the path of the sun from sunset to sunrise to noon, etc.

53. Langfeng 閬風 is the legendary location of the Hovering Gardens high in the Kunlun Mountains. See Yuan, *Zhongguo shenhua chuanshuo cidian*, 328.

54. The Palace of Spring (Chun Gong 春宮) is explained by Wang Yi as "the residence of the Green Lord of the East," who is sometimes identified as Fuxi 伏羲. It is also the name of a constellation that rules spring. See ibid., 264.

55. *Qiong* 瓊 is a term for the most precious gems, especially jade. Most scholars think that this is a tree of jade. The next line implies that its flower wilts like any other flower, meaning perhaps that it is somewhere between mineral and plant. If that is the case, this would be the first time anything close to a nonfloral ornament had been attached to the persona's belt. Yuan Ke, quoting a passage from the *Zhuangzi* that does not appear in modern editions, tells us that the *qiong* tree is the preferred perch of the *fenghuang*, or phoenix. He appears to be following Wen, *Li sao jiegu*, 47, as well as the *Taiping yulan* 太平御覽, and other sources. The translation of the passage is as follows: "In the south there is a bird called the *feng* for which Heaven produced a tree called the *qiongzhi*. It is 220 *ren* high and 30 ambits in circumference. It has precious stones for fruit" (Yuan, *Zhongguo shenhua chuanshuo cidian*, 374; see also line 335).

56. Wang Yi tells us that Fenglong 豐隆 is also known as Leishi 雷師 (Master of Thunder). According to Hong Xingzu, this divinity is also known as the Cloud God and is the object of worship in the hymn "Yunzhong jun" (Lord in the Clouds) of the *Nine Songs*. His other name is Pingyi 屏翳. He is Heaven's messenger and is also known as a diviner specializing in predicting rain. See You, *Li sao zuanyi*, 301.

57. Fufei 宓妃 is most famously represented as the spirit of the Luo River in Cao Zhi's 曹植 "Luo shen fu" 洛神賦. The earliest reference to her is here in "Li sao." Wang Yi tells us simply that she is a goddess. Later scholars identified her as the daughter of Fuxi. The Fu 宓 in her name is interchangeable with the Fu 伏 in Fuxi's name. The *fei* 妃 in her name means "consort," which has led some scholars to identify her as the consort of Fuxi. Of course her name could also mean that she is a consort named Fu, which would allow her to be the daughter of Fuxi and a consort, but whose consort is unclear. The persona in "Li sao" complains that she is the consort of many. The description of her behavior in line 225 is the same as the description of clouds in line 205, referring, I believe, both to her fickleness and her association with clouds.

58. Jian Xiu 謇脩 is not a name that occurs anywhere else. Who he or she is no one knows. Zhang Taiyan 章太炎 (You, *Li sao zuanyi*, 308) directs us to the *Erya*, which tells us that when someone plays musical stones solo. it is called *jian* 謇, and when musical bells are played solo, it is called *xiu* 脩 (Xu Chaohua 徐朝華, ed., *Erya jinzhu* 爾雅今注 [Tianjin: Nankai daxue chubanshe, 1987], 195). There are many depictions of stone and bell players on ancient artifacts, especially from Chu. I have therefore translated Jianxiu as Bell Stones.

59. Qiongshi 窮石, according to *Zuozhuan*, Xianggong, 4th year, was where Archer Yi went when the Xia showed signs of decline. Archer Yi killed the Earl of the Yellow River and stole his wife, the Lady of the Luo, according to "Tian wen." The Lady of the Luo is Fufei. Thus when she goes home to Qiongshi, she is returning to her second husband, Archer Yi.

60. Weipan 洧盤, according to Wang Yi, is a river that flows from Yanzi 崦嵫 Mountain; nothing else is known about it.

61. Yousong 有娀 is the name of an obscure and probably legendary state, whose ruler had two beautiful daughters he housed in a tower, according to "Tian wen," "Li sao," and the *Lüshi chunqiu*. One of the daughters was Jian Di 簡狄, who, according to *Shijing* 304, became impregnated by eating the egg of a swallow. In another account (*Shiji*, "Yin benji") she was impregnated by swallowing an egg dropped by a black bird that flew by while she was bathing with her legendary sage-king husband, Gao Xin 高辛. The child she bore in either case was the founder of the Shang dynasty. As it says in *Shijing* 303, "Heaven ordered the black bird to descend and bear Shang." Heaven in that case probably refers to Gao Xin, who was thought to reside there as a *di*. The black bird is a messenger from Heaven. Hawkes thinks that in "Li sao," the black bird has been transformed into a phoenix. I think this is highly unlikely. The persona of "Li sao" hopes to marry the daughters of Lord Yousong before Gao Xin does; he is not Gao Xin.

62. *Zhen* 鴆, according to Duan Yucai's 段玉裁 notes to the *Shuowen jiezi* 說文解字, is a poisonous bird whose wing, if dipped in wine, will kill the drinker. *Zhen* poisoning is written *zhen* 酖 in the *Zuozhuan*; see, e.g., Mingong, 1st year (閔公元年), *Chunqiu Zuozhuan zhengyi* 春秋左传正义, in Ruan, *Shisanjing zhushu*, 1786. *Zhen* is also known as *yunri* 運日 and always calls to herald the clearing of clouds from the sky; see You, *Li sao zuanyi*, 326. Most translators follow Qian Gaozhi 錢杲之 and others in reading *bu hao* 不好 as the *zhen* 鴆 bird's claim that Jian Di and her sister were not beautiful. Hong Xingzu and Zhu Xi, however, take it to mean that the *zhen* bird is refusing the mission because of her inappropriateness as a go-between. I follow them. See You, *Li sao zuanyi*, 324–26.

63. Translated by analogy with *you you lu ming* 呦呦鹿鳴 in *Shijing* 161.

64. I follow the Qing scholars Qian Gaozhi 錢杲之 and Xu Huanlong 徐煥龍 in taking the subject of all the verbs in lines 243–46 as the phoenix; see You, *Li sao zuanyi*, 332–33.

65. According to *Zuozhuan*, Aigong, 1st year, when Jiao (or Ao), the son of Zhuo, killed the King of Xia, his queen, who was pregnant, escaped to find refuge with the Lord of Youreng, where she gave birth to Shao Kang 少康. He later became chief herdsman of Youreng. He also had a stint working in the kitchen. Jiao eventually sent someone after Shao Kang, who then escaped to the state of Youyu. The chief of Youyu 有虞, Yusi 虞思, then gave the two Yao 姚 women to him as wives. Yao is the name of the sage-king Shun's clan. Shao Kang, after killing the

sons of Jiao, restored the Xia dynasty. See *Chunqiu Zuozhuan*, Aigong, 1st year, in Ruan, *Shisanjing zhushu*, 2154.

66. The wise king (*zhe wang* 哲王) referred to here is Shun, before whose grave the persona had the vision he has just described. The design of ancient tombs followed the plan of a house. The coffin sat in a space that corresponded to the "inner chamber," or master bedroom; in the case of a palace, the inner chambers would also be the women's quarters.

67. Tang Bingzheng has argued convincingly that *zhe zhu* 折竹 in Wang Yi's gloss on *tingzhuan* 筵篿 is in fact a mistake for *ce* 策, meaning "bamboo slips," a common divination tool; see Tang Bingzheng 湯炳正, *Chuci leigao* 楚辭類稿 (Chengdu: Bashu chubanshe, 1988), 214.

68. *Zhi* 之 has as its antecedent the vision just experienced.

69. Some scholars (e.g., Wen Yiduo, in *Li sao jiegu*, 52–53) claim that *zhan zhi* 占之 does not rhyme with *mu zhi* 慕之. That opinion has motivated a number of emendations of the text. Hawkes followed Wen Yiduo in taking *mu* as a conflation of *mo* 莫 and nian 念. Tang Bingzheng (*Chuci leigao*, 216–17) and Ma Maoyuan (*Chuci zhushi* [Wuhan: Hubei renmin chubanshe, 1985], 52–53), following the good advice of Zhu Xi, observe that the rhyming of two *zhi* 之 occurs several times in the *Chuci*. Nevertheless *mu* in its normal meaning gives little sense. I believe that *mu* in this case is another way of writing a character with the same pronunciation and the same form except that the heart radical is on the side—i.e., 慔. The meaning of this character is "to work hard, exert oneself," etc. It is a phonetic variation of the character *mao* 懋 (Bernhard Karlgren, *Grammata Serica Recensa* [Stockholm: Museum of Far Eastern Antiquities, 1957], 1109f), which also means "work hard," etc. Zhu Junsheng 朱駿聲, in *Shuowen tongxun ding sheng* 說文通訓定聲 (Wuhan: Wuhan shi guji shudian, 1983), 417, tells us that this was a common borrowing.

70. I follow Xia Dalin 夏大霖, Yao Nai 姚鼐, and You Guo'en in taking this line as the end of Ling Fen's speech. See You, *Li sao zuanyi*, 370.

71. The term *wu* 巫 originally referred to a female shaman. I suspect that the conservative shaman who wrote "Li sao" still understood it that way.

72. Zhi 摯 is the name of Yi Yin 伊尹, legendary virtuous minister of Tang 湯, founder of the Shang dynasty. Qu Yuan is punning on another meaning of the name—i.e., "take hold of." The name thus does double duty. It means "taking hold of Gao Yao" and also "Zhi and Gao Yao." Gao Yao 咎繇 (also written 皋陶) was the legendary virtuous minister of Yu 禹, founder of the Xia dynasty. The punning here corresponds to the punning in the previous line, where Tang and Yu are mentioned out of chronological order so that Tang can serve double duty as the name of the founder of the Shang dynasty and as the same word meaning "great," giving the phrase "Great Yu, the founder of the Xia dynasty."

73. See the introduction, note 4.

74. See the introduction, note 5.

75. Ning Qi 甯戚 lived during the Spring and Autumn period, and before he was discovered worked as a petty merchant. According to the legend, he was feeding a cow one day when King Huan of Qi happened to pass by. Ning Qi, seeing him, attracted his attention by singing while striking the horn of the cow. Something about the singing signaled to Duke Huan that the singer was an extraordinary person. He consequently elevated him to ministership. For a pre-Qin account, see, e.g., "Junan pian" 舉難篇, in *Lüshi chunqiu*, vol. 6 of *Zhuzi jicheng*, 253–54. For a translation of the same passage, see John Knoblock and Jeffrey Riegel, trans., *The Annals of Lü Buwei: A Complete Translation and Study* (Stanford, Calif.: Stanford University Press, 2001), 507–8. See also Jiang, *Chuci tonggu*, 2:132–37.

76. The *tijue* 鵜鴂, or "cuckoo." Some say that its cry announces the end of spring; others say it announces the beginning of fall. See You, *Li sao zuanyi*, 405–11.

77. The word *xiu* 羞 indicates a sacrificial offering of meat. Ling Fen is in effect performing a ritual sacrifice to Ling Jun.

78. Bells hung from the horse's bit were often in the shape of the fabulous *luan* 鸞 bird.

79. The Tian Jin 天津, Celestial Ford, is a group of nine stars in Cygnus near the middle of the Milky Way (the Tian He 天河, or "Sky River" in Chinese).

80. The Xiji 西極, or Western Limit, is the western edge of the world.

81. There is much controversy surrounding 承旂; the solutions of Liu Mengpeng and Zhu Ji are tempting (see especially You, *Li sao zuanyi*, 456–57). I will not introduce the various other theories here, as the specialist will already be familiar with them. Suffice it to say that I tentatively take *cheng* 承 as a substitute for *cheng* 丞, as it is used in, e.g., *Zuozhuan*, Aigong, 18th year, meaning "assistant commander" or "lieutenant." See *Chunqiu Zuozhuan*, Aigong, 18th year, in Ruan, *Shisanjing zhushu*, 1:2180.

82. Liusha 流沙, or Flowing Sands, is a riverlike desert on the verge of which the Kunlun Mountains rise. There are other places called Flowing Sands as well. See Yuan, *Zhongguo shenhua chuanshuo cidian*, 333.

83. The 赤水, or Red Waters, flow from the southeast of the Kunlun Mountains, then meander. Zhuangzi in the "Tiandi" 天地 chapter mentions them when he recounts the Yellow Emperor's trip to the Kunlun Mountains (north of the Red Waters), during which he lost his *xuan zhu* 玄珠, or "dark pearl." See ibid., 193–94. See also *Shanhaijing*, "Hainei xijing."

84. Xi Huang 西皇, the August One of the West, is usually identified as the legendary sage-king Shao Hao 少皞. See Yuan, *Zhongguo shenhua chuanshuo cidian*, 78.

85. Buzhou Shan 不周山, or Imperfect Mountain, is located to the northwest of the Kunlun Mountains. Its peak was lopped off during a battle between Zhuan Xu

and Gonggong, who were fighting for the rulership of Heaven. Gonggong angrily rammed into one of the pillars holding up the sky, damaging it—that pillar was the mountain that would afterward be called Buzhou. The force of Gonggong's impact moved the ground in such a way that the southeastern sector of China lost ground to the northwest, causing the rivers to flow southeast. See ibid., 53–54. See also *Huainanzi*, 35.

86. The Xi Hai 西海, or Western Sea, is mentioned often in the *Shanhaijing*. One passage from the "Dahuang xijing" section of that work clarifies somewhat the geography in this passage. It says, "South of the Western Sea, on the verge of the Flowing Sands, and after the Red Waters, but before the Black Waters, there are tall mountains called the Kunlun Mountains." The general direction of the journey is from southeast to northwest. See the discussion in You, *Li sao zuanyi*, 478–80. See also the discussion of this passage (on which my interpretation is based) in Jin, Dong, and Gao, *Qu Yuan ji jiaozhu*, 1:173–74.

87. My interpretation is influenced by the interpretations of Chen Benli 陳本禮 and Bi Dachen 畢大琛, who see this flying spirit episode as part of a dream. They, like most traditional commentators, recognize no distinction between the persona of the poem and Qu Yuan but at least can conceive of a nonfigurative interpretation of the sudden occurrence of the word *shen* 神. I believe, however, that here the shaman and the possessing spirit are momentarily somewhat at odds. See You, *Li sao zuanyi*, 485.

88. Reading 婾 as 偷, not as 愉. See Jiang, *Chuci tonggu*, 1:627–28.

89. *Hexi* 赫戲 means "blazing" or "effulgent," but I think that the use of *xi* 戲 (play) in place of the usual *xi* 曦 is not accidental; it is another "Li sao" pun.

90. The word *luan* 亂, which usually means "to confuse," could also be translated as "envoi," a kind of poetic epilogue. Some scholars think it can mean "to clear up confusion" or "summarize the main point." I have followed that idea only here in my translation. See Wang Yi's and Hong Xingzu's explanations in Hong, *Chuci buzhu*, 47.

91. The phrase *guo wu ren* 國無人 (there are no [states]men in the state) was frequently used in Warring States political discourse. For example, in the *Guanzi* 管子, "Mingfa" 明法 chapter, it says "The loyal minister is executed though not a criminal, but the evil minister rises though having no merit. Thus, to be someone's minister is to consider what pertains to the private individual important and to consider what pertains to one's ruler trivial. Ten will arrive at the door of the private individual, but no one will arrive at court. One hundred will concern themselves with their families, but not one will plan for the state. Though the number of those attached to him will be legion, it will not be because they honor the ruler. Though one has a complete staff of officials, it will not be because they carry the burden of the state. This is what is called *having no men in the state*.

*Having no men in the state* is not a matter of the weakness of courtly ministers. Family benefits family, but they make no effort to honor their ruler. Great minister enriches great minister, but they do not carry the burden of the state. The minor ministers use their emoluments to cultivate connections and do not see their official positions as service. Thus officialdom loses its power" (Dai Wang 戴望, *Guanzi jiaozheng* 管子校正, vol. 5 of *Zhuzi jicheng*, 259). See also the quotation of this passage in Tang Bingzheng, *Chuci leigao*, 234–36.

92. *Mo wo zhi* 莫我知 may be an allusion to *Lunyu*, "Xian wen," 35, where Confucius says the same thing. See *Lunyu zhushu* 論語注疏, in Ruan, *Shisanjing zhushu*, 2513.

93. To abandon the royal city is to leave it to the depredations of another spirit, who will surely destroy it.

94. Wu Peng 巫彭 and Wu Xian 巫咸 reside in the Kunlun Mountains according to the *Shanhaijing*. This may also refer to any place where the ritualists who consider them their ancestors are active and honored.

# CHAPTER THREE

# "Ask the Sky"

# 天問

# "Tian wen"

Sima Qian placed "Tian wen" after the "Li sao" on his list of Qu Yuan's works. Of all the canonical works of ancient Chinese poetry, it is indeed second only to the "Li sao"—in strangeness. One reason for this is that the poem is made up almost entirely of questions. There are about one hundred seventy of them, in fact, on topics ranging from the origin of the universe, the sky, the earth, the myths associated with them, early dynastic history, right down to the political situation in Warring States Chu. There is a note of skepticism, if not irony, that runs through the poem, for while some of the questions appear to be riddles with possible answers, many of the questions are either unanswerable or invite logical answers that would render self-contradictory or absurd traditional lore. As Lu Xun put it, the poem "speaks without restraint or fear saying things the ancients never dared to say" ("Molo shili shuo," quoted in Tang Zhangping and Lu Yongpin, *Chuci lunxi* [Taiyuan: Shanxi jiaoyu chubanshe, 1990], 136).

In the course of its attempt at a comprehensive questioning of received wisdom, the poem alludes to many myths and legends that were forgotten by the later tradition. It is therefore one of the most valuable sources for the study of early Chinese religion, folklore, and history.

Wang Yi explained the title in terms that Hawkes and others found ludicrous: the word order, he tells us, should be "Wen tian" which means "ask the sky," but the word order was changed because Heaven is too exalted to have the verb placed in front of it, so the verb was placed behind it. This may sound absurd, but it is only a Han schoolman's way of extracting a Confucian homily from a mere case of inversion, where the object is placed before the verb for emphasis—a common maneuver in classical Chinese. Despite his odd exegesis, I follow Wang Yi's reading and translate "Tian wen" as "Ask the Sky" or "Ask the *Sky*," a version of the almost universal response to unanswerable questions: *only Heaven knows.*

His account of the origin of the poem is another matter, for it involves making up yet another story about Qu Yuan. According to it, the poet, while in exile, used to wander about the countryside in a state of anguish, resting from time to time in aristocratic ancestral temples, on the walls of which were painted pictures illustrating ancient legend and history. Lacking anything else to do, he wrote inscriptions on the murals. These were later collected and arranged into the text of "Tian wen" that we still have today. This is at best a clumsy attempt to explain a poem whose combination of structure, content, and length seemed odd even to Han-dynasty readers.

It was thought that a poem composed almost exclusively of questions was unique in the history of Chinese literature until the relatively recent publication of a text, *Fan wu liu xing* 凡物流形, which is one of a group of Chu bamboo manuscripts discovered in 1994 and now housed in the Shanghai Museum. Part of that text consists of a long list of questions in verse, for example:

> If all things are flowing form,
> How does it take shape?
> If flowing form becomes bodies,
> How is it that it does not die?
> Once it takes shape and is born,
> How does it look about and how does it make a sound?

*Fan wu liu xing* covers much of the same territory as "Ask the Sky," in the opinion of some scholars from a Daoist point of view. It also includes a section consisting of what appear to be answers. In the confused state of the text (written on bamboo slips that got mixed up), however, it is still difficult to determine which questions go with which answers. In any event, "Ask the Sky" is now no longer considered unique. Yet the same questions asked about it are asked about *Fan wu liu xing*: who wrote it, in what context, and why compose a poem consisting primarily of questions?

**Ask the Sky**

We ask:

Deep in the past, at the very beginning of everything,
    who was there to tell us what it was like?
If up and down had not yet formed,
    from what position could one observe it?[1]

In the blear dusk before the parting of darkness and light,
    who could find beginning or end?
If no phenomenon was other than simmering chaos,
    through what sense did one experience it?[2]

Dawn breaks, night falls.
    But consider time: what is that?
There are three mixtures of yin and yang.
    Which is the original? Which are variants?[3]

Nine nested spheres is the sky.
    Who designed it?
What work that must have been.
    Who began it?[4]

Where is the rope attached that turns it?
    In what hub is the Pole inserted?
At what points do the eight pillars uphold it?
    Why is there a gap in the southeast horizon?[5]

If each of the Nine Regions has its own sky,
    How do the skies fit together,

With their complex jagged edges
    And who knows how many junctures?[6]

Where does the sky meet the land?
    Why is it divided by twelve?
How did the sun and moon find their places
    and the fixed stars their positions?[7]

If you rise from the Valley of Dawn
    and stop for the night at the Dimming Stream,
from dawn to dusk
    how many miles have you traveled?[8]

Night's brightest light has what power
    that after it dies it is reborn?
And what does it gain
    by rearing a rabbit in its belly?[9]

If Our Lady of Forked Paths had nothing to do with men,
    where did she get her nine sons?
Where dwells the Earl of Violence?
    Where are his kinder airs?[10]

Night falls when what doors close?
    Dawn breaks when what doors open?
Before the Horn Stars call for light,
    where does the effulgent spirit hide?[11]

If Gun lacked the wherewithal to stem the flood,
    why did the multitude recommend him,
all of them saying, "What is there to fear?
    Why not to let him try?"?[12]

Each biting the tail ahead, owls and tortoises formed a chain.
    Why did Gun take them as his guide?
He'd have finished the work just as everyone wished—
    why did the Sky Lord punish him?[13]

Gun was stopped for good on Feather Mountain.
  Why was he not cut open for three years?
Elder Yu emerged from his belly.
  What caused the miracle and metamorphosis?[14]

Succeeding his father, Yu shouldered the task
  and successfully completed the mission.
How did he continue his father's work
  with a different plan of action?[15]

If the deepest depths hid the source of the flood,
  how did he stop the flow?
He divided the earth into the Nine Regions.
  How did he surround them with earth walls?

Why did the winged dragon score the earth?
  Why do rivers pass to the sea?[16]

What parts of the work were Gun's planning?
  What parts were Yu's work?
When Kang Hui raged,
  why did the earth sink in the southeast?[17]

How were the Nine Regions plotted?
  How were streams and valleys hollowed out?
Rivers run east to the sea, but it never overflows:
  Does anyone know why?

East to west or south to north,
  Which is farther?
If the world is an oval, longer from south to north,
  How much longer?

On what sit the Hovering Gardens
  of Mount Kunlun?
How many miles high are the storied walls
  In nine layers around them?[18]

On Kunlun there are gates in all directions:
    Who goes through them?
When the gate in the northwest is open
    What wind comes through it?[19]

In what place does the sun not shine?
    How does the lamp dragon illuminate it?
Before Xihe lifts her child the sun,
    How do hibiscus blossoms shed light?[20]

Where is winter hot?
    Where is summer cold?
Where is the forest of stone?
    What animal can talk?[21]

Where did the hornless dragon go wandering
    with a bear on its back?[22]

The nine-headed poisonous snake
    is fast but where does it dwell?[23]

Where is the land where no one dies?
    What places have a guardian giant?[24]

When duckweed spread to the nine crossroads,
    Where did the red blooming cannabis find a home?
How big must a snake be
    To swallow an elephant?[25]

Where are the Black Waters, the Black Toe Peak,
    and Three Danger mountain,
places to go to never die?
    But where go the deathless to end their lives?[26]

Where is the fish with a human face?
    Where do the monster sparrows live?

Why did Yi shoot arrows at the suns?
   Why did the ravens shed their feathers?[27]

Yu devoted his energy to the task,
   but, when he came down to inspect all under the sky,
how did he happen to meet the daughter of Mud Hill
   and mate with her under the Towering Mulberries?[28]

Though he loved her and made her his wife
   to continue his family's line,
how is it his tastes so differed from most
   that he was content with but a morning's satisfaction?

Qi displaced Yee and became king,
   but found himself in sudden trouble.
How did Qi free himself from prison
   by simply worrying?[29]

The warriors all laid down their arms,
   refusing to harm his person.
Why was Yee's kingship stripped from him
   while the seed of Yu prospered?[30]

The Nine Songs and the dance of the Nine Variations
   Were Qi's prize for his many visits to the Sky Lord.
Why did the Lord help the son but slaughter the mother,
   scattering her body in shards on the ground?[31]

Then the Sky sent Yi the barbarian archer down
   To save the people of Xia from calamity.
Why did he shoot the Yellow River Earl
   and carry away his Lady of the Lo?[32]

Thumb ring on, he drew to the full the nacreous bow,
   and pierced with arrows the giant boar.
When he offered up this fattest of meats,
   why did the Sky Lord ignore him?

Zhuo took Madame Pure Fox,
    the benighting wife of Yi, with whom he plotted.
How was Yi, who could shoot through layers of thickest leather,
    consumed by so many mouths?[33]

Badlands cut off Gun's westward escape.
    How did he jump the cliffs?
He changed into a golden-haired bear.
    How did the shamans revive him?[34]

He had everyone plant black millet
    once they cleared away the reeds.
Why then did they cast Gun out
    hating him utterly and forever?[35]

A white nimbus encircled and veiled.
    What did it do in Cui Wenzi's house?
How did he come by the long-life elixir?
    And why could he not keep it secure?[36]

Alternating opposites is the way of heaven.
    When yang departs the body dies.
Why did the great bird call,
    and how did it lose its original form?

Ping calls and the rain comes down.
    How does he make it rise?
How does a deer stomach
    Being part bird?[37]

How do big turtles balance mountains on their heads
    While clapping their flippers
If the Big Turtle left his "boat" to walk on land,
    How could he keep his mountain from floating away?[38]

Big Turtle was at the door.
    What did he want from his sister-in-law?

How is it that Shao Kang went hunting with dogs,
    while Big Turtle lost his head?[39]

Our Lady of Forked Paths mended Big Turtle's clothes,
    and they spent the night in the lodge.
Why did the wrong head fall—hers,
    as she risked all for love?

Tang sought to bring the masses to his side.
    How did he benefit them?
After Ao capsized the boat at Zhenxun,
    what way was left to capture them?[40]

When Jie attacked Meng Mountain,
    what did he gain?
Why was Moxi so utterly unmoored?
    And how did Tang punish her?[41]

Shun lived at home with a single worry:
    Why had his father kept him a bachelor?
If Yao had not informed Shun's parents first,
    how could he marry two daughters to him?[42]

When Djou's luxury was just sprouting,
    who guessed how tall it would grow?
When he built a ten-story tower of jade,
    who foresaw where it would end?[43]

She rose to the status of Lord of the Skies.
    By what path did she get there?
Nü Wa had a body too.
    Whose handiwork was that?[44]

Shun deferred to his younger brother Elephant,
    but in the end suffered at his hands.
How could Elephant act the cur and the swine,
    yet never see danger or defeat?[45]

The state of Wu managed to last,
    expanding as far as the Southern Mountains.
Who could have predicted such a thing
    when the two men first arrived?[46]

Swan adorned and jade embedded were the vessels
    from which dined the Lord of the Skies.[47]
Why would he grant Jie the kingdom of Xia
    Only to cut off the Xia royal line?[48]

Then the Lord of the Skies came down to inspect,
    and found himself face-to-face with Yi Yin.
After Jie suffered the Tendril exile,
    why did his subjects rejoice in surrender?

If Lady Jiandi was hidden in a tower,
    how did Di Ku choose her for a wife?
When the Dark Bird delivered the gift,
    why was she delighted?[49]

In good works, Hai took up where Ji, his father
    and model of virtue, left off.
So why did he end up dying in Youhu
    herding those cows and goats?[50]

He danced the shield dance—
    why did he long for her?
Whose luscious flesh hid the ripple of her ribs?
    And how did she fatten herself?[51]

He was but a herd boy in Youyi—
    how did he meet her?
She got out before the attackers reached their bed.
    From whom had the order come?[52]

In virtue Heng took up where his father Ji left off.
    How did he obtain his brother's draft oxen?

Why did he go to administer the rewards
      instead of merely returning?[53]

Twilight Wei was next in line to the throne;
      Youdi would know no peace then.
How could she abandon her child and yield to passion
      with so many birds perched in the brambles?[54]

And the benighted brother, being as lewd as he was,
      endangered the older Hai.
How could such changeable and deceitful men
      produce such glorious and enduring posterity?[55]

Tang the Accomplished reached the Youshen kingdom
      during his eastern tour.
Why, when he begged for a mere servant,
      did he receive a lucky consort?[56]

She found an infant beside the river
      in the trunk of a living tree.
Why did they so hate him that he had to go
      with the Youshen bride as part of her dowry?[57]

The prison at the Double Source let Tang go,
      but what crime had he committed?
Failing, for once, at restraint, he praised himself before the Sky Lord.
      Who talked him into it?[58]

That morning we met with him, eager to swear the sacred oath.
      How is it we all arrived at the same time?
A kettle of hawks high in the air—
      what brings them together?[59]

King Fa hacked apart the body of Djou.
      Shu Dan did not approve.
Why, having looked deep into the heart of Fa,
      did he secure, with many sighs, the Mandate for Zhou?[60]

Heaven granted the House of Yin rule over all the lands
    as a prize for what merit?
Yet, after Yin rose, it was overthrown,
    as penalty for what crime?[61]

They wrangled to be first to send their forces.
    How did they dispatch them?
Together they sped forward to attack both flanks.
    How were they commanded?[62]

Lord Zhao came to the end of his wanderings
    when he arrived in the southland.
What benefit did he bring
    to deserve the white pheasant?[63]

King Mu of Zhou was an expert charioteer,
    but why leave no place untraveled?
Journeying to the far corners of the kingdom,
    what was he looking for?[64]

The demon couple dragged their wares in to hawk.
    What did they yell in the marketplace?
Whom did King You of Zhou punish,
    and how did he win Lady Baosi?[65]

Heaven's Mandate is changeable.
    Whom does it punish, whom does it bless?
Though he gathered his allies many times,
    Huan of Qi ended up a victim.[66]

That evil King Djou,
    who disordered his mind?
Why despise loyal ministers
    and trust slander and flattery instead?[67]

How was Bi Gan so contrary
    that it sank him?

How was Lei Kai so compliant
    that it entitled him?[68]

How can sages share one virtue
    but, in the end, have different ways?
Mei Bo was turned into mincemeat;
    Ji Zi pretended to be insane.[69]

Ji was the first son.
    Why did the Sky Lord hate him so?
When they cast him out onto the icy ground,
    why did the birds keep him warm?[70]

How is it that his archery skills
    were so uncommon that he could serve as commander?
He gave the Sky Lord such a horrific shock.
    Why was he granted glorious posterity?[71]

Bo Chang shouted his orders to the languishing masses.
    Holding the whip he acted as their herdsman.
Why did Heaven have him destroy the earth altar at Qi
    and grant him sway over the kingdom of Yin?[72]

They moved all that they owned to Qi.
    On whom else could they depend?
Yin had a woman leading his mind astray,
    but who warned him?[73]

Shou served him the minced and pickled bodies.
    The Earl of the West reported the crime to Heaven.
Why did Djou call down Heaven's punishment on himself?
    What way was that to save Yin from doom?[74]

Master Wang was in his shop.
    How did Chang know his true nature?
His knife beating time, his voice aloft,
    What about him pleased Earl Chang?[75]

Martial King Fa set forth to destroy Yin.
    Why such rage?
Charging in a chariot that bore his father's corpse.
    Why so impetuous?[76]

He hanged himself in the Northern Forest,
    for what reason?
What moved Heaven and struck the earth,
    frightening the fears of whom away?[77]

When August Heaven is about to make someone king,
    how does it alert him?
Once it charges him with the ordering rites,
    why send someone else to replace him?

At first Tang made Zhi [Yi Yin] his slave.
    Later he made him close adviser.
How did he remain Tang's minister, even after death,
    honored with sacrifices along with the royal line?[78]

Eminent Shou Meng's grandson
    suffered separation and banishment in his youth.
How is it that he grew up to become brave and fierce
    and was able to make known his dignity everywhere?[79]

Peng Keng offered up pheasant stew.
    Why did the Sky Lord relish it so?
He rewarded him with such a long life.
    Why was Peng not satisfied?[80]

Together in the center they guided the herd.
    Why did the sovereign rage at them?
Bees and ants, tiny lives—
    what made their efforts sure to succeed?[81]

They surprised a woman by picking ferns.
    How did the deer help them?

Going north they arrived at a bend in the river.
     Why were both happy to settle there?[82]

The older brother had a wild dog.
     Why did the younger brother want it?
He got it for a hundred *liang*,
     but wound up losing his income.[83]

Thunder and lightning at twilight—
     Return! Why worry?
If we do not even maintain our prestige,
     what can we expect from the Lord of the Sky?[84]

If I hide in a cave,
     what then will I have to say?

In its heyday, Chu raised great armies.
     How long could it last?

If you wake up and change your ways,
     I'll have nothing to say.

Guang of Wu struggled to be king of his state
     and was long victorious over us.[85]

Circling villages and passing through hamlets,
     she found her way to the hills
to indulge in an unseemly act.
     How could she have produced a Zi Wen?[86]

I [Zi Wen] informed him about why
     Du Ao's reign was not long.
How could one who killed his king to take the throne
     come to fame far and wide for his loyalty?[87]

# NOTES

1. "Tian wen" (henceforth TW) is not an account of the beginning of the universe; it alludes to several accounts while asking skeptical questions about them. China has several cosmogonic myths. Some have anthropomorphic agents such as Pangu 盤古, who, confronted by chaos, separated it into yin and yang (complementary opposites such as light and dark or earth and sky) with a gigantic ax. Impersonal forces such as the Dao figure in others. A recently discovered manuscript from the ancient state of Chu, called *Taiyi sheng shui* 太一生水 (The grand one generates water), posits Taiyi (Great Unity or the Grand One), which is sometimes taken as another name for the Dao, as the origin, which at the primal stage gives birth to water, which then evolves into the universe. See Sarah Allan, "The Great One, Water, and the *Laozi*: New Light from Guodian," *T'oung Pao*, 2nd ser., 89, fasc. 4/5 (2003): 237–85. The writer of "Tian wen" may also be alluding to theories such as the one found in the "Heaven and Earth" chapter of the *Zhuangzi*, which holds that in the beginning there was nonbeing. See Burton Watson, trans., *The Complete Works of Chuang Tzu* (New York: Columbia University Press, 1970), 131–32. For quotations from the relevant old commentaries on this section and the rest of the poem, see You Guo'en 游國恩, *Tian wen zuanyi* 天問纂義 (Taipei: Hongye wenhua, 1993), 12–14.

2. There are a number of similarities between this section of TW and the beginning of the "Celestial Patterns" (天文 "Tianwen"), chapter 3, of the *Huainanzi*. Here the phrase *pingyi* 馮翼 is used to describe the chaotic state before the formation of Heaven and Earth. The beginning of the "Celestial Patterns" section, in the original Chinese, uses the expression *pingping yiyi* 馮馮翼翼. The sinologist John Major generously shared with me an unpublished draft for a book chapter that demonstrates how certain sections of the *Huainanzi*, especially chapters 3 and 4, provide answers to many of the questions asked in the early sections of TW, often in the same order. The first three quarters or so of chapter 3, for example, seem to correspond intentionally with sections 1–8 of TW. See John S. Major et al., trans., *The Huainanzi: A Guide to the Theory and Practice of Government in Early Han China* (New York: Columbia University Press, 2010).

3. *Shi* 時 (time) in this passage is usually read as a substitute for *shi* 是 (this), as it was by Hawkes. By taking it as written, I am following Tang Bingzheng 湯炳正, Li Daming 李大明, Li Cheng 李誠, and Xiong Liangzhi 熊良知, *Chuci jinzhu* 楚辭 今注 (Shanghai: Shanghai guji chubanshe, 1997), 82. There is much debate about the meaning of *san he* 三合, some scholars recommending that it be taken as an alternative writing of *canhe* 參合 (combine). In this passage, *san he*, I believe, should be taken as written; it refers to the *three* (*san*) possible *combinations* (*he*) of yin and yang: (1) equal yin and yang, (2) more yin, and (3) more yang. I was

inspired by the discussion of this passage in Jin Kaicheng 金開誠, Dong Hongli 董洪利, and Gao Luming 高路明, *Qu Yuan ji jiaozhu* 屈原集校注, 2 vols. (Beijing: Zhonghua shuju, 1996), 2:298, especially their quote from the *Yuanchen ji* 元辰 紀, a text with which I am unfamiliar. I did not adopt their interpretation of *san he* as yin, yang, and heaven, however.

4. The sky in many accounts is described as a hemispherical cover over the earth. The *Yijing* tells us the sky is a sphere, though some took "sphere" to mean "hemisphere." See the commentaries on this passage by Qing scholars Xu Wenjing 徐文靖 and Jiang Ji 蔣驥 in You, *Tian wen zuanyi*, 29, where Jiang Ji is quoted citing the theory that the nine skies enclose the earth like the layers of an onion. The notion that the sky was a sphere around the earth was also held by Yang Xiong (53 B.C.E.–18 C.E.), according to Su Xuelin 蘇雪林. See Su, *Tian wen zheng jian* 天問正簡 (Taipei: Wenjin, 1992), 57, for this and other theories about the shape of the sky. See also Jin, Dong, and Gao, *Qu Yuan ji jiaozhu*, 2:298–99. This TW passage seems to allude to the idea that the sky consists of nested spheres, like an onion enclosing the earth.

5. There has been much controversy over the centuries about the meaning of these lines. Wang Yi took *guan* 斡 to mean "turn" and *wei* 維 to mean "cord." One of the main points of contention is whether this "turning cord" is the one attached to the Big Dipper's handle, which turns to indicate the seasons, or the *si wei* 四維, "four cords" or "four corners," each midway between the four cardinal directions (northeast, southwest, etc.). Wen Yiduo (1899–1946), in *Tian wen shitian* 天問釋天, pointed out that one of the ancient meanings of *guan* (or *wo*) (in the *Shuowen jiezi*, but accessible through the *Hanyu da cidian*) is a dipper (or ladle) handle. The three stars that make up the handle of the Big Dipper are called, in Chinese, the *wei xing* 維星, or "cord stars," for the ancients saw only the distance from the cup of the dipper to the first star as the handle and the rest of the stars as forming a cord.

6. The sky was once thought to be divided up into nine sections (this time not in vertical layers but in side-by-side fields known as *fenye* 分野) that correspond to the Nine Regions (九州 Jiu Zhou) of China. In effect, each region (or "province") of China had its own sky. In theory, land and sky are divided equally. In fact, the borders between the terrestrial regions are irregular. The question posed here is how could the celestial regions (*fenye*) correspond exactly to the earthly ones. The Pole is slightly off center because in ancient times the divinity Gonggong 共工 rammed against one of the pillars holding up the sky in a rage over his defeat by the god-lord Zhuan Xu in their battle over which one would become Lord of the Sky. The broken pillar was Buzhou ("Not Whole" or "Imperfect") Mountain. Since it is in the northwest, its damage caused the sky to tilt down in the northwest. This caused the Sky Pole (天極 Tian Ji), the axis around which the sky

revolves, to tilt down toward the northwest, lifting the southeastern part of the sky off the mountain-pillar supporting it there and at the same time breaking the cords binding sky to earth, causing a downward tilt in the land. The result was a southeastern gap in the contact of the sky with the earth.

7. This passage refers to how the ancient Chinese (and many other) astronomers divided so many celestial phenomena by twelve, e.g., the twelve-year cycle of the Year Star, the twelve lunations, the twelve two-hour periods of the day, etc.

8. The mythical itinerary of the sun is described here. Valley of Dawn (暘谷 Yanggu) is where the sun takes its morning bath before rising. (Some texts have 湯 and others 暘; when the two characters are used interchangeably, they are both pronounced *yang*.) The Dimming Stream (蒙汜 Mengsi) is where it rests after it sets.

9. In China one speaks of the rabbit or toad in the moon rather than the man in the moon. Hawkes preferred to follow Wen Yiduo in reading *gu tu* 顧菟 as "toad," for which there is scant support. I follow Wang Yi in taking *tu* 菟 = 兔 as "rabbit," a common substitution. *Gu* is a verb meaning "to take care of" and, by extension, "to raise."

10. Nü Qi 女岐 is a very obscure figure. Some say that she is the same as Jiuzi Mu 九子母 (Mother of Nine Sons), who is mentioned in a note by Ying Shao in the "Basic Annals of Cheng Di" (成帝本紀); see *Hanshu* 漢書, comp. Ban Gu 班固 (Beijing: Zhonghua shuju, 1962), 301. He tells us that Jiuzi Mu was painted on the walls of one of the crown prince's lodges, perhaps to express the hope for many sons. He implies that Jiuzi Mu is another name for an asterism, also known as the Wei Xing 尾星, or Tail Stars, or the Jiuzi Xing 九子星 (Nine-Son Stars), thus designated because it is composed of nine stars. Yuan Ke 袁珂, *Zhongguo shenhua chuanshuo cidian* 中國神話傳說詞典 (Shanghai: Shanghai cishu, 1985), 42, offers the ancient lore about Nü Qi and the links between her and later stories.

There are many theories about Bo Qiang 伯強, or the Earl of Violence. The most convincing identifies him with Yu Qiang 隅強, described in the *Huainanzi*, "Terrestrial Forms" (see Major et al., *Huainanzi*, 169), as a wind god who was generated by the wind from Buzhou Mountain. He is also sometimes identified with the Wind Earl 風伯 and the Winnowing Basket star 箕星. He is mentioned in the *Shanhaijing* with slightly different characters (禺彊). There he is described as having a human face and a bird's body. See Yuan Ke 袁珂, *Shanhaijing jiaoyi* 山海經校譯 (Shanghai: Shanghai guji chubanshe, 1985), 202.

11. The two Horn Stars make up the Horn constellation (角宿 Jiao Xiu) in Chinese astronomy; they are also called the Gates of Heaven (天關 Tian Guan). In Western astronomical terminology they are Alpha (or Spica) and Zeta in Virgo. It is part of a formation known in Chinese as Canglong 蒼龍 or Qinglong 青龍, which David Pankenier, a noted expert on Chinese astronomy, translates as Cerulean Dragon. The sun gradually proceeds through its horns, i.e., the Horn Stars,

which appear above the horizon sometimes in the predawn hours and sometimes in the evening. The sun's progress through the horns of the dragon seems to have been envisioned, according to TW, as the sun's entry through the Gates of Heaven. It may be that the appearance of the Horn Stars in the sky was thought of as the opening of the celestial gates, and the disappearance of those stars was thought of as their closing. The progress of the seasons could be calculated by the movement of the Cerulean Dragon constellation. See a fascinating discussion of this topic in David W. Pankenier, *Astrology and Cosmology in Early China* (Cambridge: Cambridge University Press, 2013), 38.

12. Gun 鯀 is the son of Zhuan Xu 顓頊 and the father of Yu 禹. He is connected with the main flood myth in China. According to the main sources, the sage-king Yao charged him with control of the flood. The dams and dikes he constructed failed to stem it. Yao then abdicated to Shun 舜, who, finding that Gun had failed, sentenced him to death on Feather Mountain. The two main pre-Han sources of Gun mythology are the *Shanhaijing* and the TW itself. The *Shanhaijing*, "Hainei jing," tells us that Gun was the grandson of the Yellow Emperor and that his original name was White Horse (see Yuan Ke, *Shanhaijing*, 300). That could also mean that his original form was that of a white horse. The same source (301) also tells us that there was a Great Flood and that Gun took it upon himself to fight it with the only weapon that he thought could stop it—a kind of magically self-increasing soil known as *xirang* 息壤. He was in such a hurry that he took it without waiting for permission from its owner, the Lord of the Sky (who could well have been identified as the Yellow Emperor or Zhuan Xu or Shun). The Lord of the Sky was so displeased with Gun that he commanded Zhu Rong 祝融, the governor of fire, to execute Gun on Feather Mountain (the "Hongfan" 洪範 chapter of the *Shujing* tells us it was Shun who killed Gun). Though dead and a male, Gun gave birth to Yu (the eventual founder of the Xia dynasty) after being sliced open. The Lord of the Sky then commanded Yu to stem the flood; Yu succeeded and tranquility was restored. Guo Pu 郭璞 (276–324) comments on this passage as follows: "After Gun was killed, his body did not rot for three years. Someone cut him open with a Wu knife, and he changed into a yellow dragon." According to other sources, including TW, Gun transformed into a yellow bear after the birth of Yu.

    Those who recommended Gun for the job were, among others, the Siyue 四岳, or the Four Mountains, Yao's advisers, mentioned in the *Shangshu*, "Yaodian." See James Legge, *The Chinese Classics*, 5 vols. (Oxford: Clarendon Press, 1893–1894; repr., Hong Kong: Hong Kong University Press, 1960), 3:24–25.

13. There are many recent scholars who think that *chigui* 鴟龜 refers to a creature that is a combination of owl and tortoise. There is a similar creature called *xuangui* 旋龜 in the *Shanhaijing*, but none called *chigui*. Wang Yi and earlier scholars

take *chigui* as two words—"owl" and "tortoise." One of the famous funerary flags found in the tomb at Mawangdui depicts tortoiselike creatures with owls on their backs. This may refer to the same myth that TW is alluding to. This is the only place in the literature where a collaboration between Gun, owls, and tortoises is implied.

14. The "stopped for good" (*yong e* 永遏) in this case is the execution of Gun by Zhu Rong. In some versions of the myth, Gun has his belly split open by a knife manufactured in Wu. The character *shi* 施 in the second line of the stanza has been the object of many interpretations. Most scholars follow Hong Xingzu, who records another version of the line in which *shi* is replaced by *chi* 弛, "to slacken." Many scholars extend this reading forcibly to mean "rot," a meaning not otherwise attested. This forced interpretation of *chi* is designed to accord with the part of the story where the body of Gun lies on the ground for three years without rotting. The best solution, it seems to me, is that of Fu Xiren 傅錫壬, *Chuci duben* 楚辭讀本 (Taipei: Sanmin, 1974), 81, which takes it as another way of writing *chi* 肔, meaning "to split open the belly" or "disembowel"—which accords quite naturally with another event in the story. The three characters were interchangeable.

15. According to Hong Xingzu and others, Gun's flood-control method involved damming the waters. Yu's method was channeling to drain the waters. As Sarah Allan has pointed out, the Great Flood that Gun and Yu confronted was not the result of rainfall but the overflow of water from the netherworld; see Sarah Allan, *The Shape of the Turtle: Myth, Art, and Cosmos in Early China* (Albany: SUNY Press, 1991), 69.

16. For the first line I use the textual variant cited by Wang Yi: *yinglong he hua* 應龍 何畫; see Hong Xingzu 洪興祖, *Chuci buzhu* 楚辭補注 (Beijing: Zhonghua shuju, 1986), 91. According to Hong Xingzu, the *yinglong* 應龍 is a winged dragon that figures in the *Shanhaijing*, "Dahuang dongjing," as an ally of the Yellow Emperor's in his fight with Chiyou 蚩尤, legendary leader of the Nine Li tribes of the east and a divinity associated with warfare and weapons. The war exhausted the *yinglong* so much that it could not rise again to the sky, where it normally served as a rain god. The earth was, as a consequence, plagued by drought, which was relieved only when people made likenesses of the dragon and displayed them to the sky; see Yuan, *Shanhaijing*, 248. According to Hong, the winged dragon used its tail to mark out the places where rivers, streams, and canals could be created to drain away the waters of the flood; see Hong, *Chuci buzhu*, 91.

17. Only Wang Yi tells us that Kang Hui 康回 is one of Gonggong's names (Hong, *Chuci buzhu*, 91). According to the *Huainanzi*, "Celestial Patterns" (Major et al., *Huainanzi*, 114), Gonggong fought with Zhuan Xu to see which one would reign as Lord of the Sky. Gonggong lost and in a rage smashed himself against Buzhou

Mountain. This threw the earth off balance and the sky began to tilt toward the northwest.

18. Mount Kunlun here refers to a mythical mountain and not the real Kunlun range. Wang Yi says that it is in the northwest and that it emits the primal energy and that its highest peak is called the Hovering Gardens (懸圃 Xuan Pu), which is a conduit to the heavens. The earliest mention of the Hovering (or Hanging) Gardens of Kunlun is in the *Chuci* itself—in "Li sao" and in "Tian wen." For more information we must consult later writings, e.g., *Huainanzi*, "Terrestrial Forms," tells us that they are within the gates of Kunlun and that one will develop supernatural powers if one reaches them; see Major et al., *Huainanzi*, 152–57. They have been variously imagined throughout the ages. Li Chenyu 李陳玉, for example, tells us, "They are the gardens of the spirit people and hover over the central peak, where they have contact with neither the sky nor the earth"; see You, *Tian wen zuanyi*, 126.

19. The various gates, 440 according to the *Huainanzi*, send the winds in the four directions; the winds are of various temperatures and thus is the weather of the various seasons regulated. Buzhou Mountain is located northwest of Kunlun. The wind from Buzhou Mountain comes in through the northwest gate of the Kunlun wall; see Major et al., *Huainanzi*, 156.

20. The earliest sources tell us that the lamp dragon (燭龍 *zhulong*) is a spirit of the north or northwest. *Shanhaijing*, "Dahuang beijing," tells us, "Beyond the northwest sea, north of the Red Waters, is situated Zhangwei [Screen Tail] Mountain. There lives a spirit with a human face and a serpent body, but red all over. It is a thousand *li* long, with slit eyes that stand vertically. When it closes them, night falls; when it opens them, dawn breaks. It does not eat or sleep or breathe; it just gulps down wind and rain. It can light the dark world of the dead." Here the place where the sun does not shine is the underworld of the dead; see Yuan, *Shanhaijing*, 287 and 167. *Huainanzi*, "Terrestrial Forms" (Major et al., *Huainanzi*, 167), tells us that the lamp dragon (translated there as Torch Dragon) lives north of Goose Gate but that its dwelling place gets no sunlight because it is overshadowed by Fine Feather Mountain (委羽之山 Weiyu Zhi Shan). In most sources it is described as having a human face and a dragon's or serpent's body. For other descriptions, see Jin, Dong, and Gao, *Qu Yuan ji jiaozhu*, 327.

The Ruo 若 tree is a mythical tree that grows in the extreme west. According to *Shanhaijing*, "Dahuang beijing": "In the Great Wastes there are the Hengshi Mountain, the Jiuyin Mountain, and the Dong Ye Mountains. On them grow red trees, with green leaves and red blossoms. The name of the tree is the Ruo"; see Yuan, *Shanhaijing*, 287. Guo Pu comments, "It grows on Kunlun in the extreme west. Its flowers are luminous red; they illuminate the earth." See the *Sibu congkan* 四部叢刊 edition of *Shanhaijing*, 165, at the Chinese Text Project (http://

ctext.org). Others say (see Major et al., *Huainanzi*, 157) that there are ten suns growing on the branches of the Ruo tree.

21. The *Shanhaijing* mentions mountains that are covered with snow all year-round. E.g., Mad Mountain (狂山 Kuang Shan), where "there is snow in both winter and summer." It also mentions Blazing Fire Mountain (炎火之山 Yanhuo Zhi Shan), where it is so hot that things combust upon being thrown on the ground (Yuan, *Shanhaijing*, 63, 272). It is hard to know if they are the places referred to in this passage. The "forest of stone," or Stone Forest, in this passage may refer to one or another place, such as the famous Shilin (石林) in Yunnan or the Suobuya Shilin in Hubei, but no one knows for sure. As for talking animals, myth is full of them, and of course there are certain real birds like the myna and the parrot; which one is meant here is difficult to say.

22. These lines may be a fragment (given the lack of rhyme). No one knows exactly what they refer to, but the bear brings to mind Gun, and his son Yu is in some texts associated with the dragon. On Yu and dragons, see Mark Lewis, *The Flood Myths of Early China* (Albany: SUNY Press, 2006), 103–4.

23. Jiang Ji 蔣驥 suggested that the nine-headed poisonous snake must be Xiang Liu 相柳, a minister of Gonggong's who was killed by Yu (quoted in Jin, Dong, and Gao, *Qu Yuan ji jiaozhu*, 332). *Shanhaijing*, "Dahuang beijing" (Yuan, *Shanhaijing*, 286), tells us, "One of the ministers of Gonggong was named Xiang Yao [繇, another name for Xiang Liu]. He had nine heads and the body of a snake that coiled upon itself. He nourished himself on the earth of the nine regions. Wherever he blew his breath or stopped to rest, the place became springs and bogs, the water of which was either peppery hot or bitter, so no animal could stay there. When Yu stopped the flood, he killed Xiang Liu, but his blood stank, making it impossible to grow grain, and the place flooded with water, making it impossible to inhabit. Yu stopped the place up by piling earth on it, but the earth fell away three times, so he made a pond of it. That is where the various Sky Lords built their pavilions. It is north of Kunlun." Here the poison of the snake is indicated by its malodorous blood. The paradoxical question is, if he made every place uninhabitable by his very presence, where did he himself live? See also Yuan, *Shanhaijing*, 200, and Mark Lewis's discussion of Xiang Liu in *Flood Myths*, 68–69.

24. There are many realms of immortals in Chinese myth, and we don't know which this refers to. There are also several giants. This passage is probably referring to Fang Feng 防風 (Windshield?), one of the legendary lords of the Xia dynasty, referred to in the *Guoyu* ("Luyu xia") by Confucius, who said that once when Yu held a meeting of the spirits on Guiji Mountain, Fang Feng arrived late. This angered Yu so much that he killed Fang Feng, who was a giant three fathoms tall, one of whose bones could fill a wagon. He is supposed to be tutelary spirit of

Feng 封 Mountain and Yu 嵎 Mountain. See *Guoyu*, "Luyu shang" 國語魯語上, 60–61, at the Chinese Text Project (http://ctext.org).

25. Wang Yi takes *qu* 衢 in its usual meaning, "crossroads." Hong Xingzu, quoting Liu Zongyuan's 柳宗元 *Tian dui* 天對 transform of this line (有萍九歧, "There is a duckweed with nine branches"), took it to mean "branch" of a stem or bough, a meaning found only in the *Shanhaijing*. Zuo Si 左思, in his third-century poem "Wei Capital Rhapsody," has the line *shu yu xun miping yu zhong kui* 孰愈尋靡萍 於中逵 ("How is this better than searching for spreading duckweed on a thoroughfare?" Knechtges's translation; see David R. Knechtges, trans., *Wen xuan; or, Selections of Refined Literature*, 3 vols. [Princeton, N.J.: Princeton University Press, 1982–1996], 1:433). This line is clearly modeled on Zuo Si's understanding of the TW line. Moreover, duckweed has no stems. I therefore follow Wang Yi. Hong, *Chuci buzhu*, 95, quoting the *Shanhaijing*, "Xishan jing" (Yuan, *Shanhaijing*, 22), tells us that the red (indicating high quality) cannabis flower grows on Floating Mountain. Hong's is the only plausible answer I know to the question, where can one find good cannabis during a flood?

    See *Shanhaijing*, "Hainei nanjing" (Yuan, *Shanhaijing*, 220), where it says, "When the Ba snake eats an elephant, it takes three years for the bones to come out. Eating that snake is said to guard against diseases of the heart and stomach." *Shanhaijing*, "Hainei jing" (Yuan, *Shanhaijing*, 298), says that the snake, which has a black body and green head, comes from Ba 巴 and eats elephants.

26. This interpretation is based on the Wang Yi commentary. The river called Black Waters is mentioned about ten times in the *Shanhaijing*—e.g., "Hainei xijing" (Yuan, *Shanhaijing*, 226), where it says that it springs from the northwestern corner of a mountain, and after a number of twists and turns flows south to the realm of the "Winged People." "Winged People" is another name for *xian* 仙, or "immortals," and the mountain in question, the commentator Guo Pu tells us, is Kunlun, another residence of immortals. Wang Yi comments that Black Toe (黑趾 Heizhi) and Three Danger (三危 Sanwei) are names of mountains and, according to *Huainanzi*, "Shize" (Major et al., *Huainanzi*, 201), the name of a country. Jiang Ji (You, *Tian wen zuanyi*, 164) gives much secondary evidence suggesting that Black Water, Black Toe, and Three Dangers are places that produce edible things that bestow immortality. The earliest extant source to associate immortality with these three places is, of course, TW itself. Most scholars take the last line of this stanza (壽何所止 *shou hesuo zhi*) to mean, "When does their long life end?" This is based on one of two possible interpretations of the Wang Yi commentary, which goes as follows: *Yan xianren bingming busi, qi shou du hesuo qiongzhi ye?* 言仙人稟命不死，其壽獨何所窮止也？ In English it could be translated, "The passage says that immortals are endowed with deathlessness, but when only [*du*, 'alone,' or 'contrary to what you would expect'] does it end?" In this

interpretation, *hesuo* is taken to mean "when." This, however, is an extension of its basic meaning, which is "where" or "in what place." If we take *hesuo* in its basic sense, the part of the sentence after the comma becomes, "In what place(s) alone does their long life end?" The late Qing commentator Xia Dalin 夏大霖 is one of the few who read the passage and the commentary correctly (or at least so that it renders a question that is interestingly ironical rather than self-contradictory). His comment paraphrases the lines thus: "Everyone in the world might claim that there are medicinal herbs growing near Black Waters and Three Dangers, but where, after all, are these places? Now are they not close to the mountains and rivers around the Hanging Gardens? If [those who eat the herbs] were to become immortal, then their lives would never end—anyone can see that. On the other hand, where would they go to bring [their immortal lives] to an end—has anyone ever seen that? The proverb goes, 'Everyone says that the spirits and immortals go to the heavens [to live]; but no one ever sees those in the heavens coming down here [to live]'" See You, *Tian wen zuanyi*, 164–65.

27. In Chinese mythology there is more than one fish with a human face. This one is the *lingyu* 鯪魚, which is described as having a human face, hands, and feet, and a fish's body. See *Shanhaijing*, "Hainei dongjing" (Yuan, *Shanhaijing*, 240). Some later sources say that it is so large it can swallow a boat. See Jin, Dong, and Gao, *Qu Yuan ji jiaozhu*, 336–37.

The Monster Sparrow, or Qidui 𩵋堆 (or 𩵋雀 Qique), is described in *Shanhaijing*, "Dongshan jing," as an inhabitant of Beihao Mountain that looks like a chicken, but with a white head, rat's feet, and tiger's claws. It also eats people. See Yuan, *Shanhaijing*, 99.

Yi 羿 the Archer is also known as Hou Yi 后羿. There are two main traditions about him. One depicts him as a godlike mythical figure. The other presents him as a historical figure. This passage alludes to the mythical Yi, the one who was ordered by the Lord of the Sky to save the world from certain disasters. According to *Shanhaijing*, "Hainei jing" (Yuan, *Shanhaijing*, 300), the Lord of the Sky in question was Di Jun 帝俊, who provided Yi with his main tool to deal with the disaster—a crimson bow with white-corded arrows. The main disaster according to *Huainanzi*, "Basic Warp" (Major et al., *Huainanzi*, 276), was too much heat produced by the rise of ten suns into the sky at the same time; the other disasters were caused by monsters. Yao manages to solve all the problems with his trusty bow. In the *Huainanzi* version of the story, however, it is not the divine Di Jun who commissions Yi, it is the very human Yao, who rides on Yi's success to the royal throne.

There are a number of differing accounts about where the suns came from and why they are associated with crows. In *Shanhaijing*, "Haiwai dong jing," it says, "Below there is Hot Water Valley. Above Hot Water Valley there is a *fusang* [sometimes translated as 'mulberry'] tree. This is the place where the ten suns bathe. It is located on the north side of the Kingdom of the Black Teeth. Growing in the middle of a great lake there is a great tree on the lower branches of which nine suns reside, and on the top branch of which one sun resides" (Yuan, *Shanhaijing*, 212). In *Shanhaijing*, "Dahuang dongjing," it says, "In the middle of the great wilderness there is a mountain called Nieyaojundi. On the mountain grows a tree that reaches a height of three hundred *li*. Its leaves look like those of the mustard plant. There is a valley called Warm Springs Valley. Over Hot Water Valley [its other name] grows a *fusang* tree. Just as one of its [resident] suns is returning, another one goes out. Each is carried by a crow" (see Yuan, *Shanhaijing*, 247). Other texts, such as the *Huainanzi*, "Quintessential Spirit," tell us that a crow lives in the sun and that it has three legs; see Major et al., *Huainanzi*, 242. Wang Yi (Hong, *Chuci buzhu*, 97), seemingly quoting a nonextant passage from the *Huainanzi*, tells us that when Yi hit each of the nine suns with an arrow, the crow within it died, dropping its feathers and wings as a consequence. Many scholars are of the opinion that Yi's transition from god to earthly hero took place during the Han dynasty. Karlgren thought that Yi had no connection with the ten-sun myth until the Han; see Bernhard Karlgren, "Legends and Cults in Ancient China," *Bulletin of the Museum of Far Eastern Antiquities* 18 (1946): 199–365. See some likely evidence to the contrary in Yuan, *Zhongguo shenhua chuanshuo cidian*, 303–4, and Hong, *Chuci buzhu*, 97, quote of the pre-Han *Guizang* to the effect that Yi shot down ten suns. For a fuller discussion of the Archer Yi myths, see Allan, *Shape of the Turtle*, 36.

Another tradition holds that Yi was both a good archer and the Lord of Qiong during the Xia dynasty and that he assassinated Lord Xiang of the Xia dynasty and was later murdered by Han Zhuo.

28. In the *Shangshu* 尚書, Yu tells us that after marrying the daughter of the ruler of the Tushan (Mud Hill) state, he stayed with her for only four days so that he could resume the task of stemming the flood. His main purpose in marrying her was to continue the family line. See Legge, *The Chinese Classics*, 3:84–85.

29. Qi 啟 was the son of Yu 禹, the founder of the Xia dynasty. Yee 益 (to be distinguished from Archer Yi) was one of Yu's ministers, designated by Yu to succeed him on the royal throne. Qi of course thought himself the rightful heir and sought to displace Yee. One version of the story, represented in the *Mencius*, claims that after the death of Yu, the people did not consider Yee to be up to the job, and Qi, whose virtue was augmented by his heritage, was made ruler by the approbation of the subjects. See Legge, *The Chinese Classics*, 2:358–59. Other versions say that Yu abdicated in favor of Yee, but Qi would not go along with it and therefore attacked Yee, eventually replacing him on the throne. See the *Sibu congkan* edition of *Zhanguo ce*, "Yan wang kai ji li" 燕王噲既立, 73, at the Chinese

Text Project (http://ctext.org), which says that Yu handed over the realm to Yee in name only and in fact ordered Qi to seize it from Yee. It is possible that TW is referring to yet another version.

As for "prison," one version of the *Zhushu jinian* (Bamboo annals) states, "Yee threatened Qi's rightful position, so Qi killed him"; see Legge, *The Chinese Classics*, 3:118. This happened after Qi displaced Yee and Yee tried to retake the throne. But Wang Fuzhi quotes the same source as saying that after Yee replaced Qi on the throne, he placed Qi under arrest. Qi nevertheless rose and killed Yee and succeeded his father. This information is not in the extant *Bamboo Annals*; see You, *Tian wen zuanyi*, 188–91. Qi's main "worry," according to Wang Yi, was about his moral authority. Yet according to the *Shanhaijing*, "Dahuang xijing," Qi ascended to Heaven three times and stole the heavenly music—namely, the *Jiubian* (Nine variations) and the *Jiuge* (Nine songs)—not to be confused with sections with the same names in the *Chuci*; see Yuan, *Shanhaijing*, 273. That led to his frequent revels in the fields and the consequent ruin of his state, according to the *Mozi* and "Li sao." Here TW is asking, if Qi was arrested by Yee, how was he able to escape and stage an uprising? Did heaven, which should have been displeased by his thievery, bring this about?

30. As explained in the previous note, though Yu bestowed his throne on Yee, the majority of the subjects favored Qi. This passage seems to claim that the army of Yee surrendered to Qi without a fight.

31. I emend the text from *shang* 商 to *di* 帝 with Zhu Junsheng 朱駿聲 (see You, *Tian wen zuanyi*, 209). The "Nine Variations" and the "Nine Songs" are dance music that were originally the possessions of the Lord of the Sky. *Shanhaijing*, "Dahuang xijing" (Yuan, *Shanhaijing*, 273), says that Qi (under the synonymous name Kai 開 [Open]) was the guest of Heaven three times and "obtained" the music. Guo Pu 郭璞, commenting on the passage, tells us that Qi, sending three beautiful women up to Heaven, stole the "Nine Variations" and the "Nine Songs." The *Mozi* holds that Qi's performance of the "Nine Variations" and the "Nine Songs" during long revels in the wilderness after hunting was his downfall; see Anne Birrell, *Chinese Mythology: An Introduction* (Baltimore: Johns Hopkins University Press, 1993), 85, and "Li sao." According to the myth (the earliest reference to which comes from a quotation of a no longer extant passage from the *Huainanzi* in a Yan Shigu note on the Han Wudi Annals in the *Hanshu*), Qi's mother, Madame Tushan, changed into a stone when she discovered that Yu, her husband, had changed into a bear. She was pregnant at the time, and when Yu demanded that she give him her son, she split open on her northern side and out came Qi, whose name means "open"; see Yuan, *Zhongguo shenhua chuanshuo cidian*, 332–33. See also the same source (211), quoting Qing scholar Ma Su 馬驌 (1621–1673), who quotes the largely lost *Sui chaozi* 隨巢子. *Qin* 勤, meaning "to

treat well" or "to help" goes as far back as the *Shijing* and also occurs in the *Zuozhuan* and the *Guoyu*. I follow Wang Yi in taking fen 分 as referring to the postpartum fragments of Madame Tushan.

32. The calamities that Archer Yi confronted were ten suns and a number of monsters. The only calamity that the *Shanhaijing* ("Haiwai nan jing") mentions is Zaochi 鑿齒, or Chisel Teeth, with whom he fought and over whom he triumphed (Yuan, *Shanhaijing*, 185). Archer Yi's killing the River Earl and taking his wife, the Lady of the Luo, is not mentioned in other texts. His shooting the giant boar is mentioned in the *Huainanzi*, "The Basic Warp" (see Major et al., *Huainanzi*, 276). "Mound Pig" is another way of translating Feng Xi 封豨, also translatable as "Giant Boar"). His offering its meat to the Sky Lord and being ignored by him is not mentioned in texts other than TW. But if Di Jun 帝俊 was the Sky Lord under whom Yi shot down nine of the ten suns as recounted in the *Huainanzi*, then Di Jun's reaction is understandable, for the suns were the sons of Di Jun (Yuan, *Zhongguo shenhua chuanshuo cidian*, 303). The only problem is that the *Huainanzi* has Archer Yi removing the nine suns on the order of Yao rather than Di Jun. In the "Li sao," however, his shooting the giant boar was not an aspect of his heroism but a sign of his addiction to hunting, which he pursued to the detriment of his subjects. Some think that the main calamity that Archer Yi removed was the third ruler of Xia, Tai Kang, who, spending most of his time hunting in the wilds, neglected his subjects, according to the *Shangshu* (see Legge, *The Chinese Classics*, 3:156–61). As for Yi's killing the River Earl, Wang Yi quotes a "Commentary" (on what text he does not reveal) that relates that the River Earl changed into a white dragon and swam close to the shore. Yi caught sight of him, shot at him, and hit him in the left eye. The River Earl reported this to the Lord of the Skies, saying, "Kill Yi for me." The Lord of the Sky said, "How is it you were shot?" The River Earl said, "At the time I had changed into a white dragon and had gone on an excursion." The Sky Lord said, "If you had maintained your spirit powers, how could Yi have gotten to you? You are now but a common beast; you ought to be shot by people—he did what was appropriate for sure. What crime did Yi commit?" Wang Yi also tells us that Yi had an erotic dream about the Beauty of the Luo—i.e., the wife of the River Earl. See Hong, *Chuci buzhu*, 99.

The events in the life of the Xia-dynasty Archer Yi are related in *Zuozhuan*, Xianggong, 4th year; see Legge, *The Chinese Classics*, 5:424. According to that account, he took the throne of the Xia dynasty after saving its subjects (presumably from the neglect of Tai Kang). Like Tai Kang, he lapses into a hunting addiction and begins to depend too much on Han Zhuo 寒浞, the estranged son of the Lord of Boming 伯明. As a trusted minister, Han Zhuo had the run of the court and of Archer Yi's household. Thinking that he deserved the kingship, he plotted with Yi's household, including Yi's wife, to assassinate Yi when he returned home from his hunting. Members of the household decided to chop up Yi's body, cook it, and serve it to his sons in the bargain. The sons of course could not bear to eat their father. They were subsequently killed. One of the Xia ministers escaped and eventually returned to assassinate Han Zhuo.

Madame Pure Fox seems to be one of Archer Yi's wives. The words *xuan qi* 眩妻 (bewitching or benighting wife) may be a pun on *xuan qi* 玄妻 (black wife), who some say is the same as Pure Fox (純狐 Chun Hu). In *Zuozhuan*, Zhaogong, 28th year (Legge, *The Chinese Classics*, 5:724–727), she is described as having hair so smooth, black, and glossy that one could use it as a mirror (I do not think Legge was correct to translate *jian* 鑒 as "cast a light."). Her son, by Hou Kui, was Bo Feng, whose immoderation gained him the name Feng Zhu 封豬, which means Big Swine. He was supposed to have been killed by Hou Yi. It is difficult to determine whether Black Wife is the same as Pure Fox or whether Big Swine is the same as the giant boar.

33. Zhuo is Han Zhuo, referred to earlier, a younger member of the Boming family. Lord Han of Boming ejected him from the state for his slanderous tongue. Archer Yi took him in and made him a minister.

Han Zhuo worked hard to undermine Archer Yi by gaining influence, through deception and bribery, over Yi's subjects and encouraging him in his hunting addiction, with which the subjects were not pleased. Han Zhuo eventually turned Yi's subjects against him, and, having won over Yi's wife, Pure Fox, convinced the members of Yi's household to assassinate him, cook him, and eat him, as noted.

Archer Yi is supposed to have killed a giant boar in the course of his destruction of the nine suns. The suns were supposed to have been the sons of Di Jun, who is the Sky Lord who assigned Yi the task of keeping them in line. Yi's killing of them may not have pleased him, and he therefore accepted no offerings from him. His later fate may have been the Sky Lord's doing.

34. Gun's transformation into a yellow bear is recounted in *Zuozhuan*, Zhaogong, 7th year, Legge, *The Chinese Classics*, 5:617. After being killed at Feather Mountain, he changes into a "yellow bear" and jumps into the deep Feather Pool. Hong Xingzu thought that in fact "yellow bear" (黃熊 *huang xiong*) is another way of writing "golden three-footed tortoise" (黃能 *huang nai*), a mythical creature. He nevertheless mentions that people on the east coast of China never use bear meat or turtle meat when they offer sacrifices at temples dedicated to Yu, and he wondered, "Could this mean that Yu was transformed into both creatures?"; see Hong, *Chuci buzhu*, 100–101. The idea that Gun was revived (probably in the form of a yellow bear) by shamans occurs nowhere else. The shaman ancestors live on one of the peaks of the Kunlun Mountains (also known as Shaman Mountain, Lingshan 靈山) in the west. See Yuan, *Shanhaijing*, 270.

35. Another aspect of the Gun myth not found elsewhere. I am influenced by Wang Fuzhi here. See You, *Tian wen zuanyi*, 235.

36. (Refers also to next stanza.) According to Wang Yi, Cui Wenzi 崔文子, a Daoist adept, studied the science of becoming immortal with Wang Ziqiao 王子喬. During the process, Wang Ziqiao changed into a nimbus around the sun and in that form delivered the elixir of immortality to Cui Wenzi. Cui Wenzi, not understanding what it was, panicked and struck the nimbus with a halberd. Thereupon the elixir fell to the ground. When he looked down at it, he found the body (some say the shoe) of Wang Ziqiao. Cui Wenzi placed the body in his house and covered it with an old basket. In a moment the body changed into a large bird that began screeching. When Cui Wenzi removed the basket to look, the large bird flew out and away; see Jin, Dong, and Gao, *Qu Yuan ji jiaozhu*, 359–60, and Hong, *Chuci buzhu*, 101.

37. The first couplet is about Ping Yi 屏翳 (Screen Shade), who causes rain and has the alternative name 蓱號 (Duckweed Howl). The second is about Feilian 飛廉, the Wind God, whose body is a combination of bird and deer.

38. There are two myths about different things whose names sound the same here. The first couplet (as Wang Yi tells us) deals with the story of the Giant Man from the Kingdom of the Dragon Earl, where dwell immortal sages who can fly from mountain to magic forested mountain. But the five mountains in the realm were not rooted in the earth and were liable to be carried away by the tide. The immortal sages therefore asked the Lord of Heaven to do something about this, and he ordered one Yuqiang to create fifteen giant turtles to carry the five mountains on their heads, each team of five taking turns every sixty thousand years; however, there was a giant in the Dragon Earl's kingdom who managed to catch six of the turtles, which he promptly killed, fired, and turned into divination tools. This left three sets of three turtles to hold the mountains steady; thus two of the mountains drifted away into the great sea in the north; see A. C. Graham, trans., *The Book of Lieh-tzu: A Classic of Tao* (New York: Columbia University Press, 1990), 97–98. The word for these turtles is *ao* 鼇 in Chinese. There is also the story of a strongman named Ao (澆 or 敖), who was so strong that he could walk dragging a boat (some say carrying it on his back) on land (Yuan, *Zhongguo shenhua chuanshuo cidian*, 291). He was the son of Han Zhuo and seems to be connected with the discovery or use of armor, the word for which is the same as the word for "shell." The shell connection seems to connect the strongman Ao with the *ao* turtles. The boat in the last couplet is both the boat that Ao dragged on land and the shells that keep the turtles afloat. It seems to be saying, "Of course Ao did not abandon his boat on land. If he did, how could *ao* [i.e., the amphibious turtles] keep the mountains out of the destabilizing waters." See more detailed discussions about this passage, especially that of Wen Yiduo, in Jin, Dong, and Gao, *Qu Yuan ji jiaozhu*, 362–64.

39. (Refers also to next stanza.) When Yi 羿 took control of the Xia government, he set up Zhong Kang 仲康 as puppet ruler. When Zhong Kang died, his son Xiang 相 became ruler. When Yi out and out declared himself king, he exiled Xiang, who took refuge with the Lord of Zhenxun 斟鄩. When Han Zhuo assassinated Yi, he sent soldiers to attack Zhenxun, and they killed Xiang there. Xiang's wife, Queen Min 緡, escaped to the domain of the Lord of Youreng 有仍 and there gave birth to Shao Kang 少康. Shao Kang grew up in Youreng, where he became chief of the shepherds. Shao Kang, fearing the depredations of Han Zhuo, eventually fled to the domain of Lord Youyu 有虞, in whose kitchen he worked. Si 思, the Lord of Youyu, gave his two daughters, who were surnamed Yao 姚, the same surname as Shun's. Eventually one of the former Xia ministers assassinated Han Zhuo, and Shao Kang was set up as King of Xia. Shao Kang restored the Xia dynasty after the Yi usurpation; see Legge, *The Chinese Classics*, 3:169–70 and 5:792–94.

Nü Qi 女岐, according to Wang Yi, was the sister-in-law of Ao (Big Turtle). According to a note by Shen Yue on the *Bamboo Annals* (see Legge, *The Chinese Classics*, 3:120–21 [Annals of the Bamboo Books]), Shao Kang sent a spy to seek out Ao (spelled "Keaou" by Legge; pinyin "Jiao") (*Zuozhuan*, Aigong, 1st year, also says this.) One of Ao's sons had died early, leaving a widow named Nü Qi. Ao took a liking to her and put on strong armor to go to her house and pretend that he needed something from her. Nü Qi mended his lower garments, and they spent the night together. Shao Kang's spy, Ru Ai 汝艾, sent someone to kill Ao as he slept, but the assassin mistakenly killed Nü Qi instead. Later the same spy killed and beheaded Ao after siccing dogs on him during a hunt, which may have been conducted by Shao Kang. Some scholars accept this; others don't. The *Zuozhuan*, Xianggong, 4th year, Legge, *The Chinese Classics*, 5:424, says that Zhuo had two sons by Yi's wife, Ao (or 浇 Jiao), and Yi 豷. It also says that Shao Kang killed Ao in the state of Guo 過 and Lord Shu 杼 killed Yi in the state of Ge 戈. The state of Qiong 窮 (Archer Yi's state) was, as a consequence, destroyed. These passages about Nü Qi and Ao allude to parts of the Ao story that have long been lost. Note that TW calls the woman sister-in-law, whereas in the *Bamboo Annals* it is his daughter-in-law.

40. In the *Jinben zhushu jinian*, Di Xiang 27th year, it says, "Ao attacked Zhenxun and fought a great battle at the Wei [潍] River. There he capsized the boats and destroyed them." Later Han Zhuo sent Ao to assassinate Xiang, the ruler of Xia, who had taken refuge in Zhenguan and then Zhenxun; see *Zhushu jinian*, Di Xiang 帝相, Legge, *The Chinese Classics*, 3:121–22. See also *Zuozhuan*, Aigong, 1st year, Legge, *The Chinese Classics*, 5:794. Unlike many interpreters after Zhu Xi, I do not read Tang 湯 as Kang 康, as he did. Nor do I read Tang 湯 as Ao 浇, as Wen Yiduo did. Mine is a combination of Wang Yi's and Wang Fuzhi's

interpretations. See You, *Tian wen zuanyi*, 263–65. Tang is the founder of the Shang; Ao's temporary overthrow of the Xia dynasty is an unfortunate foreshadowing of Tang's fortunate permanent overthrow of the Xia with his defeat of its evil last ruler, Jie 桀. In the former instance, the masses were captured by force; in the latter, they were "captured" by virtue.

41. The *Zhushu jinian* (see Legge, *The Chinese Classics*, 3:126–27) tells us that Jie, the last ruler of the Xia dynasty, attacked Meng (蒙 or 岷) Mountain and captured two women, Wan 琬 and Yan 琰; he then abandoned his queen, Moxi 末喜, whom he shut up in the Yao 瑤 stone tower (the jade tower of Legge's translation). Moxi had been as much a sybarite as her husband, but after being abandoned, Moxi conspired with Yi Yin 伊尹, who eventually overthrew the Xia. The story of Moxi is in the *Lie nü zhuan*; Anne Behnke Kinney, *Exemplary Women of Early China: The "Lienü zhuan" of Liu Xiang* (New York: Columbia University Press, 2014), tells us that after Tang defeated Jie, he set him afloat in a boat with his wife, Moxi. They escaped to Nanchao and died there. See also Yuan, *Zhongguo shenhua chuanshuo cidian*, 259.

42. See *Shangshu*, "Yaodian," for the statement, "There is a bachelor in the world; his name is Yu Shun." This is the recommendation of some of the same advisers who recommended Gun to stem the flood. Yao decides to test Shun, who is the son of perverse and immoral parents. In the same section Yao, seeing that Shun has passed the test, decides to give Shun his daughters in marriage; see Legge, *The Chinese Classics*, 3:26–27. For the idea that Yao did not inform Shun's parents about the marriage, see *Mengzi*, "Wanzhang shang" 345–47. There Mengzi claims that Yao did not inform Shun's parents about his plan to marry his daughters to him because it was clear that the parents would not have permitted it.

43. Djou 紂 (usually "Zhou," but here spelled differently to distinguish it from the Zhou dynasty) was the bad last king of the Shang dynasty, noted for his extravagance and complex debauchery. Before his predilections became entirely clear, one of his ministers noticed with some alarm that the king had had ivory chopsticks made for himself. The minister decided it was a sign of bad things to come. Djou's palace building soon followed. The *Han Feizi* tells us, "In ancient times King Djou had ivory chopsticks made, causing fear in the heart of Viscount Ji [or 箕子]. He thought, 'Ivory chopsticks would certainly not go with earthen soup cauldrons. Next will come cups made of rhino horn and jade. And with ivory chopsticks and cups of rhino horn and jade the king will certainly not eat bean soup; it will have to be meat of yaks, elephants, and leopard fetuses. And while eating those, one certainly cannot wear short cloth coats and eat under a thatched roof; he will have to have nine layers of embroidered cloth and broad mansions with high towers. I fear how it will end; therefore I have horror of the beginning.' After five years Djou built the meat park, set up the roasting pillars,

climbed the wine dreg hill to look down on the wine pool. As a consequence, Djou was destroyed. Thus the Viscount of Ji knew that calamity would come to the empire when he saw the ivory chopsticks. Thus they say, 'Seeing the small is called knowing clearly.'" See the *Sibu congkan* edition of *Han Feizi*, "Yulao" 喻老, 21, p. 140, at the Chinese Text Project (http://ctext.org).

44. Nü Wa 女媧 makes her first appearance in the extant ancient literature here. There are a number of later accounts as well. Guo Pu, in his comment on *Shanhaijing* (see the *Sibu congkan* edition of *Shanhaijing*, "Dahuang xijing," 145, at the Chinese Text Project [http://ctext.org]), tells us that she became Lord of the Sky. In the *Fengsu tongyi* 風俗通義, she, along with Fuxi 伏羲 and Shen Nong 神農, constitute the Three Augusts (三皇 Sanhuang). "August" is there defined as "heavenly" or "celestial" sovereign; see the *Sibu congkan* edition of *Fengsu tongyi*, "Sanhuang," 33, at the Chinese Text Project [http://ctext.org]). She is also credited with the creation of human beings. She began this project by molding people out of earth (of course), but, growing weary of the process, she finished the job by dragging ropes through the mud. The ones made of yellow earth became the upper classes, and the ones made of mud became the lower classes. See Birrell, *Chinese Mythology*, 35. The TW question here seems to imply that the questioner is concerned about the basic philosophical objection to theological creation stories—the problem of infinite regress. If Nü Wa created human bodies, who created hers (which the *Shanhaijing* describes as having a human head and the form of a snake from the waist down)?

45. Elephant (象 Xiang), in league with his parents, mistreated his half brother, Shun, but Shun never wavered in his filiality and loyalty. See Yuan, *Zhongguo shenhua chuanshuo cidian*, 357, and Mencius, "Wangzhang shang," Legge, *The Chinese Classics*, 2:346–48.

46. Tai Bo 太伯 and Zhong Yong 仲雍 were two sons of the legendary founder of the Duchy (later the kingdom) of Zhou, Gugong Danfu 古公亶父, grandfather of one of the founders of the Zhou dynasty, King Wen. When they perceived that their father would hand the throne over to their younger brother, Ji Li 季歷, they fled south, where they tattooed their bodies and cut their hair after the manner of the tribes there. Adoption of such customs made both of them ineligible to become rulers of the Chinese. The people of the southern region, however, respected them, and Tai Bo was accepted as the ruler of the people of Wu, and his brother Zhong Yong succeeded him. See Sima Qian 司馬遷, *Shiji* 史記 (Beijing: Zhonghua shuju, 1992), "Wu Taibo shijia," 31:1445–46.

47. Despite the fact that the Shang royal house diligently offered sacrifices to Heaven, the throne went eventually to Jie, who brought the dynasty to ruin.

48. (Refers also to next stanza.) Yi Yin 伊尹 was the chief minister of Tang, the founder of the Shang dynasty. When the kingdom of Shang was still under the

suzerainty of Xia, Jie acceded to the Xia throne and proceeded to live a life of profligacy and rule by cruelty. Tang sent Yi Yin to advise King Jie to reform himself, but to no avail. Yi Yin in the end encouraged Tang to rebel. Tang, following this advice, led his armies against the Xia and defeated King Jie at a place called Mingtiao 鳴條 (Singing Tendrils). After that Jie was exiled to Nanchao, where he eventually died (*Shiji*, "Xia benji," 2:88–89).

49. Jiandi 簡狄 was one of the daughters of the mythical Lord of Yousong 有娀, who built a high tower to house, and isolate, her and her sister; see John Knoblock and Jeffrey Riegel, trans., *The Annals of Lü Buwei: A Complete Translation and Study* (Stanford, Calif.: Stanford University Press, 2001), 162. When she was already one of the wives of Di Ku, a black bird dropped an egg in front of her, which she swallowed, thereby becoming pregnant with Qi, the first hereditary ruler of the Xia dynasty; see *Shiji*, "Yin benji," 3:91.

50. According to the *Shanhaijing*, "Dahuang dongjing" (Yuan, *Shanhaijing*, 247), "There is a place called the Kingdom of Yinmin, where the royal surname is Gou and the primary food is millet. There is a person there named Wang Hai who holds in each hand a bird, each of whose heads he is in the process of eating. Wang Hai is the ruler of the Yin [or Shang] dynasty. At one time he entrusted his draft cattle to the ruler of the Youyi 有易 people and the River Earl." The ruler of Youyi ends up killing Wang Hai because Wang Hai had had improper relations with the ruler's wife. Wang Hai's son and successor, Shangjia Wei 上甲微, attacks the Youyi to avenge the death of Wang Hai, inflicting heavy losses on them. The River Earl comes to their aid and helps the rulers of Youyi to escape and set up another kingdom elsewhere. Wang Guowei 王國維 found the name Wang Hai 王亥 (see Wang Guowei, *Yin buci zhong suo jian xian gong xian wang kao* 殷卜辭中所見先公先王考 [Shanghai: Cangsheng mingzhi daxue, 1916]) represented on the oracle bones and determined that he was a distant ancestor of the Shang royal house and recipient of many sacrifices. His father is called Ming 冥 in the *Shiji* etc., but Ji 季 in the oracle bones. Wang Hai seems to have consulted Ji in divination and offered him sacrifices. Wang Guowei concludes that the Ji of the oracle bones is the Ming of the received texts. Wang Guowei also cites Guo Pu's commentary on the *Bamboo Annals*, which claims that Prince Hai wandered through a place called Youyi herding cattle and sheep and ended up staying there. Later because of some sexual misconduct (presumably with the ruler's wife or daughter) he was killed by the ruler of Youyi, Mian Chen. Aside from being what some consider the first herdsman, he appears to be associated with the first use of oxen etc. for pulling wagons; see You, *Tian wen zuanyi*, 311–13.

51. See *Zuozhuan*, Zhuanggong, 28th year (Legge, *The Chinese Classics*, 5:113–15), where it says, "The *lingyin* of Chu, Zi Yuan, wished to seduce Lady Wen, so he built a lodge next to her palace and performed the Wan dance." The Wan is also

known as the Shield Dance. Wen Yiduo thinks that Wang Hai is performing the Shield Dance for similar purposes vis-à-vis the wife (some say daughter) of the ruler of Youhu (which most scholars think is a miswriting for Youyi; see You, *Tian wen zuanyi*, 333–34). See also Jin, Dong, and Gao, *Qu Yuan ji jiaozhu*, 383. According to the Guo Pu's comment on *Shanhaijing*, "Dahuang dongjing," Wang Hai seduced the daughter or wife of the ruler of Youyi. For this reason, his son Shang Jiawei borrowed an army from the Earl of the Yellow River and attacked Youyi, which he destroyed and whose ruler, Mian Chen 緜臣, he killed; see the *Sibu congkan* edition of *Shanhaijing*, "Dahuang dongjing," 130–31, at the Chinese Text Project (http://ctext.org).

52. The *Shanhaijing*, "Haiwai dong jing," refers to (Wang) Hai as Shu Hai 豎亥, i.e., Herd Boy Hai. I am following Tang Bingzheng's very commonsensical approach in assuming that it was Hai who died and the woman (Mian Chen's wife or daughter) who escaped here, and that the order to kill them came from Mian Chen, the ruler of Youyi (Tang et al., *Chuci jinzhu*, 107).

53. Heng 恆 was a younger brother of Hai's. During the Shang the younger brother often succeeded the older brother on the throne. After the death of Hai, Heng may have ruled. We know little about him. Wang Guowei claims to have found Heng's name in the oracle bone inscriptions; see You, *Tian wen zuanyi*, 333–34. See Tang et al., *Chuci jinzhu*, 107, and Jin, Dong, and Gao, *Qu Yuan ji jiaozhu*, 385, for why *pu niu* 僕牛 should be taken as *fu niu* 服牛, meaning "draft oxen."

54. Hun Wei (昏微, or "Twilight Wei") was Shangjia Wei, Hai's son. He borrowed the army of the River Earl to avenge his father; see Tang et al., *Chuci jinzhu*, 107. No one is sure about what the last two lines of the stanza refer to. They may be blaming the woman of Youyi for yielding to passion with his father and thus becoming the ultimate cause of Shangjia Wei's destruction of her state. If the lines refer to her abandoning her child, they could support the idea that Hai had an affair with Lord Youyi's wife. The birds perched in the brambles could refer to the real birds that might have witnessed their lovemaking, or, figuratively, to the people who might have found out about their affair and gossiped. Youdi 有狄 seems to be another version of Youyi 有易; *di* and *yi* were interchangeable characters in ancient times. See Jin, Dong, and Gao, *Qu Yuan ji jiaozhu*, 387.

55. Scholars are in disagreement as to what this passage refers to. Shangjia Wei, though the son of the immoderate Hai and the nephew of just-as-bad Heng, seems to have extended the royal line that eventually blossomed into the Shang dynasty. The question that these stanzas seem to be asking is how could such bad ancestors produce such good descendants.

56. According the *Lüshi chunqiu*, "Ben wei" (本味, or "Fundamental Tastes"), when Tang heard about the talents of Yi Yin, who was serving as royal cook in Youshen (有侁 or 莘), he sent an envoy to request that he be sent to him. The ruler of

Youshen, however, would not permit it. Yi Yin himself wanted to serve Tang. Tang then requested a wife from Youshen, and the ruler offered his daughter and sent Yi Yin as part of the slave contingent in the bridal entourage. See Knoblock and Riegel, *Annals of Lü Buwei*, 307.

57. According to the *Lüshi chunqiu*, "Ben wei" section (see note 56), when the princess of Youshen was picking mulberry leaves, she found a baby in the trunk of a mulberry tree. When she presented it to the ruler, the ruler ordered a cook to raise it. When they inquired to find out the reason that the baby found himself in a tree, someone said that the mother dwelled on the banks of the Yin River. When she became pregnant, she dreamed of a spirit who told her, "When water comes out of the mortar, go east and do not look back." The next day she saw water come out of the mortar and she told her neighbors. She went east, running ten *li*, but then she looked back and saw that her town had disappeared underwater. She then changed into a mulberry tree. For this reason, Yi Yin was named Yin (meaning "officer") of the Yi River. Wang Yi tells a different version of the story. When Yi Yin's mother was pregnant, she dreamed that a spirit told her that when frogs grow in the mortar and stove to immediately leave and don't look back. After a short time frogs began growing in the mortar and stove. So she left and ran east. When she looked back at her town, it was submerged in water. The mother drowned and became a mulberry tree. After the water receded, a small baby was heard crying on the shore. Someone took it and raised it; see *Lüshi chunqiu*, "Ben wei"; Knoblock and Riegel, *Annals of Lü Buwei*, 307.

58. In the "Basic Annals of Xia" in the *Shiji* it says that Jie summoned Tang and imprisoned him in the Tower of Xia. Other sources have an evil minister putting Jie up to this. His desire to attack Jie arose from his perception of Jie's general tyranny, but being imprisoned for no apparent reason seems to have been the last straw; see *Shiji*, "Xia benji," 2:88. Double Spring may refer to the Tower of Xia. In the *Shangshu*, Tang calls the people together to attack Jie and tells them that he has been appointed by Heaven, which in effect means that he has recommended himself to Heaven for the task of replacing the evil Jie. See Legge, *The Chinese Classics*, 3:173–76.

59. This appears to shift time to the Zhou dynasty. According to the "Basic Annals of the Zhou" in the *Shiji*, the various lords spontaneously assembled in the second month on the *jiazi* day in the morning to take an oath to follow King Wu to attack Djou, the evil last ruler of the Shang; see *Shiji*, "Zhou benji," 4:122–23. The hawk imagery seems a poetical way to describe the army. The *Shangshu* also describes the unplanned convergence of eight hundred princes to fight and bring down Djou. See Legge, *The Chinese Classics*, 3:298.

60. Shu Dan, or Uncle Dan, is the very virtuous Duke of Zhou. The "Zhou benji" and a number of other sources describe the cruelty with which King Wu (one of

whose names is Fa) treated the body of Djou. Djou, seeing that his forces had turned against him, climbed up the Deer Tower, dressed himself in all his best jade, and immolated himself. King Wu, after declaring victory, shot three arrows into Djou's corpse, hacked it with a sword, cut off its head with a battle-ax, and hung the head from a flagstaff. He did the same to Djou's main consorts. See *Shiji*, "Zhou benji," 4:124–25.

61. Yin is another name for the Shang dynasty.

62. These lines may refer to the Zhou forces attacking the forces of the last Shang king.

63. In the *Zuozhuan*, Xigong, 4th year (Legge, *The Chinese Classics*, 5:139), King Zhao 昭 is said to have drowned in a defective boat that sank while crossing the Han River during a tour of the south. *Shiji*, "Zhou benji, zhengyi" (the "Corrected Meanings" [正義] commentary by Sima Zhen 司馬貞 [fl. 745]), 4:134–35, says the boatman hated him and had intentionally given him a defective boat. According to Mao Qiling 毛奇齡, quoting an unknown (except to him) passage of the *Zhushu jinian*, the people of Chu sent a message to King Zhao of Zhou telling him that they wished to give him a white pheasant. Zhao, believing them, went south but suffered harm. The harm was death by drowning; see You, *Tian wen zuanyi*, 376. In the extant *Bamboo Annals*, King Zhao is said to have died in the nineteenth year of his reign by drowning in the Han River while campaigning against the state of Chu. Just before he and his army sink into the river, the sky clouds over and the pheasants and rabbits manifest terror (Legge, *The Chinese Classics*, 5:149). This is the only extant text that associates pheasants and King Zhao and the south. The same text tells us that he had attacked Chu three years before and had encountered a large rhinoceros while crossing the Han River. This prompted Wen Yiduo to advise changing "pheasant" to "rhino" in TW. David Hawkes took the advice but ignored the adjective "white." In the *Sibu congkan* edition of the *Shangshu dazhuan* 尚書大傳, *juan* 4, 56 (available online at the Chinese Text Project [http://ctext.org]), the presentation of the white pheasant is related. The people of Yueshang presented the pheasant, it appears, as a sign that they were pledging allegiance to Zhou because of the good rule of the Duke of Zhou and King Cheng. The TW text is probably not talking about Zhao receiving a pheasant but the Duke of Zhou and King Cheng receiving one for maintaining peace. Zhao, however, did not deserve one, and may have suffered drowning for waging war.

64. King Mu 穆 was the son of King Zhao. He is reputed to have traveled widely and to have conducted many military campaigns. The histories tell that he had an expert charioteer named Zao Fu 造父. In mythology, such as in the *Mu Tianzi zhuan* 穆天子傳, he seeks to become an immortal by traveling to Mount Kunlun to visit the Queen Mother of the West.

65. *Shiji*, "Zhou benji," 4:147, tells us that King You 幽 of the Zhou wanted to make the son of Baosi 褒姒, his new favorite, the crown prince. To do this he would have to demote the current crown prince, his son by Empress Shen. The Grand Astrologer tried to dissuade him by relating a few things he knew about Baosi's background. According to him, during the Xia dynasty two dragons appeared in the king's court and announced that they were the incarnations of two previous rulers of the state of Bao. The nonplussed king called for a divination. The oracle advised that the king request that the dragons give him some of their saliva. After this was done, the dragons disappeared, but their saliva remained. It was gathered up, stored in a casket, and hidden away. After the downfall of the Xia, the casket was transferred to the rulers of Shang. After the Shang fell, it came into the possession of the rulers of Zhou. During all that time it was never reopened. At the end of the reign of King Li of the Zhou it was opened and out flowed the saliva onto the grounds of the palace, where it stuck and could not be removed. King Li 厲 ordered that his palace women strip naked and scream as loud as they could. Thereupon the saliva changed into a black lizard, which immediately crawled into the women's quarters. A palace maid who was still a little girl encountered it, and by the time she was of marriageable age she became pregnant as a result. Though a virgin, she gave birth but abandoned the child in fear. In the time of King Xuan 宣 of Zhou there was a children's song that had the line "Mulberry bows and quivers will surely destroy the kingdom of Zhou." Someone informed King Xuan that there happened to be a couple selling these items in the market. The king dispatched his agents to arrest and execute them, but the couple fled to the state of Bao in fear. On the way they heard the cries of the little girl who had been abandoned. They took her and raised her. This was Baosi, who eventually became the queen of King You of Zhou. Her influence on the king led to his downfall. An alternative account has it that Baosi came to be the wife of King You another way. The Lord of Bao had committed a crime, and somehow he got the couple selling arrows and quivers to give the girl to King You to weaken his resolve to attack and punish the state of Bao. (For this and other accounts, see Yuan, *Zhongguo shenhua chuanshuo cidian*, 432–33.) She was famously morose, but one of the few things that made her smile was watching the army rush to the palace when the king sent out false alarms. On one such occasion the army did not respond to the king's call, although the kingdom was in fact under attack. King You was thus defeated.

66. Duke Huan of Qi 齊桓公 was one of the Five Hegemons. His prime minister was the famous Guan Zhong 管仲. Guan Zhong advised Duke Huan to banish from the palace four men whom he considered dangerous. Duke Huan at first resisted, for they were some of his favorites, but in the end he complied. After Guan Zhong's death, he invited them back and gave them official positions, but they

indeed turned out to be scoundrels. They staged a coup, had his residence walled in, and starved him to death; see Knoblock and Riegel, *Annals of Lü Buwei*, 383–84; Jin, Dong, and Gao, *Qu Yuan ji jiaozhu*, 401; and the *Sibu congkan* edition of *Guanzi*, "Xiaocheng," 124–26, at the Chinese Text Project (http://ctext.org).

67. The dissolute Djou, the evil last king of the Shang dynasty, was misled by the proverbial femme fatale Daji 妲己 and deceived by bad ministers, such as the flattering Fei Lian 飛廉 (also known as 費中 Fei Zhong) and the slandering Wu Lai 惡來; see *Shiji*, "Yin benji," 3:105–9.

68. Bi Gan 比干 was the minister and uncle of Djou. He was so loyal that he risked his life to advise Djou to reform. Djou eventually killed him and had his heart cut out to see if, as some used to say, the heart of the sage has seven apertures; see *Shiji*, "Yin benji," 3:105–9. Lei Kai 雷開 was a corrupt minister who won Djou's favor through flattery.

69. Mei Bo was a marquis under the reign of Djou. When he criticized Djou, Djou had him chopped up and his flesh pickled in brine; see Knoblock and Riegel, *Annals of Lü Buwei*, 532. Ji Zi 箕子 offered criticism but feigned insanity as he did so and thus avoided anything crueler than being reduced to slavery by order of Djou. He secretly played the *qin* 琴 to vent his sorrow; *Shiji*, "Yin benji," 3:108.

70. Ji 稷 or Hou Ji 后稷 (Lord Millet) is honored as the progenitor of the Zhou royal house; see *Shijing* 245 (生民 "Shengmin"). Jiang Yuan 姜嫄, his mother, is supposed to have gotten pregnant by stepping on the footprint of the Lord of the Sky (identified in this case as 帝嚳 Di Ku), though she was thought barren. The poem tells us that Hou Ji was abandoned soon after his birth and was even thrown on the icy ground. Certain birds, however, used their wings to keep him warm. Here I read 竺 as 毒 (*du*, "to hate"), a common substitution; see discussion of this in Jin, Dong, and Gao, *Qu Yuan ji jiaozhu*, 405.

71. Ji 稷, the progenitor of the Zhou royal house, is usually thought of as an agricultural culture hero, but in this passage there seems to be a trace of another talent. His military prowess is alluded to in the *Sibu congkan* edition of Wang Chong's *Lunheng* 論衡, "Chu bing" 初稟, 118, available at the Chinese Text Project (http://ctext.org), where it says that Qi 棄 (another name for Hou Ji) served Yao (who may once have been thought of as the Sky Lord) in the capacity of *sima* 司馬, which is equivalent to something like minister of war. If this passage is about Hou Ji, then it may reflect a tradition outside the mainstream; see Jin, Dong, and Gao, *Qu Yuan ji jiaozhu*, 406–7. What the Sky Lord found shocking in this case is probably the way Hou Ji was conceived.

72. Bo Chang 伯昌 is one of the titles of King Wen of Zhou, whose name is Ji Chang 姬昌. He originally received his title Earl (伯 Bo) of Yongzhou under the rulership of the Shang dynasty. In that capacity he was also known as Earl of the West (西伯 Xi Bo). After carefully building alliances among the people suffering under the

reign of King Djou of Shang, he was able to stage a successful revolution. The earth altar at Qi 岐 (northeast of Qi Mountain in Shaanxi province) was the original place where the Zhou ruling family sacrificed to the spirits of the earth, thus affirming their power. As their power grew, however, they had to move their earth altar to Feng 豐 (northeast of Chang'an county in Shaanxi) and destroy the old one at Qi; see *Shiji*, "Zhou benji," 4:117–18.

73. This appears to allude to the story of King Tai (who was also known as Gu Gong and Tan Fu), the grandfather of King Wen, who was so loved by his subjects that they followed him even when he decided to avoid fighting invading barbarians and flee to establish another kingdom at Qi; see ibid., 113–14. King Wen's reputation for treating prospective retainers well was also such that many went to live with him. Yin is another name for the Shang dynasty and here stands for Djou, its last king. He was led astray by Daji, one of the Chinese archetypes of the femme fatale. Equivalence is apparently being suggested here between King Wen and his grandfather and King Djou and the barbarians.

74. According to the *Lüshi chunqiu*, "Xing lun" (see Knoblock and Riegel, *Annals of Lü Buwei*, 532), Djou killed the Earl of Mei 梅伯 and the Marquis of Gui 鬼侯 and served their flesh to various lords, including Wen, future king of the Zhou dynasty, at a ceremony in the ancestral temple. According to the *Shiji*, "Yin benji," 3:106–7, Djou killed King Wen's son and made a soup of his flesh, which he served to the unwitting King Wen.

75. Master Wang (師望 Shi Wang) is Lü Wang 呂望 or Jiang Taigong 姜太公. He was King Wen's greatest adviser and commander in chief. Legend has it that he was discovered in the Shang capital, Chaoge 朝歌, working in a butcher shop by the future King Wen. Chang 昌 is one of King Wen's names. Master Wang's singing seems to have first caught the king's attention. It is also said that the king's diviner predicted that such a person would appear to ensure the success of the king's reign. "Li sao" also alludes to this story; see Wang Yi's commentary in Hong, *Chuci buzhu*, 114. For more on the scattered and fragmentary sources about this figure, see Yuan, *Zhongguo shenhua chuanshuo cidian*, 157, 290–91; and Birrell, *Chinese Mythology*, 260–61.

76. Fa 發 was the name of King Wu of Zhou, who was one of the sons of King Wen. Most of the sources that deal with this event say that when King Wu attacked Djou, he carried the corpse of his father into battle; see, e.g., *Huainanzi*, "Integrating Customs," Major et al., *Huainanzi*, 412; see also Jin, Dong, and Gao, *Qu Yuan ji jiaozhu* 409–10. Other sources prefer, without much justification, to think that the "corpse" in this case is a spirit tablet, to which one sacrifices in the ancestral temple.

77. No one is entirely sure what this stanza is about. Xu Wenjing, among others, believes that Bo Lin 伯林 is another way of writing Bei Lin 北林 "North Forest,"

which was in Henan and is mentioned in *Zuozhuan*, Xuangong, 1st year. This is part of the place where Guan Shu 管叔 (also known as 管叔鮮 Guan Shuxian), the younger brother of King Wu, was enfeoffed. After the death of King Wu and during the regency of the Duke of Zhou 周公, Guan Shu, Cai Shu (Du) 蔡叔(度), and Huo Shu (Chu) 霍叔(處) allied themselves with remnants of the defeated Shang royalty and staged a rebellion. After the Duke of Zhou put down the rebellion, according to *The Lost Book of Zhou*, Guan Shu hanged himself; see *Yi zhoushu* 逸周書, *juan* 48 (作雒解 "Zuo Luo jie"), 119–20, available at the Chinese Text Project (http://ctext.org). Other sources say simply that he was killed. One of the pretexts for their rebellion was the unfounded claim that the Duke of Zhou intended to usurp the throne. After the rebellion, King Cheng, the initially underaged heir to the throne, grew suspicious of the duke. The sky, in response, sent forth thunder, lightning, and wind, making the grain lie flat and tearing up the trees. Then a metal-bound coffer came to light in which a prayer offered by the duke when King Cheng was gravely ill indicated that he had requested that the spirits cause him to die rather than the king. This cleared up all doubt about the duke, whereupon the grain and trees were made by Heaven to stand up again. I have followed Xu Wenjing; see You, *Tian wen zuanyi*, 422–23.

78. For an interesting study of Yi Yin, see Roel Sterckx, *Food, Sacrifice, and Sagehood in Early China* (Cambridge: Cambridge University Press, 2011), 65–76; see also Birrell, *Chinese Mythology*, 129. The claim that Yi Yin was offered sacrifices along with the Shang royal house is borne out in the oracle bone inscriptions. For Yi Yin in oracle bone inscriptions, see Mayvis Marubbio, "Yi Yin, Pious Rebel: A Study of the Founding Minister of the Shang Dynasty in Early Chinese Texts" (Ph.D. diss., University of Minnesota, 2000).

79. He Lü 闔閭 (r. 514–496 B.C.E.) was King of Wu during the late Spring and Autumn period. Wu prospered under his rule. He appointed Wu Zixu 伍子胥 as his general and declared war on the state of Chu. He once attacked the Chu capital of Ying and destroyed it. His grandfather was King Shou Meng 壽夢, who had four sons: Zhu Fan 諸樊, Yu Ji 餘祭, Yu Mei 餘昧, and Ji Zha 季札. After the death of Shou Meng, Zhu Fan became king. Later Zhu Fan passed the throne to Yu Ji. Yu Ji passed the throne to Yu Mei. Yu Mei should have passed the throne to Ji Zha, but Ji Zha was not interested in becoming a king. So Yu Mei passed the throne to his own son, Liao 僚. He Lü was Zhu Fan's oldest son. Since Yu Mei had broken the tradition of fraternal succession, He Lü thought that retrospectively he had the right to be king, so he had King Liao assassinated. He Lü retrospectively, here, thinks of himself as having been ostracized and banished (*Shiji*, "Wu Taibo shijia," 31:1445–77).

80. Peng Keng 彭鏗 is Peng Zu 彭祖, who is supposed to have lived some eight hundred years. According to the *Zhuangzi*, it was even longer; see Watson, *Chuang*

*Tzu*, 82n12. The "Chushi jia" of the *Shiji* tells us that he was one of the six sons of Lu Zhong. The *Liexian zhuan* 列仙傳 of Liu Xiang 劉向 tells us that he was an important officer in the Yin (Shang) court and that he was the grandson of Zhuan Xu 顓頊. Wang Yi tells us that despite the fact that he lived over eight hundred years, he still regretted the shortness of life. According to *juan* 1 of the *Shenxian zhuan* 神仙傳, Peng Zu felt sorrow that in his unusually long life he had seen his many wives and children die and that he had learned so little that he had nothing to teach; see Yuan, *Zhongguo shenhua chuanshuo cidian*, 378. He is also supposed to have been a good cook, but that reputation seems based mostly on this TW passage. It is clear from Wang Yi's comment that his text had 悵 instead of 長. I have translated accordingly.

81. These lines appear to refer to the uprising against King Li 厲王 of the Western Zhou, thus the reference to the strength of bees and ants, a metaphor for a peasant uprising. According to the *Shiji*, after the rebellion the Duke of Zhao and the Duke of Zhou jointly took the reins of power, thus "guiding the herd" (metaphor for ruling) together from the center. King Li fled to the state of Zhi 彘 after the uprising and died there. According to other sources, a long period of drought ensued. Diviners were consulted, and it was concluded that the problem was caused by the spirit of King Li. Dukes Zhou and Zhao decided to appease the angry spirit of the king by setting up his son, Crown Prince Jing 靖, as King Xuan 宣王. See Legge, *The Chinese Classics*, 3:153–54.

82. These lines appear to be about Bo Yi 伯夷 and Shu Qi 叔齊, who lived under the Shang dynasty. After the Shang was overthrown by King Wu, who established the Zhou dynasty, the two brothers refused to eat crops grown under his rule, and they fled to Shouyang 首陽 Mountain, which is located in the north of Shanxi in a place called Hequ 河曲, which means River Bend. The Yellow River meanders in circles around this county, thus the name. (The *huishui* 回水 in the text, therefore, would seem to mean not "whirlpool" but "[re]turning waters" [or "river"]; see Watson, *Chuang Tzu*, 322–23.) There their diet consisted of ferns. One day, however, a woman pointed out to them that the ferns were in effect crops grown under the rule of the Zhou. They therefore stopped eating even ferns and died of hunger. The story alluded to here appears to be the same as that alluded to in a "Five Ministers" commentary on *Wen xuan* 文選, *juan* 54 (辨命論 "Bianming lun"), which has it that when they stopped eating even ferns, a compassionate white doe came along and suckled them. See Zhou Gongchen's 周拱辰 comments on these lines in You, *Tian wen zuanyi*, 449, and the discussion in Jin, Dong, and Gao, *Qu Yuan ji jiaozhu*, 417.

83. There several very different explanations of this passage. I am adopting the one offered by Wang Yi; see Hong, *Chuci buzhu*, 117. According to it, the older brother in question here is the Earl of Qin. His younger brother was Prince Qian 鍼.

*Zuozhuan*, Zhaogong, 1st year, says that Qian was favored by his father, Duke Huan. Later he fled to Jin because he somehow displeased his mother (see Legge, *The Chinese Classics*, 5:578–79). According to Wang Yi's comment on this passage, Qian coveted his brother's dog and offered one hundred cash for it, but the brother would not give it up. The brothers began feuding, and Qian ended up fleeing to Jin, losing his title and income. No one knows the basis of Wang Yi's comment. There is no account of a conflict between the brothers over a dog in the *Zuozhuan*.

84. (Refers also to next three stanzas.) There are many theories about these lines. Many scholars think that Qu Yuan wrote them to bewail the fate of Chu and bemoan the ineffectuality of one or another of the kings of Chu.

85. Wu Guang 吳光, Prince Guang of the state of Wu, as King of Wu was known as He Lü, as previously noted.

86. 環閭穿社, 以及丘陵, 是淫是蕩, 爰出子文 is the text that both Wang Yi and Hong Xingzu saw. The text that is in the standard editions is unreadable, so I emend it, as do most others, according to Wang and Hong. Zi Wen 子文was the name of an incorruptible minister who served King Cheng 成of Chu (r. 671–676). According to *Zuozhuan*, Xuangong, 4th year, Ruo Ao 若敖married a woman from Yun. She gave birth to Dou Bobi 鬬伯比. When Ruo Ao died, he went with his mother to be raised in Yun. Dou Bobi was a member of the Chu royal family. He was raised in the domain of the Viscount of Yun. As a youth he had illicit relations with his cousin, the daughter of the Viscount of Yun, who then gave birth to Zi Wen. The woman abandoned the child in Meng Marsh, where he was raised by a tiger. The Viscount of Yun was hunting when he saw the child and, fearing for him, brought him home. Discovering that the child was in fact his grandson, he then married his daughter formally to the father, Dou Bobi, and the child was accepted into the family; see Legge, *The Chinese Classics*, 5:297.

87. Du Ao 堵敖 is one of the names of Xiong Jian 熊艱, also known as Zhuang Ao 莊敖, third king of Chu (r. 676–672 B.C.E.). In the fifth year of his reign he decided to do away with his younger brother, Xiong Yun 熊惲. Xiong Yun, learning of this, fled but eventually returned, assassinated Du Ao, and usurped the throne. Xiong Yun, who came to be known as King Cheng of Chu, gradually developed a reputation for generosity and loyalty.

# CHAPTER FOUR

# Nine Cantos

# 九章

# Jiuzhang

The word *zhang* 章 in the title means, among other things, a section of a suite of songs, music, poetry, or other writing. I therefore translate it as "canto." Zhu Xi noticed that Sima Qian never mentions the *Nine Cantos* but listed one of its sections, the "Ai Ying" 哀郢 (Mourning Ying), as one of the works of Qu Yuan. Even the Han scholar-poet Yang Xiong (53 B.C.E.–18 C.E.), who lived into the Later Han dynasty, mentions the first poem, "Xi song" (I deplore pleading), and the fifth poem, "Huai sha" (Bosom full of sand), of the series but never *Nine Cantos*. These and other pieces in the *Nine Cantos* seem to have appeared later than "Mourning Ying" and were grouped into a series by some later editor, believed by many to be the Han scholar Liu Xiang, for it is in his writings that the title first appears. His purpose may have been to use them as lyrics for musical performance.

The *Nine Cantos*, with the exception of "Hymn to a Mandarin Orange Tree," are remarkably similar in content. They describe the strained relationship between a minister and a ruler in terms very reminiscent of the "Li sao." The minister and the ruler are therefore almost unanimously taken to be Qu Yuan and a Chu king, either Huai or Qing Xiang. Some of the poems describe or allude to exile and suicide. Because all the poems were traditionally ascribed to Qu Yuan, scholars for centuries have looked to them for biographical material not supplied by the *Shiji* biography or poems like the "Li sao" or the *Nine Songs*.

1

"I DEPLORE PLEADING"

惜誦

"XI SONG"

This work begins as courtroom testimony in verse. The plaintiff
addressed appears to be the king, who has accused the speaker, Qu Yuan
or a Qu Yuan–like person, of disloyalty. Early Chinese writings suggest
that the state of Chu had a highly developed legal system, but details
were not forthcoming until the discovery of tomb no. 2 at Baoshan in
1987. The tomb occupant, who was a legal officer named Shao Tuo, was
buried in 316 B.C.E. with over two hundred bamboo slips containing
among other things records of court cases. They reveal that Chu courts
required witnesses to take an oath before the spirits to tell the truth,
which functioned somewhat like swearing on the Bible in the West. As
Susan Weld, a specialist in ancient Chinese law, has put it,

> A possibly distinctive aspect of Chu justice may be related to the
> region's reputation for religious excess and eccentricity. While the
> legal documents now available from both Qin and early Han
> emphasize the use of careful interrogation—backed by torture if
> necessary—as the way to secure truth in judicial proceedings, tor-
> ture is not apparent in Shao Tuo's documents. Instead judges and
> officials seem to have resorted to the judicial oath, relying, perhaps,
> on their subject's deep belief in the existence of, and the court's
> access to, a complex pantheon of ancestors, ghosts, and spirits.[1]

The persona in the poem appears to lose his case and in the end
resigns himself to exile.

**I Deplore Pleading**

I deplore pleading my own case to draw your sympathy,[2]
   Unleashing my outrage as I reveal my heart.
But, I swear, to speak thus is to do my all for you.
   Raising my hand I call the Blue Skies to be my witnesses.

Let the Five Lords arbitrate,
  Let the Six Spirits verify the evidence,
Let the mountains and rivers be the jury,
  And let Gao Yao pass the final verdict![3]

I served you, My Lord, with complete loyalty and sincerity.
  Yet, once I left the herd, you treated me like a wart.
For by neglecting to flatter I had turned my back on the crowd,
  Expecting a wise lord to understand.

Where my words walk my deeds follow.
  My face is the image of my heart.
Who better to judge me than my lord,
  With me, my own proof, always at his side?

Lord first, self last—what I thought only right
  Was the very thing the crowd loathed.
A mind on my lord's welfare and nothing else
  Made me everyone's enemy.

He of the unwavering heart
  Finds no protection.
He who has no family other than his lord
  Is on the road to ruin.

To think that I am disloyal in your eyes—
  I who forgot my own poverty
To serve you with so undivided a mind
  That I lost my way to the gates of your favor.

What crime is loyalty that I should be punished for it?
  That possibility never crossed my mind,
Nor that I would stumble and fall to the crowd's laughter
  As I walked the road they would not travel.

I was caught in a tangle of blame and slander
  I could not unravel,

My true feelings lying so low they could not surface,
    Blocked from view, I was helpless to clear my name.

My melancholy heart despaired,
    For no one cared to see what was really within me.
Surely there is too much to say to wrap in a parcel and send you—
    I would lay my heart before you, but have no way.

No one will understand if I retreat into silence.
    No one will listen if I step up and shout,
Ever thwarted in a maze,
    My heart sinks, confused and stunned.

I once dreamt I was a spirit waiting for a ferryboat
    In midair, stalled on my skyward rise,
So I had the God of Whetstones interpret the dream, and he said,[4]
    "It means your goals are lofty, but you have no allies.

You will end up in peril, alone, at odds with everyone."
    And he advised, "Though you long for him, you cannot depend on
    your lord.
Hot air from so many mouths will melt even metal.[5]
    The danger was there from the start.

"'If the soup burns your tongue, you blow on the cold cuts too—
    Why not change your goals
Rather than try to climb skyward without a ladder,
    As you are doing now—and always have?

"You so shock the crowd they turn against you.
    How can you think them your friends?
You serve the same lord as they, but for different reasons.
    How can you count on their support?

"Never forget the filial son, Shensheng of Jin,[6]
    Whose father believed slander and thought ill of him.
And Gun[7] who walked the unswerving path of the stubborn,
    And so never achieved his goal."

When he said my devotion would bring only resentment,
　　I ignored what seemed an excessive view,
But, "Nine broken arms will make you a doctor"—
　　Only now do I know his words are true.

Crossbows cocked overhead,
　　Nets spread underfoot—
Traps they've set to amuse my lord.
　　I would run for cover, but there is no cover.

Should I linger waiting for my luck to change,
　　Risking more trouble and worse accusations?
Or should I fly high for a perch far away—
　　Would my lord even ask where I'm going?

Should I run wild down the wrong path?
　　Perhaps I could bear it with a will less strong.
But, given who I am, a writhing agony would knot my heart
　　And tear the rib cage from my spine.

Pound magnolia, knead basil,
　　Grind the Shen pepper for food on the road.
Broadcast lovage[8] seeds, and plant chrysanthemum—
　　I want them to fragrance my grains in spring.

Fearing you do not trust the sincerity of these sentiments,
　　I say it over and over to make myself clear—
As I go into hiding, I gather these beauties,
　　Wishing, though distant, to never forget you.

2

## "CROSSING THE YANGTZE"

涉江

## "SHE JIANG"

Many scholars in China think that this poem is by Qu Yuan and that the place-names in it are reliable information about the itinerary of his exile in the south. On the basis of that assumption they proceed to speculate about at what point in his life the poem was written. There is little agreement, however, either about the course of the journey or the date of the poem. There are also scholars who think that Qu Yuan could not have written it. The main argument for that view is the presence of a number of typically Han elements in the poem. The wish to live forever in the third stanza is redolent of the very Han cult of the immortals (仙 *xian*); and referring to the south as "savage" seems to reflect Han, or at least not Chu, attitudes.

The poem alludes to the "Li sao," especially in the first stanza, as well as to the *Nine Songs*. The poetic persona seems to be Qu Yuan. Perhaps it was sung in a drama by someone playing that role. I agree with Hawkes that it is at least partially made up of fragments from other works.

### Crossing the Yangtze

In my youth I loved these strange clothes,[9]
And the love has not faded although I am old—
A sword's long glimmer drags from my waist,
On my head a cloud-piercing headdress towers,
And from my neck hang the moonlight gem and the precious *lu* jade.[10]

But when mud flowed into the waters of these times,
    the world forgot my value,
So I'm galloping high and not looking back.

Dragons, both green and white, pull my chariot,
    And when I roam with Lord Chonghua[11] in the *yao*-stone[12] gardens,
And climb the Kunlun Mountains[13] to eat the flower of jade,[14]
    I will live as long as Heaven and Earth,
And glow as bright as the sun and the moon.

Though I lament that no one knows me in the savage south,
    I will cross the Yangtze and Xiang[15] Rivers at dawn,
Look back as I mount the banks of the River Islet of E,[16]
    And sigh in the last breezes before autumn turns to winter,

As I walk my horses on the hillsides,
and halt my chariot in the Square Forest.[17]

Boarding a small boat on the Yuan[18] I float upstream.
Long oars of Wu strike the waves in unison,
But the lingering boat will not go forward,
and sits caught still in a whirlpool.
At dawn I set forth from Wangzhu
to spend the night at Chenyang.[19]
As long as I keep an upright heart,
What wound is exile in far wilds?

Yet entering the Xu River[20] I hesitate,
Lost, not knowing where I'm going,
As I go deep into darker and darker forest,
discovering the places where gibbons live.

Below the sun-blocking height of the mountains,
lost valleys of rain-filled gloom.
And above the high borderless realm of hail and snow,
no sky roof other than cloud swell.

Lamentable my joyless life here,
Living alone in the remotest part of the mountains—
Lacking the heart to change and herd with the vulgar,
Assuring me misery till the end of my days.

Jieyu[21] shaved his head.
Sanghu[22] went naked.

The loyal will be employed—
not necessarily.
The worthy will be put to use—
not necessarily.

Master Wu[23] met calamity,
Bi Gan's[24] flesh was minced and brined.

If such men suffered even under the ancient kings,
What do I expect my complaints will accomplish today?
Yet I hold to the Way and will not waver,
Certain to pass my days in the dark of the dark.

Luan:

As the simurghs and phoenixes
Distance themselves day by day,
Swallows, sparrows, wrens, and crows
Make their nests in the palace halls.
Winter daphne and magnolia
Die in the forest thickets.
The stench advances,
The fragrant cannot abide.

Yin and yang exchange places—
The times are out of joint.
Despairing, the loyal heart stands alone—
I'm getting out without a second thought.

3

"MOURNING YING"

哀郢

"AI YING"

"Ying" in the title of this poem is the Chu royal city, which was located northwest of Jiangling county in modern Hubei province. In 278 B.C.E. it was conquered and destroyed by the Qin army under the generalship of Bai Qi, and the Chu court fled east and established a new capital at Chen, which was located in Huaiyang county in modern Henan. The reigning king of Chu at that time was Qing Xiang. Most scholars assume that these events form the background of the poem and that its author is Qu Yuan. Controversies arise when they attempt to square the historical background with the author's biography. According to it, King Qing Xiang banished Qu Yuan, and Qu Yuan committed suicide before Chu went into decline with the defeat of 278 B.C.E. That means that the Qu Yuan of the biography could not have known about the fall of Ying. Indeed, the fall of Ying is never mentioned in the biography.

The poem is one of two poems in the series that do not imitate the "Li sao," although it is written in *sao* meter.

Those who insist that Qu Yuan wrote the poem revise the biography by having Qu Yuan in exile and still alive when Ying is sacked; the news about it is too much to bear, and he therefore commits suicide. The speaker of the poem tells us that he has not been back to Ying in nine years. Some scholars therefore conclude that the poem's beginning describes how the poet imagines the fall of Ying, and that the rest of the poem is for the most part a recollection of how he first left the city to go into exile years before. The problem with this approach is that there are no clear markers dividing imaginary parts from recollected parts. Added to these difficulties is the fact that parts of the poem appear to come from elsewhere or at least share parts with other poems. Of course many of these problems evaporate if we simply exclude the Qu Yuan biography from consideration and admit the possibility that the poem was written by someone else.

**Mourning Ying**

August Heaven,
    Your Mandate mixes blessing and curse.
      Why make the high families endure
    These shocking hardships,
And the common people separate and scatter,
    Losing each other,
Fleeing east,
    Right in the middle of spring?

We left the ancestral land for the long journey
    as refugees on the Long and Summer Rivers,[25]
through the gates of the royal city, with aching hearts.
    On a *jia* day[26] at dawn we set forth,
away from Ying and our old neighbors,
    despairing to know where it would end.

And I lifted both oars from the water to linger,
  grieving I would never see my lord again,
and watched the tall catalpa trees[27] pass sighing
  in a hailstorm of tears.
Drifting west past Summerhead,[28]
  I looked back, but saw no Dragon's Gate,[29]
and my heart, bewildered, tore in my breast
  wondering where on the vast land to set foot,
as wind and waves tossed me downriver,
  a stranger thenceforth on wide water.

I ride Yanghou's[30] swelling waves
  suddenly soaring I know not where,
my heart tied in knots too tight to unravel,
  helplessly trammeled and tangled in longing.

I turn the boat to float downstream,
  stern to Lake Dongting,[31] prow to Long River,
leaving behind our home since unremembered time,
  to arrive in the east this aimless day.

Yes, the soul's wish to return—
  how stop it for even an instant?
My back to Summershore,[32] my heart longing west,
  mourning the old city daily more distant.

I climb a high mound to see how far away it lies,
  small ease for my melancholy,
and look back, grieving, to tranquil joys in a lost country,
  missing the ancient river-land ways.

Time to face Lingyang[33] (where am I going?),
  to cross the broad southern waters (where am I going?).
How can it be that our mansions are reduced to hills,
  How can it be that the eastern gates are overgrown with weeds?

So long has my heart been cheerless.
      Worry gives way only to sadness,
thoughts go the long distance back to Ying,
      across the Yangtze and Xia I may not cross.

Hard to believe what time has passed,
      nine years ago I left and never went back,
and melancholy builds with no way out,
      locked in despair, a bitter taste in my mouth.

Parading their skin-deep charms they won your favor,
      But they were weak inside—on them you could not lean.
Yet when I approached to give you my all,
      They blocked my way with anything they could find.

The lofty ways of Yao and Shun[34]
Approached the glory of the skies.
Why do the slanderers in their envy
falsely label them unkind?

You've come to hate the quiet beauty of the unflauntingly loyal,
and delight in the high martial spirits of the others,
The crowd, sprinting into your presence day after day,
while the beautiful drift farther and farther away.

Luan:

I let my gaze wander the vast unpeopled land.
When will I have one chance to return?
Birds fly back to their old country,
The fox dies facing his natal hills.
Exiled indeed for no crime,
Could I night or day ever forget home?

# 4

## "EXPRESSING MY LONGING"

## 抽思

## "CHOU SI"

Wang Yi claimed that the *Nine Cantos* were written during the reign of King Qing Xiang—that is, after the death of Qu Yuan's first king, King Huai. Scholars have therefore looked to these poems for about two thousand years for certain details about Qu Yuan's life. The chief problem with this poem in that regard is that it tells us that the speaker of the poem is in exile north of the Han River, whereas most of the tradition, including that subscribed to by Wang Yi, claims that King Qing Xiang exiled Qu Yuan to the south. Qing scholars noticing this decided that this poem, and possibly others in the series, must have been written during the time of King Huai. The place of Qu Yuan's banishment, and even whether Qu Yuan was banished at all at that time, are left unclear in the *Shiji* biography. Later scholars fill in those lacunae with this poem, saying that Qu Yuan was banished to the north by King Huai. I agree with Hawkes that certain features of the poem, especially its division into "song" sections, argue against authorship by Qu Yuan and for later composition by someone who intended it to be performed, perhaps in a kind of drama. The "Li sao"–style lover's complaint conceit is especially apparent in the first part of the poem.

### Expressing My Longing

A thicket of grief entangles my heart.
My every lonely sigh sharpens the pain.
This intricate binding of longing will not loosen,
And so I endure the endless night.


I grieve when the autumn wind changes the shape of things.
Why is everything blowing away as far as the eye can see,[35]
Bringing to mind time after time Lure Leaf's wrath
That wounded my heart with sorrow on sorrow?

I want to stagger to my feet and run away wild,
But seeing your subjects suffering I compose myself,
And gather my trifling thoughts to set forth,
And lift them up as offering to you, Beautiful One:

Once, My Lord, you gave me your word
That you would meet me at dusk,
But midway you took another road.
How could I have known you desired someone else?

You flaunted your goodness and beauty before me,
Revealing your splendors to my eyes alone,
Yet not one thing you promised you ever delivered—
Why, then, seek reasons to rage against me?

I hoped to explain myself when the opening came,
But my heart pounded so, I did not dare.
Sad and hesitant I hoped to face you,
But my heart hurt so, I held my tongue.

One by one I lay these facts before you,
But, Lure Leaf, you pretend you cannot hear
The sincere man who never flatters,
Always a threat in the eyes of the crowd.

Could it be that what I warned about
From the beginning you have forgotten now?
Why do I take such joy in frankness?
I hope to bring back the beauty of Lure Leaf.

If you look to the Three and the Five[36] as models,
And take Peng and Xian[37] as your ideals,
Then what goal will you fail to reach?
And your fame, known far and wide, will not fade.
Goodness is no mere matter of surface.
Reputation is not to be built on air.
What return is there for those who do nothing?
What harvest for those who grow no fruit?

The little song says:

I have emptied my heart before the Beautiful One,
Night and day, with no one there to judge my case.
She paraded her beauty before me,
Belittling my words, ignoring my advice.

The lead singer's song:

A bird from the south
Flew north of the Han River and perched on a tree.
Though fine feathered and beautiful,
A solitary life it leads in a strange land.

A single bird apart from the flock,
With no good go-between at her side—
In the hearts of far-away bird land her image daily fades.
She would be willing to plead her own case, but finding no way,
She faces the distant northern mountains and weeps,
And gazes down on flowing waters and sighs.

I yearned for these short nights of early summer,
Yet dusk to dawn is long as a year.
Despite the distance from here to Ying,
My spirit goes there many times a night.

Not knowing which roads were crooked or straight
My spirit takes the moon and stars as guides,
Looking for a direct route, but seeing none,
Back and forth it wanders till it finds the way back.
And why is my soul so doggedly faithful?

The hearts of others are not like mine,
My go-between is useless, she cannot make the match,
And still you have no idea who I am.

Luan:

Against the long rush of the rapids,
Against the current of the Jiang and Tan Rivers,
Turning my madman's eyes everywhere, I head south,
To ease my heart for now.

But a strangely gnarled rock towers before me,
Hobbling my resolve,
I hesitate, I waver,
And advance cautiously.

Now with lingering doubts,
I spend the night in Beigu,[38]
Agitated and confused,
For in fact I'm but a wretched vagabond,

A sad, sighing, bitter soul,
A spirit yearning for someone far away,
But the journey is too long and I live in an unknown place,
And there are no matchmakers here.

I made this song of my yearning
For a moment's diversion,
But my sorry heart will not sing along—
To whom, then, will I tell these things?

5

## "A BOSOM FULL OF SAND"

懷沙

## "HUAI SHA"

Tradition has it that this poem is Qu Yuan's suicide note. In Sima Qian's biography, Qu Yuan composes (or recites) a slightly different version of it just before he jumps into the Miluo River. This takes place after a dialogue with a fisherman, who advises him to be less adamant and more adaptable. The episode involving the fisherman appears almost word for word in the *Songs of Chu* under the title "The Fisherman," with a somewhat different ending—no "Bosom Full of Sand," no suicide, just the fisherman floating downstream singing his Daoist advice. In the biography the story is presented as fact; in the anthology it is presented as parable. All of this renders the claim that "Bosom Full of Sand" is a real suicide note, or even the work of Qu Yuan, suspect.

The title refers to the practice of filling one's robe above the sash with sand in order make sure one's body sinks in water. It was one of many methods available to those who preferred suicide by drowning. Some say that the title means "yearning (*huai*) for sand (*sha*)," "Sand" being one of the ancient names for the place that is now known as Changsha (Long Sands) in Hunan. The fact that there is little in the way of longing for any particular place in the poem would seem to disqualify that interpretation.

### A Bosom Full of Sand

Summer's virile fire rising,
Plants and trees teeming, teeming,
My heart wounded and keening,
As I speed on the torrent to the south land.

My eye wanders unpeopled vastness,[39]
Its silence broad and tranquil,
while grief's cords bind me tighter,
And my pain and poverty deepen.

Yet looking within I find consolation,
In a heart that though wronged maintains its control.

They whittle the square to make it round,
But eternal laws can't be ignored.
Altering principles with which we began
Is what the noble-minded abhor.

If it was clearly marked and mindfully inked,
The plan as drawn we do not revise.
A sincere heart on an unswerving path
Is what the great extol.
If Craftsman Chui[40] had not taught how to cut wood,
Who could make wheels round or arrows straight?

Texts written in the blackest ink are hidden from view,
Because the blind find them hard to read.
And when Lou Li[41] squints but slightly,
The purblind think he cannot see.

They change white to black,
Invert the up and make it down.
They keep the phoenix in a bamboo cage,
While chickens and ducks dance through the air.

They mix jadestones and pebbles in a pail,
Level them off to weigh on the same scale.
It is surely the stupidity of the cabal
That blinds their eyes to any worth in me.

Struggling under a heavy weight
I've fallen into an uncrossable bog.
The *jin* jade is in my hand, the *yu* jade,[42] behind my lapels—
To whom will I show them now?

A pack of village dogs barking,
Barking at what before they've never seen—
Rejecting the extraordinary, suspecting the outstanding
Is always the way of mediocrities.

Mine is the simplest grain in the plainest wood, but deep.
The crowd does not care for my unusual pattern.
I am an abandoned pile of timber and lumber,
You do not know what you have in me.

Yet I redouble my benevolence, fortify my integrity,
And with careful magnanimity increase my inner wealth.
But Chonghua[43] is no longer with us—
Who now understands behavior such as mine?

Long is the history of worthies who find no good ruler,
And who knows why?
Long gone are Tang and Yu[44]—
Too distant even to yearn for.

So I will break this bond and drop my anger,
Restrain and steel myself.
Though I suffer, my dream will never change,
Let it be an ideal for others to follow.

I proceed on my way and stop in the north,
The dimming sun on its downward path.
I'll let go of my worries, find play in grief,
My only limit, the great end.

Luan:

Yuan and Xiang, wide, surging rivers,
swiftly flowing their separate ways,
This long road hidden in the forest,
Takes me to the far unknown.

My character and will
Keep me lonely and friendless.
With Bo Le[45] no longer with us,
Who can judge a good horse?
The span of each person's life
Is measured in advance.
With heart set, but mind wide open,
What have I to fear?

But the blades keep cutting and the tears keep flowing,
And I sigh and endlessly sigh.

In this world's muddy waters no one knows
Who I am, nor will they let me speak my heart.
Death, I know, cannot be refused,
And so I will not grudge it a life.
Let me clearly announce to the noble spirits,
I will emulate you.

# 6

## "LONGING FOR THE BEAUTIFUL ONE"

思美人

## "SI MEIREN"

David Hawkes thought this poem might be made up of two fragments,
for it appears to break in the middle with the words "Spring opens,"
which may be a clumsy attempt to write a song using various elements
from the "Li sao." Here, just as in the "Li sao," the relationship between
lovers is a metaphor for that between minister and ruler; plants stand
for people, the wagon and the road it travels symbolize the state and
how it is ruled, and Peng and Xian figure as embodiments of spiritual
and moral integrity. The suddenly shifting images and scenes are also
rather similar to those in the "Li sao" as well as the *Nine Songs*.

### Longing for the Beautiful One

Longing for the beautiful one,
I stand staring wide-eyed, brushing away tears.
The matchmaking has failed, my way is blocked,
And I can't send my words, even bound in a parcel.
For me, the speaker of plain truth, only trouble and resentment,
And to be stuck in a bog I cannot escape.
Night and day I speak my heart out loud,
But my dream sinks in the bulrushes and never reaches you.
I would send you my words on a floating cloud,
But when I ask Fenglong,[46] he will not take them.
I would have homing birds convey my message,
But of course they fly too high and fast to stop for such a task.

Gao Xin's[47] spirit power was so great
That the Mysterious Bird delivered his engagement gift to Jiandi.[48]
I would discard my principles to follow the vulgar,
But I'm ashamed to change course and thwart my own will.

Year after year I have suffered these wrongs.
Yes, I am full of anger, but my heart is still unchanged.
I would rather bear the suffering for the rest of my life—
What other course could I even entertain?

I know there is no smooth ride in old wheel tracks,
But I refuse to take another route.
Though my wagon has capsized, and the horses have fallen,
My heart will always long for this one road.

So, bridling Qi and Ji, I'll yoke them to the wagon again.
Zao Fu[49] will drive them for us.
Let us move forward slowly, don't rush.
Wait, for the time being, for the right moment.

I point to the west side of Bozhong Mountain,[50]
Let us meet there in the red and golden dusk.

Spring opens, growing season
Begins with the rise of the slow white sun.
I'll steal a moment of play to clear my heart,
To forget my worries along the Yangtze and the Summer Rivers.[51]

In the great thicket I pick fragrant angelica,
And gather evergreens on the islet, root and all,
Regretting I was born too late to meet the ancients—
With whom will I enjoy these sweet-smelling herbs?

The people here untangle knotweed to string through garden vegetables,
And work them into double sashes.
Banquet makings they luxuriantly wind around their waists,
And, of course, they wither and fall.

I tarry forgetting my worries, for now,
Watching the strange ways of the southerners,
Who when glad in their hearts,
Pretend to be fighting mad.

Where fragrant herbs and mud mix,
Fragrant flowers will surely rise above it.[52]

Their luxurious fragrance will carry far,
For what fills within will gradually waft out.
If you maintain integrity and character,
You will be widely known, though you live out of view.

Let creeping fig[53] be my matchmaker?
I'm afraid to lift my foot to climb the tree.
Depend on lotus to be my go-between?
I dread hoisting my robe to muddy my feet.

I find no joy in climbing so high,
And am incapable of sinking so low.
Indeed it is my nature to never submit,
So I pace the ground and do not act.

I will follow the plan exactly as first drawn.
My principles will never change.
I will live in exile, if that is my fate, for I am nearing my end.
I hope to use the time before sunset
To travel through the south alone,
For I long to see Peng and Xian.[54]

7

## "I LOOK BACK IN SADNESS"

惜往日

## "XI WANG RI"

This is one of the poems that even premodern scholars doubted was written by Qu Yuan. As far back as the Song dynasty it was noticed that this poem, like "I Grieve When the Whirlwind" (Bei hui feng), holds up Wu Zixu as an exemplary figure. Wu Zixu, however, defected from Chu to Wu and thus would seem an inappropriate hero for a member of the Chu royal family like Qu Yuan. On the other hand, one text excavated from the Chu tomb at Guodian presents Wu Zixu as a hero.[55] It is difficult to say at this point how sensitive Chu royals of the fourth century B.C.E. were about the case of Wu Zixu.

Another reason for doubting that Qu Yuan wrote it is that it appears to follow closely the *Shiji* biography. Finally, as Galal Walker has observed, it borrows too much from a later work, "Mourning Ying," to be considered an early work.

**I Look Back in Sadness**

I look back in sadness to the days when I was trusted,
    When I received your order to brighten the times,
To continue the sage-kings' task of enlightening the ruled,
    And clear up difficulties in interpreting the law.

The kingdom was prosperous and strong, the law was enforced.
    After you entrusted governance to me, your loyal slave, you daily
    rejoiced.
My heart was where you kept the royal secrets,
    And, even when I erred, you did not punish me.

But though a heart so simple and honest never leaks,
    It attracted slander and envy.
You dealt with me angrily,
    For you never distinguished the true from the false.

They sealed your ears and eyes,
>    Confused you with empty claims—deceived you.
You drew no line between fact and fiction—
>    You simply sent me far out of sight—and out of mind.

You believed the filth of slanderers.
>    Blinded by furious visions you punished me.
Why did they cover me, your blameless, upright slave,
>    With so much slander and abuse?
Because I was reliable as the sun and the moon,
>    And it put them to shame,
Now I hide from them in a dark place.

I look into the depths of the Yuan and Xiang Rivers,
>    Steeling myself to jump in and drown.
And though my body and name in the end disappear,
>    I'd regret if my lord had never known the truth.

Without standard to measure or eye to see
>    You've let fields of fragrant herbs become the darkest swamp.
Where can I show my love and regain your trust
>    So that I can die in peace or stop living in vain?

The only one barred at the gateway and hidden from view,
>    Your honest slave is at a loss.

I have heard that Baili[56] was held captive,
>    That Yi Yin[57] worked in the kitchen,
That Lü Wang[58] was a butcher in Zhaoge,
>    That Ning Qi[59] sang as he fed oxen.
If they had not met the likes of Tang, Yu, Huan, or Duke Mu,
>    Who in the world would know of them?

The King of Wu so believed slander he couldn't tell sweet from bitter,
>    But when Wu Zi[60] died, his worries began.
Only after Jia Zi's[61] loyalty reduced him to dry bones standing
>    Did Duke Wen of Jin wake up and go to find him,

And when he found him, he renamed the place for him,
    and declared it sacred,
To repay a debt so vast.
    And missing the friend who had never left his side,
He donned white hemp and wept.

Some are so loyal they will die for you,
    Some, so skilled in deceit, you will never doubt.

Not examining the facts
    You believed the slanderer's empty claims—
Now the flowers are mixed with the mud,
    And who even in the light of day can tell them apart?

Why do fragrant herbs die early?
    Because they take no precautions when fine frost falls.
You must be handicapped by hearing loss
    To allow slanderers and flatterers to gain ground by the day!

Even in the past there were those who, jealous of the worthy,
    Claimed that basil and galangal were not good belt charms.
Envious of the fragrance of the beautiful and refined,
Momu[62] made herself alluring and thought herself beautiful.
    Even if you have the beauty of a Xi Shi,
Envious slanderers will enter and displace you.

I wish to set forth the facts that show that behind my actions
    There was no intention to offend.
It should be clear, in the light of day, that I was dealt with unjustly,
    As clear as the constellations in the night sky.

Try not falling from a chariot drawn by thoroughbreds
    running wild without bridle and bit.
Try controlling a raft racing downstream
    with no oars.
Is it any different when you ignore the law
    and try to rule on whim?

I would prefer escape by sudden death
    To seeing the next inevitable catastrophe.
If I do not drown myself before finishing my plea,
It is because I pity my benighted lord in his confusion.


## 8

### "HYMN TO A MANDARIN ORANGE TREE"

橘松

### "JU SONG"

There are many theories about this poem. Most are based on the assumption that it is a work by Qu Yuan, which inevitably leads to attempts to locate what part of his political career it describes. Because it has no hint of the bitter disappointment we see in many of the other works attributed to him, some scholars assume that it was composed during his youth when his hopes and aspirations were still fresh and unthwarted. Some of those who subscribe to this theory even claim that Qu Yuan wrote it to praise himself. Others think that it was written when he was still an officer at court and that the poem is a kind of self-defense against slander. Still others think that it was written after his exile to the south, where he was inspired by the sight of mandarin orange trees growing there.

The poem becomes much more interesting if we concentrate less on questions of authorship and politics and examine the lore behind its rhetoric. Wang Yi, his attempt at forcing it into the Qu Yuan story notwithstanding, provides a very good clue to its rhetoric. He cites an old Chinese belief according to which the mandarin orange tree (*Citrus reticulata*) grows south of the Yangtze River, but, if it is planted north of the Yangtze, it changes into the hardy orange (*Poncirus trifoliata*), which has similar leaves and blossoms but bitter fruit.[63] He, however, began the tradition of thinking that the tree in the poem is growing in the south. I take the opposite view.

After the fall of Ying, the Chu capital, in 278, the capitals of Chu were all north of the Yangtze River. The tree that is being praised for its steadfastness is a mandarin orange tree that has "crossed the river"—that is, most probably one that has been transplanted from south of the Yangtze to one of the northern capitals. But, contrary to traditional lore, it has not changed into a hardy orange tree, thus becoming a metaphor for steadfast moral integrity. (I say "northern capital" because I take the first line as indicating that the tree was transplanted by royal command.) The hymn may have been written to celebrate its first fruiting.

At first glance the poem is unlike the other poems in the *Nine Cantos* and elsewhere in the *Chuci*. It is short and joyous, whereas most other poems ascribed to Qu Yuan are long and sad. On closer inspection, however, we observe a use of floral metaphor very similar to that of "Li sao" and other poems in the *Chuci*.

### Hymn to a Mandarin Orange Tree

The Lord August delights in planting,[64]
    So, orange tree, you came to serve.
You accepted his order but never changed,
    You who were born in the southern kingdom.[65]

Deep and firm, hard to move,
    The better to focus your will.
Your green leaves and white blossoms,
    Abound to our joy,
Up tiers of sharp-thorned branches
    Your round fruit spiral.
Shades of green and gold combine,
    Patterns appear and glisten.
Rich color lined with plain white pith,
    like one to entrust with a mission.

Adorned in so many happy ways,
    You are splendor without peer.[66]
We sigh before your youthful will.
    Something in you, different from the rest,
Stands alone and abides.
    How could we not delight in it?

So deep and solid, so hard to uproot,
    A spacious heart that seeks no gain.
You stand upright and apart from the world,
    Having crossed the river without yielding to the flow.

Lock your heart, guard yourself,
    Allow no trespass,
Maintain your virtue selfless
    As the sky and the earth.

With you we would pass the withering years,
    Friends always,
With your pure unflaunting beauty,
    straight and strong in your orderly grain,

And fit, though young,
    to teach the old,
You act as Bo Yi[67] would—
    Let us raise you as our model.

9

## "I GRIEVE WHEN THE WHIRLWIND"

悲回風

## "BEI HUIFENG"

This poem was originally counted, as were all the other poems in this series, as one of the works of Qu Yuan. By the Song dynasty opinion had begun to change. Some scholars recognized stylistic divergence between the poem and many of the other poems attributed to Qu Yuan. Many noticed similarities between it and "Xi Wang ri," "Yuan you," "Ai Ying," and poems elsewhere in the anthology. Nevertheless there are still many scholars who think that it was written by Qu Yuan.

    "I Grieve When the Whirlwind" is a difficult poem. It is not clear whether it was written that way or whether later editors added parts to it that left it garbled. Its last two lines, for example, appear to have been lifted from "Mourning Ying." Another possibility is that the original order of some of the bamboo slips onto which it was transcribed was lost.

Especially difficult is the long dream sequence that seems to begin with the phrase "in a waking dream." That is one of the possible meanings of a word that is usually translated as "to wake up." My reason for using the alternative and rare meaning is that the word comes after a passage describing a sleepless night. At the end of the dream sequence the "beautiful woman," who appears to stand for an out-of-favor courtier, suddenly wakes up. But that awakening occurs after she has stopped to "rest" near the mythical place from which winds originate. Thus it is unclear whether she is awakening from her "rest" (which may or may not involve sleep) or from her waking dream. Or is it meant to be a clever device where falling asleep in a dream signals awakening from a dream, corresponding with the waking up in a dream that marks the end of sleeplessness earlier in the poem.

The dream itself outdoes the "Li sao" in obscurity and should be ranked as one of the ancient predecessors of surrealism. Its imagery shows the influence of the Han cult of the immortals (*xian*), whose adherents believed the absorption of certain forms of *qi*, through breathing, eating, osmosis, and even certain sexual practices, conferred superhuman powers and even immortality. This is especially obvious in the latter part of the dream sequence. The stanzas describing turbulent river waters, right after the dream sequence, give the impression of lines to be sung in a dramatic performance where someone playing Qu Yuan contemplates suicide. Interestingly, the end of the poem seems at least rhetorically to deny the value of suicide. Is this evidence that there was a non-suicidal version of Qu Yuan? Or, perhaps, that the persona of the poem is not meant to be taken as Qu Yuan?

### I Grieve When the Whirlwind

I grieve when the whirlwind harasses the basil.[68]
    Sorrow tangles my heart, I bleed inside,
For a tiny thing is losing its life,
    While an invisible singer leads the song.

How is it that I look back, longing, to Peng and Xian,
    Hoping that their aspirations and high moral principle never be
    forgotten?
What wavering heart can ever be disguised?
    How long can the empty and false endure?

Birdsong or beast cry is signal to the flock,
    but even the sweetest herb will stink when worn in a shoe.[69]
Scales form on each fish to mark its kind,
    but the flood dragon's markings are hidden.

Thus sow thistle and shepherd's purse[70] never live in the same field,
    but thoroughwort and angelica are fragrant
even when they grow where no one goes—
    For the beautiful, no matter how the times change,
are always their own measure.

Wherever they find themselves, those who see far
    will always love the freedom of floating clouds.
But what is it like, you might ask, when the lofty and far-sighted
    find themselves at a loss?
That I will humbly explain in this poem:

Consider a beautiful woman lonely and longing for her lover,
    picking fragrant pepper to eke out a living,
sighing, constantly sighing,
    living hidden and careworn,

feeling chill after chill of crisscrossing tears,
    she lies awake until dawn, yearning
through a long night of slow hours,
    with no way out of flooding sorrow.

Then, in a waking dream,[71] she wanders everywhere,
    A moment of freedom that brings her hope.
But when she feels the pain of deep sighing regret,
    she cannot stop the choking sobs.

Braiding her yearning, she makes bellybands for her horses,
    and breast bands[72] woven of bitter sorrow,
and breaks a hibiscus branch for sunshade,
    and would go wherever the whirlwind goes.
But no whirlwind appears, being only a phantom,
    and her heart leaps like boiling water.
So she calms herself, arranging her robes and belt charms,
    And in deep despair continues her journey.

The year speeds away as though dropped from a cliff,
    and sun-slow time will soon bring the season
when club rush and asarum wither and fall,
    and flowers are too weak to even lean on each other.

Pity her longing heart that cannot be cowed,
    proof that her words mean just what they say:
She would sooner escape by sudden death
    than bear her heart's constant sorrow.

The orphan moaning as she wipes away tears,
    the banished going out to never come back—
Who can think on such things without pain?
    Peng and Xian suffered such, they say!

She climbs the rocky heights to scan the far distance.
    Now begins the journey through vast silence,
where she casts no shadow and makes no sound,
    where she cannot hear or see or think,

where she bears the weight of sadness with no relief,
    and sorrow binds and never slackens,
and a bridled heart cannot break free,
    And anger within her tangles and knots.

In the borderless silence,
    in the vast featureless void,

the voice of the formless wind moves her nevertheless,
　　　but the pure ones, though here, are helpless.

Through immeasurable space,
　　　shadowy, indistinct, ungraspable,
she suffers constant sorrow,
　　　joyless even as she flies through dark skies.

Riding the great waves and flowing with the wind,
　　　she finds refuge where Peng and Xian dwell,
here she climbs to the edge of a steep cliff,
　　　and perching herself high on the pale arc of a female rainbow,[73]

She unfolds the male rainbow's colors against blue space.
　　　Then, suddenly she is stroking the sky,
and drinking thick dew from a floating spring,
　　　and rinsing her mouth in a freezing flurry of frost.

Seeking shelter she stops at the ice-cold Wind Cave,[74]
　　　when she suddenly falls on her side and wakes up bewildered.

She leans on a Kunlun boulder overlooking the mist,
　　　that covers Min Mountain[75] and the clear Long River.
She is startled by the sound of rapid waters crashing on stones,
　　　and the violent surge of waves in her ear.

The lawless churning flow,
　　　the vast borderless chaos,
wave upon wave pressing in from no beginning,
　　　an undulating rush to what end?

Turning over and over, up and down,
　　　flying far to the left and right,
tossing and rising in front and behind,
　　　arc and trough faithfully coupling.

She observes the continuous production of fiery vapor,
　　　watches mist condensing into rain,

laments the fall of snow and frost,
    and hears the sound of the ramming tide.

She uses her time to come and go,
    Wielding a curved whip of yellow jujube,
seeking the remains of Jie Zhitui,
    Looking for Bo Yi's exiled footprints—
the ones who adjusted, but did not abandon, their precepts,
    the ones who engraved an unfading thought on their hearts.

I say:
I resent the thwarted hopes of the past,
And fear the horrors to come.
I will float on the Yangtze and Huai and sail out to sea
Following Zixu[76] for the pleasure of it.

I will look toward distant islets on the great Yellow River,
And sadly recall the noble path of Shentu Di[77]
Who having tried many times
To set his heedless ruler straight,
Jumped into a river with a stone on his back,
Accomplishing what?

My heart tied in knots too tight to unravel,
I am helplessly trammeled and tangled in longing.

## NOTES

1. Susan Roosevelt Weld, "Chu Law in Action: Legal Documents from Tomb 2 at Baoshan," in *Defining Chu: Image and Reality in Ancient China*, ed. Constance A. Cook and John S. Major (Honolulu: University of Hawai`i Press, 1999), 96.
2. Here, with Tang Bingzheng, I read *song* 訟, "bring a case to court," for *song* 誦, which can mean a number of things, including "chant," "remonstrate," and "complain." The two characters are interchangeable. See Tang Bingzheng 湯炳正, Li Daming 李大明, Li Cheng 李誠, and Xiong Liangzhi 熊良知, *Chuci jinzhu* 楚辭今注 (Shanghai: Shanghai guji chubanshe, 1997), 124.
3. The sky was often conceived of as plural in China. The Five Lords were the gods of the five directions, Taihao (East), Yandi (South), Shao Hao (West), Zhuan Xu

(North), and Huang Di (Center). The Six Spirits are variously explained. Zhu Xi tells us that they are the spirits of (1) sun, (2) moon, (3) stars, (4) water and drought, (5) the four seasons, and (6) cold and heat. Gao Yao was a minister of the sage-king Shun. He was his chief justice and known for his wisdom and fairness. He is sometimes thought of as the inventor of law.

4. The God of Whetstones (厲神 Lishen) rules untimely death but is also the spirit who possesses and empowers shamans specializing in dream interpretation. The shaman thus possessed will be addressed by the spirit's name.

5. "Hot air from so many mouths" seems to be a metaphor derived from blast furnaces used for smelting, such as the ancient one discovered at Daye 大冶 in Hubei, where a continuous stream of air was produced by the coordinated application of many bellows.

6. Shensheng 申生 was the heir apparent of Duke Xian of the state of Jin (晉獻公 Jin Xiangong) during the Spring and Autumn period known for his filial piety. He was the son of the duke's principal wife, Qi Jiang 齊姜. The duke, however, fell under the spell of Li Ji 驪姬, one of his concubines. She induced him to demote Qi Jiang and make her his principal wife instead. Li Ji of course wanted to have her own son Xiqi 奚齊 designated heir apparent. Toward this end she arranged to have Shensheng and two of his three half brothers sent away to defend the borders of Jin from barbarian raiders. In the meantime, Shensheng's mother died. Li Ji convinced him that he could appropriately offer sacrifices to his mother while still on the frontier, and that the customary offering of sacrificial food to his father could be accomplished when he returned to the capital. Before Duke Xian received the food, Li Ji had it intercepted and poisoned. Duke Xian as usual had it tested before he touched it. The poisoning was of course blamed on Shensheng, who in turn hanged himself, unable to bear revealing the truth about his stepmother to his father; see *Zuozhuan*, Xigong, 4th year, in James Legge, *The Chinese Classics*, 5 vols. (Oxford: Clarendon Press, 1893–1894; repr., Hong Kong: Hong Kong University Press, 1960), 141–42.

7. Gun 鯀 in Chinese mythology is the father of Yu, the founder of the Xia dynasty. The sage-king Yao charged him with stopping the Great Flood, but he failed. Yao then had him executed on Feather Mountain, where his corpse lay for three years without decomposing. Finally someone cut him open and out came Yu. The corpse then turned into a turtle, dragon, or bear, depending on the source, and jumped into a deep lake.

8. Lovage (江離 *jiangli*) is *Ligusticum chuanxiong*, a plant that grows in both Europe and Asia. Its leaves and roots are edible and its seeds can be used as a spice. It tastes somewhat like celery.

9. The "strange clothes" described here are similar to those mentioned in "Li sao" and are presumably those of a shaman.

10. The moonlight gem emits a moonlike light even in the dark. It is not clear what *lu* 璐 jade is, save that it is fine jade.

11. Chonghua 重華 is one of the names of the sage-king Shun, whose spirit was consulted in the "Li sao" at his burial place on Jiuyi 九疑 (Nine Doubts) Mountain near Changsha.

12. *Yao* stone 瑤 is a white jadelike stone.

13. There are two Kunlun 崑崙 mountain ranges, one real, one legendary; this is the legendary one, where spirits and powerful shamans live.

14. Flower of jade 玉英 is jade of magical purity.

15. The Xiang 湘 River, in Hunan, is a tributary of the Yangtze.

16. The River Islet of E (鄂渚 Ezhu) was probably an islet in the Yangtze near Wuchang in Hubei. E was where King Xiong Qu of Chu enfeoffed his middle son, Hong.

17. No one knows for sure what the Square Forest is.

18. The Yuan 沅 is a river in Hunan and another tributary of the Yangtze.

19. Wangzhu 枉陼 was a place along the Yuan River, south of Changde county in modern Hunan. Chenyang 辰陽 was west of Chenxi county in Hunan.

20. The Xu River 漵浦 flows past the old site of Chenyang and into the Yuan River. It is difficult to tell whether the journey described here is real or imaginary. The journey bears some resemblance to the spirit journeys described in the *Nine Songs*.

21. Jieyu 接輿, also known as the Madman of Chu, was a famous hermit who feigned madness rather than serve a corrupt ruler. The *Analects* describes an incident in which he stood in the road and sang a song to Confucius as he passed by in a chariot urging him to give up trying to change the world. Some legends tell us that he wore his uncut hair loose and flowing; others say that he shaved his head.

22. Sanghu 桑扈 is possibly Zi Sanghu 子桑扈, mentioned in the *Zhuangzi*, or Zi Sang Bozi 子桑伯子 in the *Analects*. He, like Jieyu, showed his disapproval of power politics by becoming a hermit. The *Zhuangzi* tells us that he was so poor he had nothing to eat. The *Confucius Family Sayings* (孔子家語 *Kongzi jiayu*) tells us that he was so unconventional that he refused to wear clothes.

23. Master Wu (Wuzi) is Wu Zixu 伍子胥, who was originally from Chu but, when King Ping of Chu executed his father, defected to Wu, where he helped King Helü defeat Chu at the battle of Boju. When the Wu forces took the Chu capital, Wu Zixu desecrated the tomb of King Ping of Chu. Wu Zixu also served the next king of Wu, Fuchai, but less successfully. That king took offense at Wu Zixu's opinion that Yue was a threat to Wu and ordered him to commit suicide. He had Wu Zixu's body wrapped in a leather sack and thrown into the Yangtze River; see Sima Qian 司馬遷, *Shiji* 史記 (Beijing: Zhonghua shuju, 1992), 66.2180. Bi Gan 比干 served Zhou Xin, the last king of the Shang dynasty.

24. When Bi Gan 比干 criticized the king for his cruelty, the king executed Bi Gan and had his heart torn out; see *Shiji* 3.108.

25. The Long River (長江Changjiang) is better known as the Yangtze River in the West. The Summer River (夏 Xia) branches off from it and runs parallel until it empties into the Han River. The river is full in summer and dries up in the winter, thus the name.

26. In ancient China a series of ten signs were used to designate a ten-day week. These were known as the ten stems. *Jia* 甲 is the first day of the week. Its use here is as vague as saying "on a Monday."

27. Catalpa trees seem to have been a favorite tree in Ying. Some say that they were planted near grave sites.

28. Summer Head (夏首 Xiashou) is where the Summer River branches out from the Yangtze southeast of Ying in modern Shashi in Hubei. To reach the Yangtze River from Ying one could go west on the Summer River.

29. The Dragon Gates were the two eastern gates in the wall around the city of Ying.

30. Some say that Lord Yang was the Lord of Lingyang (陵陽侯 Lingyang Hou) who drowned himself in the river and thus became the god of the waves; see *Huainanzi*, "Surveying Obscurities," in John S. Major, Sarah A. Queen, Andrew Seth Meyer, and Harold D. Roth, trans., *The Huainanzi: A Guide to the Theory and Practice of Government in Early Han China* (New York: Columbia University Press, 2010), 214.

31. Lake Dongting is in northern Hunan on the southern bank of the Yangtze. Four rivers, the Xiang, Zi, Yuan, and Li, flow into it. Here the journey passes the place where the Yangtze River and Lake Dongting connect.

32. Summer Shore (夏浦 Xiapu) is also known as Xiakou 夏口, or Summer Mouth. It is modern-day Hankou, where the Han River enters the Yangtze, near Wuhan.

33. Some say Lingyang refers to a place in Anhui; others say it refers to a prince by that name who became a god of the waves, referred to as Lord Yang in the preceding.

34. Yao and Shun, the sage-kings, were thought by some to be fathers who mistreated their sons because neither chose his son, but only the ablest person, to succeed him to the throne.

35. "As far as the eye can see"—I follow Wang Siyuan in my interpretation of *huiji* 回極, reading it as *siji* 四極; see Wang Siyuan 王泗原, *Chuci jiaoshi* 楚辭校釋 (Beijing: Renmin jiaoyu chubanshe, 1990), 164–65.

36. The Three and the Five are variously identified. Some say that the phrase stands for the Three Augusts (Fuxi, Nü Wa, Shennong,) and the Five God-Lords (Huang Di, Zhuan Xu, Di Ku, Di Yao, Di Shun). Wang Yi says that they are the Three Kings (Yu of the Xia, Tang of the Shang, King Wen of the Zhou) and the Five Hegemons (Duke Xuan of Qi, Duke Wen of Jin, Duke Mu of Qin, Duke Xiang of Song, King Zhuang of Chu).

37. Peng Xian 彭咸 in the next line is parallel with Three and Five (三五 Sanwu) in the first line, suggesting that Peng Xian should be read as Peng and Xian. There

is no basis for taking these two lines (about the Three and the Five and Peng and Xian) as having two separate subjects, other than an ambiguous note by Wang Yi.

38. Beigu 北姑 is presumably a place-name, but that is all anyone knows about it.

39. South China during the Warring States period did not extend as far as Guangdong, Guangxi, Guizhou, Yunnan, etc. "Southern" meant Hubei, Hunan, Anhui, etc. The southern regions, many of which were occupied by Chu at its height, were viewed by northerners as underpopulated.

40. Craftsman Chui 倕 is the mythical inventor of such things as measuring instruments, musical instruments, and woodworking techniques.

41. Li Lou 離婁 is a mythical figure endowed with supernormal vision who is said to have lived in the time of the Yellow Emperor.

42. *Jin* jade 瑾 and *yu* jade 瑜 are obscure. They are simply defined as types of fine jade.

43. See note 11.

44. Tang 湯 was the founder of the Shang dynasty, and Yu 禹 is the founder of the Xia dynasty.

45. Bo Le 伯樂 is a legendary expert on horses; see *Liezi* 列子, vol. 3 of *Zhuzi jicheng* 諸子集成 (Shanghai: Shanghai shudian, 1987), 8.8b.

46. Fenglong 豐隆 is the cloud god or the thunder god, also mentioned in "Li sao."

47. Gao Xin 高辛, also known as Di Ku 帝嚳, is often counted as one of the five legendary sage-kings or god-lords. He is the legendary ancestor of the Shang royal house.

48. The Mysterious Bird, or Dark Bird (玄鳥 Xuanniao), dropped an egg while in flight, and Di Ku's consort, Jiandi 簡狄, ancestress of the Shang dynasty, ate it. It appears to have made her pregnant with Qi 啟, who grew up to help the sage-king Shun control the Great Flood, after which he was rewarded with the Shang domains.

49. Zao Fu 造父 is a legendary expert charioteer who served King Mu of the Zhou 周穆王. He drove when King Mu went to visit the Queen Mother of the West.

50. Bozhong 嶓冢 Mountain is located in Xi prefecture, in modern Gansu (see *Hanshu* 漢書, comp. Ban Gu 班固 [Beijing: Zhonghua shuju, 1962], 28B.1610). It is the place where the Qin state began. Here it refers to the west, where the sun is setting, metaphor for the late years of a person's life.

51. See note 25.

52. A similar image is used in "Li sao." It is similar to the lotus flower, in Buddhist symbolism, rising over the mud from which it grows.

53. Creeping fig (*Ficus pumila*) is *bili* 薜荔 in Chinese, a parasitic plant that grows clinging and climbing up trunks and boughs of trees.

54. It is difficult to tell whether the author of this poem thought of Peng Xian as one person or two.

55. Scott Cook, *The Bamboo Texts of Guodian: A Study and Complete Translation* (Ithaca, N.Y.: Cornell University Press, 2012), 463.

56. Baili refers to Baili Xi 百里傒, who was the chief minister of the Duke of Yu 虞 during the Spring and Autumn period. After the state of Yu was conquered by Jin, the Duke and Baili were taken captive. When the ruler of Jin married his daughter to Duke Mu of Qin (659–620 B.C.E.), he sent Baili along as a slave in her retinue. Baili escaped on the way but was captured by Chu troops. Duke Mu, having heard that Baili was a talented and intelligent man, reclaimed him from Chu by offering five black ram hides. He then made him his chief minister (*Mengzi*, "Wanzhang shang," and *Shiji*, "Jin benji," 39:1647).

57. Yi Yin 伊尹 was chief minister of Tang, the founder of the Shang dynasty. He started out as a slave and, before rising to chief minister, served as a cook.

58. Lü Wang 呂望 is also known as Lü Shang 呂尚 and Jiang Taigong 姜太公. He worked as a butcher in the city of Zhaoge and fished on the banks of the Wei River. King Wen of Zhou could tell he had extraordinary talent immediately upon meeting him and gave him high office. Later he helped King Wu of Zhou overthrow the Shang dynasty.

59. Ning Qi 甯戚 was a native of the state of Wei during the Spring and Autumn period who used to express his thoughts in song while feeding his cattle. When Duke Huan of Qi heard him, he was so moved that he gave him high office.

60. Wu Zixu 伍子胥 was originally a subject of King Ping 平 of Chu (r. 528–516 B.C.E.). He fled to Wu after the king killed his father and elder brother. Once in Wu, he became a military adviser to King Helü 闔閭, helping him defeat Chu after a number of military engagements between the two states between 511 and 504 B.C.E. He is reputed to have desecrated the tomb of King Ping when he returned to Chu with the triumphant Wu army. He did not fare so well under the next Wu king, Fu Chai 夫差, who, under the influence of Wu Zixu's enemies, turned against him and eventually required that he commit suicide. See *Shiji*, "Wu Zixu liezhuan," 66.2171–83.

61. Jie Zhitui 介之推 was a faithful official of Chong'er 重耳 (also known as Duke Wen of Jin) during the Spring and Autumn period. When Chong'er fled Jin after his father turned against him, he went into a nineteen-year exile, during which time Jie Zhitui and a number of others remained his faithful followers. When Jie Zhitui returned to Jin to take the throne, all the followers lined up to receive their rewards—except Jie Zhitui. Chong'er therefore neglected to reward him. Meanwhile Jie Zhitui retired to Mian Mountain with his mother. Chong'er, finally realizing that he had overlooked Jie Zhitui, went to look for him. Jie, however, refused to come down from the mountain. Chong'er tried to force him by setting fire to the mountain on three sides, leaving one side free for Jie's escape, but Jie embraced a tree instead and allowed himself to be consumed by the flames. His charred corpse was discovered still standing, its arms around the

tree. Later, Chong'er renamed Mian Mountain Jie Mountain and made it a sacred precinct (*Zuozhuan*, Xigong, 24th year; Legge, *The Chinese Classics*, 5:191); *Shiji*, 39.1662.

62. Momu 嫫母, was the very ugly secondary wife of the Yellow Emperor. See Hong Xingzu 洪興祖, *Chuci buzhu* 楚辭補注 (Beijing: Zhonghua shuju, 1986), 152.

63. For a story that alludes to the lore, see *Yanzi chunqiu*, "Nei pian za xia" 晏子春秋, 內篇雜下, quoted in Jin Kaicheng 金開誠, Dong Hongli 董洪利, and Gao Luming 高路明, *Qu Yuan ji jiaozhu* 屈原集校注, 2 vols. (Beijing: Zhonghua shuju, 1996), 2:608.

64. Many translators take *shu* 樹 in its later meaning, "tree." Zhu Xi advised reading the character according to its usual Warring States period sense, "to plant." He also read Houhuang 后皇 (Lord August) not as "Heaven and Earth," as did Wang Yi, but as an epithet for a Chu ruler. I follow Zhu Xi. (He thought, however, the Chu ruler was King Huai. I do not.) Accordingly, I take *fu* 服 to mean "serve" rather than Wang Yi's "acclimatize."

65. The southern kingdom may be southern Chu or another kingdom further south.

66. Reading *chou* 儔 (same kind) rather than the interchangeable *chou* 醜 (ugly).

67. Despite recognizing the cruelty of the last king of the Shang dynasty, Bo Yi and his brother Shu Qi refused to eat grain grown under the reign of the Zhou king who finally overthrew the Shang. They retired to Shouyang Mountain and starved to death instead. By producing mandarin oranges rather than bitter hardy oranges, the mandarin tree demonstrates that it maintains its character despite being transplanted from south to north, just as Bo Yi maintained his loyalty despite change of regime. See the introduction to this poem for the lore behind this interpretation.

68. The Chinese is *hui* 蕙, which is *Ocimum basilicum* L., not orchid, as Hawkes has it.

69. *Ju* 苴 is the straw lining of a shoe. Thus the phrase *cao ju bi* 草苴比 means "herb and straw shoe lining put together."

70. Sow thistle (*Sonchus oleraceus*) is *tu* 荼, and shepherd's purse (*Capsella bursa-pastoris*) is *ji* 薺—a bitter vegetable and a sweet vegetable, respectively.

71. The difficulty in this passage emerges when we consider the fact that the woman is described in the preceding stanza as having passed a sleepless night. This stanza begins with the word *wu* 寤, which normally means "to wake up." Hawkes tried to solve the problem by translating *wu* as "rising," but the character cannot refer to the physical act of getting out of bed without having slept—it must involve waking up. There is, however, a rare meaning of *wu*, which may be active here, i.e., as an abbreviation for *wu meng* 寤夢, "to have a waking dream." The woman seems to wake up from this waking dream later in the poem.

72. The words *xiang* 纕 and *ying* 膺 can both refer to horse accoutrements, as well as

items worn by humans. The equine reference appears to be the intended one here.

73. This is referring to the phenomenon of the double rainbow. The primary rainbow, with its bright colors, is referred to as the male rainbow (虹 *hong*) in Chinese. The fainter, secondary rainbow that appears over it is called *ni* 霓, or *cini* 雌霓, "female rainbow."

74. Fengxue 風穴 can also be translated as "Wind Hole." Located in the north, it is where the winds of winter come from; see John S. Major et al., trans., *The Huainanzi: A Guide to the Theory and Practice of Government in Early Han China* (New York: Columbia University Press, 2010), 6.5, p. 221.

75. The name of the mountain is also written Min 岷. There is a mountain by that name in Sichuan. It was believed, inaccurately, that the Yangtze River started there.

76. On Wu Zixu, see note 60.

77. Shentu Di 申徒狄 was a fearless minister who criticized the brutality of Djou, the last Shang king. Unheeded, he drowned himself in the river, hugging a stone to his chest; or, according to some versions, holding a stone on his back. I have filled out the stanza here to make it intelligible in translation.

# CHAPTER FIVE

# "Wandering Far Away"

# 遠遊

# "Yuan you"

"Wandering Far Away" was thought to be the work of Qu Yuan until the Qing dynasty, when some scholars began to have doubts. They observed that the quest to attain immortality that runs throughout the poem has more in common with the Daoist cult of the immortals, popular during the Qin and Han dynasties, than with the world represented in works such as the "Li sao" and the *Nine Songs*, where the immortals never appear.

Other scholars noticed similarities between "Wandering Far Away" and "The Great Man Rhapsody" (大人賦 "Daren fu") of the Han poet Sima Xiangru 司馬相如, speculating that he was the author of "Wandering Far Away" and that it was an early draft of "The Great Man Rhapsody." Others thought that the former was influenced by the latter. Hawkes thought, and I think rightly, that "The Great Man Rhapsody" derives from "Wandering Far Away," of which the author remains unknown.

The poem is loosely modeled on the spirit flights of the "Li sao," with only the faintest hint of the political dissatisfaction. The "flight" in the "Li sao" is a vision or waking dream, where the spirit of the main persona wanders through another dimension, a spirit world that, in the modern view, could be seen as a combination of internal and external reality. A similar melding of internal and external geographies appears in "Wandering Far Away," which is generally recognized as the first *youxian* 遊仙 ("wandering immortal" or "wandering among immortals") poem, a genre, often allegorical, that depicts journeys into the realms of the immortals. The imagery of such poems is symbiotically connected with the visions of paradisiacal realms described in certain Daoist scriptures, which are sometimes interpreted as symbolic of internal states.[1] In "Wandering Far Away" the shamanic spirit flight of the "Li sao" is translated into the spirit flight of later Daoism. It is a straight path from there to the flying poetry of Li Bai.

**Wandering Far Away**

Grieving at a dead end in a degenerate time,
I wished to be weightless, to ascend and wander far away,
But with no such power among my feeble gifts,
What would I ride to float to the sky?

I was sinking into a bog, overwhelmed by filth,
In stifling sadness—who was there to turn to?
Wide-eyed, sleepless nights I lay alone,
Till morning light fell on my cowering soul.

Ponder the endless cycles of Earth and Sky,
Lament how we fret our lives away.
Our past is lost—
Our future, unknown.

I paced the floor, yearning for far-off realms,
Feeling abandoned, hopeless, my heart awry,
My thoughts confounded and adrift on an anchorless sea,
And I sank deeper and deeper into gloom.

Then suddenly my soul flitted out and away,
And did not return, as my earthbound body withered.
And with the inner eye my only guide,
I set forth to find the source of primordial energy.

Detached, clear, and calm I felt joy,
Contentment born of a placid lack of intention.
I had heard the stories of Red Pine's[2] miraculous life,
And now wished to walk his path of purity.

There is nothing higher than the powers of the perfected ones,
Nothing more beautiful than those who anciently attained Transcen-
    dence,
Vanishing into unity with cosmic process,
Leaving but name and legend to age with the days.

We wonder at Fu Yue[3] who lives among the stars,
And envy Han Zhong's[4] attainment of Oneness.
Their serene, dignified forms gradually grew more distant,
Until they broke free of the human herd and went beyond.

There their energy changed as they rose higher,
Until their yang spirit bolted[5] as their yin spirit marveled,
And sometimes in the distance they seem to appear,
Shimmering back and forth across the night sky.

They transcended the dust and cleansed themselves of care,
Never to return to the cities they knew.
Freed of crowding threats they had no fear,
Of a world where none could guess where they had gone.

I dread the endless cycles of celestial time,
The effulgent spirit's beaming westward march.
Snow falls thin to thicken where it falls,
And I mourn that the most fragrant plants will wither first.

For a moment I wandered aimless, distracting myself
From thinking of the years, my many fruitless years.
With whom could I enjoy the fragrance left?
When dawn came I confided my heart to the wind—
Long gone in distant time is Gaoyang,[6]
To whom could I look for a model?

And I say again:

As untarrying springs and autumns speed by,
Why stay here, where I've lived so long,
Where the Yellow Lord is beyond my reach?
I will follow Wang Qiao[7] for the fun, for the play.

Taking in the six energies,[8] I drink the dew of northern midnights.
I rinse my mouth with the light of southern noons,
And hold in my mouth the reddish sunrise air.
Thus will I keep my spirit pure,
Absorbing the subtle, expelling the gross.

Drifting on a mild southern breeze,
I arrive at South Nest[9] to spend the night
Where Master Wang with open doors receives me.
And I sought from him the secret of primordial energy.[10]

And he said:

The Way can be learned,
But cannot be taught.
It is so small it has no inside,
So vast it has no outline.
Maintain your spirit unconfused,
And it will become what it is.
The primordial energy is very numinous,
Accumulate it at midnight,
Attend to this in a state of utter emptiness,
In a state prior to Nonintention.
All things are thereby completed—
This is the gateway to its power.

Having heard this most precious teaching I set forth,
Eager to put it into practice.
I followed the Winged People[11] to the Cinnabar Hills,[12]
And stayed in the old country of the Undying.

In the morning I washed my hair in Hot Water Valley,[13]
dried myself in the warmth of nine afternoon suns,[14]
and drank the elixir spraying from the Flying Springs.[15]
Then I placed the flower of *wan* and *yan* jades[16] in the bosom of my
    robe,

And my complexion took on the glistening texture of the jade.
Vigor surged through me as my essence grew pure,
For I was shedding my grosser elements and becoming light as gauze,
And my spirit power flowed freely.

I admired the flaming aura of this southern region,
And loved the cinnamon trees that bloom there in winter,
But its creatureless mountains were deserted,
And its uninhabited wilds were silent,
So I lifted my altered spirit and mounted the sunset clouds,
Which concealed me as I journeyed higher.

I ordered the celestial gateman to open the sky gates.
He pushed them open and stared at me.
I called Fenglong[17] to be my guide,
To find where the spirit of Great Subtlety[18] resided.

Reaching the highest and clearest sky I entered the Sky Lord's palace.
Arriving at Venus I surveyed the Pure Capital.
In the morning I set out from the Heavenly Court,[19]
And by evening was looking down upon Mount Yuweilü.[20]

I mustered my ten thousand chariots,
And at a leisurely pace we proceeded abreast,
Driving teams of eight undulating dragons,
Serpentine waves of streamers above us.

Rainbow pennons with yak-tail crests rose high,
Their many colors blinding,
Over the bobbing heads of yoke dragons,
And the muscular writhing of trace dragons.

Around the chariots, a bustling horde of cavalry
Proceeded shoulder to shoulder in an endless motley wave.
I grasped the reigns and raised the whip,
And led them to Goumang's[21] realm.

We passed Tai Hao[22] and turned right.
Feilian[23] went ahead to scout,
As the glow of the sun preceded its rise,
We crossed the Sky Pool[24] and moved forward.

When the Wind Earl[25] sped ahead to herald my arrival,
Dust fled the airy path leaving it clean and cool.
Phoenixes winging overhead served as my banners,
As I met Rushou[26] in the realm of the Western Lord.[27]

I used a comet as my ox-tailed and feathered flag,
And held the handle of the Broom Star[28] for signal banner.
Up and down in colored bands
Flowed the waves of the startled mists we rode.

But as the darkening hour obscured the way,
I summoned the Black Warrior[29] to serve as rear guard.
And had Wen Chang[30] behind command those in my train,
Selecting and assigning spirits to protect my chariot.

On the endlessly long journey,
We slowed as we climbed to a higher place.
I had the Rain God[31] serve as bodyguard on my left,
And the Thunder God[32] on my right.

I was ready to escape the world and never look back,
To break the bonds and soar.
Joy filled my heart and pride,
And, for the moment, lost in my own happiness,

I was wandering aimlessly through clouds and blue sky,
When I caught sight of that old home of mine.

My charioteer fell homesick and my heart grieved,
The draft beasts looked back and would not go on.

Images of fond old times filled my mind with longing,
Deep in sighs I wiped my tears away.
But breaking my hovering delay I rose higher,
Suppressing the thoughts for a time, controlling myself.

I pointed to the God of Fire[33] and we galloped straight toward him.
I was on my way to the Southern Doubts.[34]
Seeing the vastness of the world beyond my homeland,
I let myself float as though on open seas.

Zhu Rong gave warning and the road was cleared of people.
News was relayed, *luan* birds welcomed Fufei,[35]
Musicians played "Xian Pond"[36] and "Holding Clouds,"[37]
And the two daughters of Yao[38] performed the "Nine Shao" song.[39]

They had the Xiang River spirits play the many stringed *se*.
And when they had Ruo,[40] the ocean god, dance with the River Earl,
Black dragons and monsters of the sea surfaced and joined in,
Their forms bending and coiling.

The voluptuous rainbow women added their charm,
And the *luan* birds soared and hovered above.
Music and joy were everywhere, endless,
And I lingered—how could I leave then?

We gave free rein to our dragons and the procession ran wild,
Arriving at the Gate of Winter[41] at an extreme end of the sky,
And we overtook the speedy winds at Clear Spring,[42]
And followed Zhuan Xu[43] through the piled-up ice.

We visited Mysterious Dark[44] taking a side road.
As we charioted through high heavens we looked back,
And I summoned Qian Ying[45] to audience with me,
And he guided me onto level road.

I traversed the four wilds,
And traveled all over the six directions,
So high I could see through the seams between the skies,
Then I looked down toward the abysmal sea.

Below me was only landless depth,
And above me, skyless space.
I looked but saw the blur of nothing,
I listened but heard the muffled silence of nothing.
I had transcended Nonintention and arrived at perfect purity,
A short distance from the Great Beginning.[46]

## NOTES

1. For a translation of "Yuan you" that is informed by a deeper knowledge of religious Daoism than mine, see Paul W. Kroll, "On 'Far Roaming,'" *Journal of the American Oriental Society* 116, no. 4 (October–December 1996): 653–69.

2. Red Pine (赤松 Chi Song) is one of the most famous of the immortals (仙 *xian*).

3. Fu Yue 傅說 was raised from poverty to the position of prime minister by King Wuding of the Shang dynasty. One of the legends about him is that when he died, his spirit rose to the sky on a star.

4. Han Zhong 韓眾 (not to be confused with Han Zhong 韓終, the Qin-dynasty wizard) is a figure described in a quote in Hong Xingzu 洪興祖, *Chuci buzhu* 楚辭補注 (Beijing: Zhonghua shuju, 1986), 164, from a nonexistent passage in the *Liexian zhuan*. There he is described as an expert herbalist who picked medicinal plants that he made into a concoction for a king who refused to take it. Taking it himself, he became an immortal.

5. A person was believed to have two souls in ancient China, the *hun* 魂 (also known as 神 *shen*), which was yang and associated with mental and spiritual faculties and which rose to heaven upon death, and the *po* 魄 (also known as 鬼 *gui*), which was yin and connected to the body.

6. Gaoyang is Zhuan Xu, a *di* 帝, or god-lord, the ancestor of a number of royal families, including the royal family of the kings of Chu.

7. Wang Qiao, also known as Wang Ziqiao 王子喬, is an immortal whose fame is on par with that of Red Pine.

8. These are the *liu qi* 六氣, which are variously defined. Wang Yi, quoting the now lost *Lingyangzi Ming jing* 陵陽子明經 (The bright scripture of the Master of Lingyang), lists the six energies: (1) morning clouds (朝霞 *zhaoxia*)—i.e., the reddish-gold air at sunrise—to be absorbed in spring; (2) sinking dimness (淪陰 *lunyin*)—i.e.,

the reddish-gold air just after the sun has set—to be absorbed in fall; (3) evening mist and dew (沆瀣 *hangxie*)—i.e., the air at midnight in the north—to be absorbed in winter; (4) high noon (正陽 *zhengyang*)—i.e., the air of noontime in the south—to be absorbed in summer; and (5) and (6) the dark golden airs of Heaven and Earth (天地玄黃 *tiandi xuanhuang*). Three of these energies are mentioned in this stanza: evening mist and dew ("dew of northern midnights"), high noon ("light of southern noons"), and morning clouds ("reddish sunrise air").

9. South Nest is Nanchao 南巢, a non-Chinese southern state.

10. This is the *yiqi* 壹氣, or the "one energy" that underlies everything. Some say the term is synonymous with Dao.

11. The Winged People (羽人 Yuren) are the *xian*, or immortals.

12. The Cinnabar Hills (丹丘 Dan Qiu) are where the *xian* live. It is always bright there, day or night.

13. Hot Water Valley (湯谷 Tanggu) is where the sun bathes and where the *fusang* tree grows.

14. Nine suns grow on the *fusang* 扶桑 (handhold mulberry) tree's lower branches, but on the top branch there is a tenth sun.

15. No one knows for sure, but some scholars claim that the Flying Springs (飛泉 Feiquan) confer immortality.

16. No one knows for sure what the *wan* 琬 *yan* 琰 jades are, but any "flower" of jade indicates that it is jade so fine and pure that it has magical powers.

17. Fenglong 豐隆 is the god of clouds.

18. Great Subtlety (大微 Dawei) is the name of a star, and the celestial palace, where the Sky Lord lives.

19. The Pure Capital (清都 Qingdu) with its Heavenly Court (太儀 Taiyi) is located near Venus (Taibai 太白)

20. Yuweilü 於微閭 is a mythical mountain in the northeast that produces extraordinary jade.

21. Goumang 勾芒 is the god of the wood element and is located in the east.

22. Tai Hao 太皓 is the god-lord of the east.

23. Feilian 飛廉 is the wind god.

24. Sky Pond is Xianchi 咸池, or Xian Pond, a star, or god, located in the west.

25. Wind Lord (風伯 Fengbo) is another name for Feilian.

26. Rushou 蓐收, located in the west, is the god of metal and autumn.

27. Western Lord is Shao Hao 少昊, the god-lord of the west.

28. Broom Star is Huixing 慧星, a general term for comet.

29. Black Warrior (玄武 Xuan Wu) is the sky god of the north.

30. Wen Chang 文昌 is a star cluster and also the name of the god of officials.

31. Rain God is Yushi 雨師.

32. Thunder God is Leigong 雷公.

33. God of Fire is Zhu Rong 祝融 in the following. He is the god of summer and the ancestor of the royal family of Chu.

34. Southern Doubts (南疑 Nanyi) is Nine Doubts Mountain 九疑, where Shun is buried.

35. Fufei 宓妃 is the daughter of Fuxi 伏羲, a god-lord. She drowned in the Luo River, and her spirit became its goddess.

36. Xian Pond is the same name as the star mentioned in note 24, but here it refers to music that originated in the court of the sage-king Yao.

37. "Bearing Clouds" (承雲 "Cheng Yun") is music that is supposed to have originated in the court of the sage-king Huangdi.

38. Ehuang 娥皇 and Nüying 女英 were the two daughters of the sage-king Yao. They are also the Xiang River spirits.

39. "Nine Shao" (九韶 "Jiu Shao") song is music from the court of Shun.

40. Ro or Ruo 若 is the god of the Northern Sea in the "Autumn Floods" (秋水 section of the *Zhuangzi*).

41. Gate of Winter (寒門 Hanmen) is the celestial gate of the North Pole.

42. Clear Spring (清源 Qingyuan) is a mythical body of water in the north. It is also thought of as the place where winds are stored.

43. Zhuan Xu 顓頊 is god-lord of the north and winter.

44. Mysterious Dark is Xuanming 玄冥, a water spirit.

45. Qian Ying 黔嬴 is the god of creation and change.

46. Great Beginning (太初 Taichu) is where one finds the primordial energy.

# CHAPTER SIX

# "The Diviner"　卜居　"Bu ju"

# and

# "The Fisherman"　漁夫　"Yufu"

The idea that the following pieces are the work of Qu Yuan began during the Han dynasty. The earliest appearance of "The Fisherman," however, is as part of *The Records of the Grand Historian* (史記 *Shiji*) biography of Qu Yuan, which is to say that Sima Qian, or whoever composed the biography, considered it less literature than history. "The Diviner" first reappears as literature alongside "The Fisherman" in a catalogue of the works of Qu Yuan compiled by Liu Xiang (57–6 B.C.E.). The earliest extant edition of the *Chuci* by the Han scholar Wang Yi (d. 158 C.E.) included them as well. Serious doubt about the authorship of the works arose during the Song dynasty, and today almost no one thinks they are by Qu Yuan. Both stories read like parables, but their viewpoints differ. "The Diviner" expresses sympathy with Qu Yuan's plight in tragic tones. "The Fisherman," taking a subtly ironic stance, reads like the type of Daoist story one finds in works such as the *Zhuangzi*, where figures similar to Qu Yuan, such as Confucius, are satirized. Both stories mix verse and prose, verse being in fact preponderant in "The Diviner." Some literary historians therefore think of them as representing an early stage in the development of the *fu* 賦, or rhapsody, which is rhymed prose.

## "THE DIVINER"

卜居

## "BU JU"

Qu Yuan had been exiled for three years, and during that time never managed to have audience with his king again. He had done everything he could think of to serve his king with the utmost loyalty, but slanderers stood in his way. Distressed and confused he did not know which way to turn, so he went to visit the Grand Diviner Zheng Zhanyin and said, "I am in a quandary, and am looking to you to help me solve it." Zhanyin thereupon took out his divining stalks[1] and dusted off a tortoise shell, saying, "I await your instructions."

Qu Yuan said:
Should I be sincere,[2] straightforward, and loyal, or should I be an end-
    lessly accommodating social butterfly?
Should I remove the grass[3] with a hoe and vigorously plow the field,
    or should I make the rounds visiting the important people in
    order to establish my name?
Should I speak with full candor and thus place myself in danger, or
    should I consort with the vulgar and lead a life of no goals other
    than wealth and status.
Should I rise above the crowd to preserve my authenticity, or should I
    become a trembling, false-faced toady fit only to serve women?
Should I remain honest and straight and keep myself clean, or should
    I become smooth talking and slippery as a leather band used to
    measure the thickness of columns?
Should I hold my head high like a colt that can run a thousand miles,
    or should I float like a duck on the stream bobbing up and down
    with the waves just to save my skin?
Should I run abreast with the Qis and Jis, or should I walk in the tracks
    of the nags?
Should I fly wing to wing with golden swans, or fight over food with
    chickens and ducks?
Which way will end well, which will not? Whom do I leave, whom do
    I follow?

The world is filthy, drenched in muddy water.
They take the wing of a cicada as heavy, and thirty thousand catties as
    light.
The keynote bell they break and discard, but make a thunderous noise
    beating clay pots.
The liars are on the rise and honest gentlemen are out of sight.
I'm left with only silence or sighs—who appreciates my purity?

Zhanyin thereupon put down his divining stalks and declined to perform the divination, saying, "There are places where a foot rule is too short and an inch rule is too long. There are times when one finds oneself inadequate, when one's knowledge does not clarify. There are instances where divination is useless, and the spirits have no power. Go by your heart, follow your will. My tortoise shell and divining stalks cannot advise you."

## "THE FISHERMAN"

漁夫

## "YUFU"

After Qu Yuan was sent into exile, he wandered the banks of the rivers and lakes singing as he walked and looking lean and haggard. A fisherman seeing him asked, "Are you not the High Officer of the Three Districts?[4] How did you come to this pass?"

Qu Yuan answered, "This world is a muddy river; I alone am clean. It is a mob of drunkards; I alone am sober. That is why I was sent into exile."

The fisherman answered, "The sage does not get bogged down in externals, and is thus able to adapt as the world changes. If the people of the world are in muddy waters, why not make waves by stirring up even more mud? If every one is drunk, why not make wine dregs your food and clear wine your drink? Why get yourself banished for thoughts too deep and deeds too lofty?"

Qu Yuan said, "They say that if you have just washed your hair, you should dust off your hat. If you have just taken a bath, you should shake out your clothes. Why cover a clean body with dirty things? I would rather enter the flowing river and let the bellies of fish be my burial ground than let my gleaming purity be sullied by the filth of the vulgar world."

The fisherman smiled ever so slightly. Tapping his paddle he began to leave. As he did so he sang the following song:

> When the Canglang waters[5] are clear,
> I can wash my hat strings.
> When the Canglang waters are muddy,
> I can wash my feet.

And so he departed and never conversed with Qu Yuan again.

NOTES

1. Yarrow stalks, slips of bamboo, or coins are used in divination techniques associated with the *Book of Changes* (易經 *Yijing*) and other such texts. The tortoise shell is one of the oldest Chinese divination tools. The diviner would interpret cracks that appear on its surface after firing.
2. From this point, Qu Yuan's speech is entirely in verse.
3. This may not be meant literally. Agricultural metaphors evoking the cultivation of plants and herbs are used extensively in "Li sao" and elsewhere and refer to reforming corrupt government.
4. The Chinese for this title is San Lü Dafu 三閭大夫. It is generally thought to mean an officer who is in charge of the various affairs of the three branches (屈 Qu, 景 Jing, and 昭 Zhao) of the Chu royal family. The three branches presumably resided in three different districts. The title is applied to Qu Yuan nowhere other than in this story.
5. This song, sung by a boy and interpreted by Confucius, appears in slightly different form in *Mengzi*, "Lilou A"; see James Legge, *The Chinese Classics*, 5 vols. (Oxford: Clarendon Press, 1893–1894; repr., Hong Kong: Hong Kong University Press, 1960), 2:299.

# CHAPTER SEVEN

# Nine Variations

# 九辯

# *Jiubian*

*Nine Variations*, like *Nine Songs*, is a title borrowed from myth. It refers to music said to have been brought back to earth by Qi, the son of the founder of the Xia dynasty, after one of his visits to heaven. These poems are traditionally attributed to Song Yu 宋玉, believed to be a student of Qu Yuan's. Little is known about him. The *Historical Records* by Sima Qian lists him among the great poets of Chu who lived after Qu Yuan, the others being Jing Cuo 景差 and Tang Le 唐勒. Jing Cuo's poems are believed to be lost, but there are some people who think "The Great Summoning" (大招 "Da zhao") is his work. Four poems are attributed to Tang Le, but these are not included in the *Chuci*. Besides the *Nine Variations*, some sixteen works in the *fu* form are attributed to Song Yu, including "Fu on the Wind" (風賦 "Feng fu") and "Gaotang fu" (高唐賦). Song Yu, like Qu Yuan, served the Chu court. Indeed, *Nine Variations* are variations on themes that belong very much to court life: falling out of favor with one's sovereign and the concomitant demotion and exile.[1] In most of these poems the exile's landscape is the wilderness and his season is autumn. Sadness that is peculiar to autumn is associated with Song Yu's work, these poems in particular.

**1**

How sad the weather autumn brings—
bleak, wind-beaten grass and trees wither,
pitiful as wayfarers climbing a hill
to see off a friend going home
on the water.

Vast hollow clarity—
sky higher, air cleaner,
mute and lucid,
rain floods recede, rivers clear.
Melancholy and many sighs
as the cold comes near to strike.

Thwarted and hopeless,
I leave the old to face the new,
in straits,
a poor scholar out of work,
with no tranquil thought,
an outcast
finding lodging, but no friend,
heartsick,
in secret misery.

The swallow flutters good-bye.
The cicada silenced loses its voice.
Honking geese migrate south,
where the jungle fowl twitters sorrow.

Alone, I lie awake until dawn,
lamenting the crickets' midnight campaigns.
Relentless time, more than half gone,
Stuck in a bog with nothing to show.

**2**

Alone in the boundless wilds,
    with no way out of sorrow,
lives a beautiful woman
    whose heart was not glad
to leave her family in a distant land
    to come here, a stranger,
and now, a vagabond,
    where will she go?

She longs for you only, Lord.
    You cannot change her.
If this you refuse to know,
    what can she do?
Her resentment builds,
    Her longing deepens—
Her heart so vexed by dread,
    she neglects her food.

I desire but one meeting
    to speak this thing on my mind,
but they are so at odds,
    my heart and yours,
that when I left in the carriage you readied,
    only to return,
you would not see me.
    It cut me inside,
as I leaned on the carriage wall,
    and sighed through its lattice window,
and so many tears crossed down my face,
    they wet the carriage rail.

I rage that I cannot
    stop it.
I am delirious,
    lost!

How do I end
    this hidden misery?
My frenzied heart pounds,
    but always for you.


3

August Heaven granted each season its share,
But sadness comes in cold autumn only.
White dew already falls on all the grasses,
*Wutong* and catalpa suddenly cast down their leaves.

Sunlight dims,
As we enter the endless night.
Gone is vigor's fragrant luxury.
Sad dejection arrives
in ill health, with scant means.

To autumn's warning of white dew
Winter adds rigor of pitiless frost,
Damping the broad cheer of early summer.
Now beasts hide in burrows, where food is buried deep.

Brittle leaves colorless
On the tangled uproar of branches,
And the brightest leaves soon to fade
On the dull and lifeless boughs.
And the bare-branched trees dolefully tower
Their bodies worn and scarred.
Think how they burgeoned only to shed,
How much sadder, though, had they died before that.

I'll grasp the reins but lay down the whip,
And wander this time for the pleasure.
The fleeting year is soon to close,
Not much of life, I fear, is left.

I mourn my birth in the wrong world,
My stumble into appalling times.
Standing alone, I look for peace
In this westward room
while the cricket sings.

But my heart quakes in dread—
Why does it dwell on so many things?
I will look to the moon with a long sigh,
and walk with the stars until dawn.

4

I mourn the basil with its many-tiered flowers,
Whose fluttering flags once crowded the royal greenhouse,
Why did storm winds carry away
its fruitless clustered petals?

I thought, My Lord, you would wear this basil[2] only,
But you cannot distinguish its fragrance from others.
Hurt that its uncommon thoughts do not reach you,
It will soar even higher and leave you.

My heart in wretched misery
Harbors but a single wish—a meeting with you to clear my name.
Guiltless estrangement is too much to bear,
Pain redoubling stuns me to the core.

Do I not long for you with my every thought?
Yet you hide behind nine layers of doors
Where fierce dogs yapping wait to greet me.
Even gates and bridges are locked against me.

August Heaven sends too much autumn rain.
Queen Earth, when again will you manage to dry?
Alone I live in this overgrown swamp,
Constantly sighing as clouds go by.

**5**

What skill the vulgar wainwrights[3] display!
  Ignoring ink string, misusing their tools,
Accepting no thoroughbred to pull their wagons,
  Going their way whipping nags instead.

Have the times produced no horse to call Qi or Ji?[4]
  The fact is, a thoroughbred needs a skillful driver.
The horse seeing no such man holding the reins,
  Shies and bolts over the horizon.
Wild ducks and geese gorge on grain and water plants,
  While the phoenix[5] soars high above them.

Make mortise round and tenon square—
  Hard put you'll be to fit them together.
The other birds have nests in high places,
  Yet comfortless lone phoenix finds nary a perch.

How could I bite the bit and never speak,
  Having once enjoyed your flowing bounty?
Jiang Taigong[6] revealed no splendor before his ninetieth year,
  For only then did he meet a fitting lord.

Where have the Qis and Jis gone?
  Where do the phoenixes perch?
The world trades ancient for vulgar, and so begins decline.
  Today when horses are judged, the fat ones always win.

So Qis and Jis hide themselves never to reappear,
  And phoenixes fly high—never down to perch.
If even beasts know virtue and yearn for it,
  Why wonder that the best will not stay here?

A thoroughbred is never so eager that it will pull any wagon,
  A phoenix, never so hungry that it will eat anything.
Not knowing the truth you push me away, Lord,
  I would give you my all, but how can I now?

Would that I could cut our hearts' ties in silence,
But I cannot forget what kindness you showed me.
Grieving in solitude will break me,
How far will my misery go?

**6**

When dew and frost, cold and cruel descended together,[7]
My heart still hoped it would not come to pass,
But when the blizzard came with hail and snow,
I knew my fate was sealed.
(Though I still await a fluke that might save me)
I will die in the vast plains with the wild grass.

I would have gone directly to him to plead my own case,
But the roads were blocked; I could not get through.
I would have galloped the length of a highway,
But never found the one to take,
So I lost my bearings midroute.

I force myself to study the art of chanting the *Songs*,[8]
But I am doltish and unschooled.
Surely I'll never master them,
I admire the spirit of Shen Baoxu,[9]
But I'm afraid his time and ours are not the same.

What skill these vulgar craftsmen display,
Compass and try square they destroy and chisel as they please.
I alone, staunch in my craft pride, do not follow them,
For I wish to honor teachings the departed sages bequeathed.

To be glorified while living in a dirty world
Would never bring my heart joy.
Instead of renown among those who have no principles,
Give me poverty, if only to keep me high and apart.

Feed me only food that has not been stolen,
Keep me warm only in clothes honestly come by.

I admire an air handed down by a singer of the *Songs*,
For it describes my enemies, who do "nothing but eat."[10]

Yes, I'll wear a threadbare robe with no border,
And wander grasslands that never end,
Without a cloak to keep me warm,
And perhaps drop dead and miss sunny spring.


## 7

Late fall, long silent nights,
My heart grieves, outrage hobbles me,
So many years I've lived, so many days,
Only for despair and secret sorrow.
The season turns, harvest ends,
Light and dark exclude me from their circle.

Sun dims on the downslope,
Moon, for wear, loses shape,
Another year runs its short course,
As old age slackens the bowstring.

My heart rocked happy in days full of hope,
But now, hopeless frustration
Brings desolation and woe by the heartful,
And sigh upon heavy sigh.

Endless time goes by with the sun.
I am old and find no shelter in this vast space,
Longing to speed my lord's relentless progress,
Through the dust of a dead end I pace and pace.


## 8

How they flood the skies, the floating clouds,
Running in packs that block the light of this moon.
She would show you her shining devotion,
But overcast skies she cannot shine through.

I wish the gleaming sun would light the path,
But darkening clouds stand in the way.
I have no self-interest doing my all for you,
Yet some have smeared such filth on me.

The lofty deeds of Yao and Shun[11]
Approach the glory of the skies.
Why do the treacherous in their envy
falsely label them unkind?

If dark spots mar the brightness
Of even the moon and sun,
What to expect of one ruling a state,
With its intricate vexations?

## 9

You drape yourself in a magnificent tunic of lotus leaves,[12]
But it is too wide to close with a sash.
Proud of your beauty now you vaunt your warriors' skills,
Turning your back on the upright advisers at your side,
Whose beauty in your eye, as they stammer foreboding, fades,[13]
But you delight in the high martial spirits of those others,
The crowd that sprints into your presence day after day,
While the beautiful drift farther and farther away.

The peasants have left their plows for lazy pleasures,
The farmlands may soon be overgrown with weeds,
Trammeled by private interests the work of the realm drags.
I fear the looming calamity.

The whole world dazzled by your radiance thunders its support,
Ever blind as to who really merits praise or blame.
As you don your adornment today, look in the mirror—
Later you may need it as a hideaway.

I would send you a message by one of the shooting stars,
But moving so fast they are hard to find.

And floating clouds always block them in the end—
It is gloomy down here without their light.

## 10

Because they elevated the worthy,
Even the lowly and obscure ones,
Yao and Shun[14] could rest easy on high pillows.
If indeed no one in the realm had cause to resent you,
Where would your heart have come by such terror?

When Qi and Ji[15] are in the harness and the chariot flows like water,
Why would the driver ever use the heavy whip?
If indeed a city's inner and outer walls are unstable,
Even with two layers of armor, how will you survive?

I have nothing to show for my care and caution,
Save rancor and sadness and poverty.
I was born, it seems, just to pass between earth and sky.
My projects have failed, I'll leave no mark.

I would willingly have withdrawn never to appear again,
Were it not for my wish to spread my name all over the world.
I wandered far and wide, yet never met one who understood me—
To put my self through so much pain was simple stupidity.

Over the boundless grasslands,
Where will my restless soaring end?
The state has a good horse, but you don't know how to drive him.
Why do you so feverishly search elsewhere?

Ning Qi[16] sang near the oxcarts.
When Duke Xuan heard, he understood.
If none can now judge a horse as did Bo Le,[17]
Who would they send to appraise me?

Stop weeping and think.
Only by applying your mind will you succeed.

If you devote your will to proving your loyalty,
The chaotic and envious will only stand in your way.


**11**


I wish you would let me take my unworthy carcass away from here,
Set me free to let my mind play among the clouds,
To fly where the primal essence congeals into the solar and lunar
  spheres,
While I pursue the spirit crowds.


Pale rainbows on light wings would draw my chariot across the sky,
Leaving even the myriad spirits behind,
While the Vermilion Bird[18] fluttered on my left,
And the green dragon[19] leapt on my right.


The thunder god would be there booming in my train,
And Feilian[20] would clear the way before me.
In front would be the jingling of light carriages,
Behind would be the rumble of heavy covered wagons,
And undulating cloud banners would fly
Over the cavalry of my airborne retinue.


But my plan would remain fixed and unchangeable,
I would wish to do good by carrying it out,
And relying on the help of August Heaven,
I would return to serve while my lord enjoys health.


NOTES

1. The word 辯 *bian*, "debate," aside from being interchangeable with 變 *bian*, "variation," is also interchangeable with 貶 *bian*, "demotion." The title *Jiu bian* could also mean *Nine Demotions*.
2. *Hui* 蕙 (*Ocimum basilicum*), or "basil," appears to stand for the valuable but less assertive, more scholarly advisers among the king's ministers, in this case the poetic persona himself.
3. Craft imagery such as this was commonly used in the rhetoric of ancient Chinese

political theorists in essays and speeches meant to persuade rulers to adopt their systems and policies.

4. These are mythical wonder horses that can run a thousand Chinese miles in a day—stock symbols of capable and loyal ministers

5. This is a not very accurate but almost universal translation of 鳳凰 *fenghuang*, a mythical bird that presages the advent of a sage-king. It is often used for those whose moral integrity keeps them so aloof from their contemporaries that they are continually out of step—and unemployed. The symbol was applied to Confucius in the *Analects* by Jieyu 接輿, the madman of Chu. The bird is auspicious but does not rise again from its own ashes.

6. According to legend, Jiang Taigong 姜太公 only revealed his talents as a military strategist at the age of ninety, when he met King Wen of the Zhou dynasty.

7. This poem appears to be about someone who is being sent into exile.

8. This appears to refer to the *Book of Songs* (詩經 *Shijing*), which every educated person was supposed to be familiar with, especially those involved in literature or politics and diplomacy. One wonders if such a great poet as Song Yu could have written these lines to describe himself.

9. Shen Baoxu 申包胥 was one of the great ministers of Chu, who served under King Zhao during the Spring and Autumn period. When the state of Wu, with the help of Wu Zixu, took Ying, the Chu capital, Shen Baoxu traveled on foot through rough terrain to Qin. There he stood in the Qin ducal court and wept for seven days and seven nights. That moved the Duke of Qin to send his army to drive the Wu army from Chu.

10. This is a phrase from Ode 112 of the *Shijing*. The full verse is as follows: 彼君子兮 不素餐兮 *bi junzi xi bu su can xi*, "That nobleman is not one who does nothing but eat."

11. Both these sage-kings abdicated in favor of talented, unrelated men rather than to their sons. Later advocates of strict adherence to hereditary succession criticized their behavior as unbefitting a father.

12. In the "Li sao" lotus leaves are held up as a symbol of purity maintained in difficult times or in immoral society because they grow out of mud and rise clean to the surface of the water. Here the lotus-leaf tunic may mean a false reputation for goodness, especially if it is accomplished by surrounding oneself with people of fine moral repute. In Chu rhetoric, especially florid in the "Li sao," flora are often used as symbols or metaphors for types of people. Here the lotus-leaf tunic, representing people of moral integrity, is only a means to an end.

13. My interpretation of these lines is based on Hu Nianyi 胡念贻, *Chuci xuanzhu ji kaozheng* 楚辞选注及考证 (Changsha: Yueli chubanshe, 1984), 228 and 164.

14. Here again are legendary sage-kings (mentioned in note 11), now praised for their ability to recognize talented and virtuous people, regardless of social status, and put them to good use.

15. Here again are the legendary wonder horses Qi and Ji (mentioned in note 4), symbolic of talented ministers. Employed appropriately they allow the ruler to govern the state (represented by the chariot) easily.

16. Although a man of Wei, Ning Qi 甯戚 sought office in the court of Duke Huan of Qi but failed. He then worked as a traveling merchant and habitually sang near his oxcarts. One night Duke Huan was passing by and heard him. Mysteriously moved by the singing, he granted him a ministerial position; see John Knoblock and Jeffrey Riegel, trans., *The Annals of Lü Buwei: A Complete Translation and Study* (Stanford, Calif.: Stanford University Press, 2001), 507.

17. Bo Le 伯樂 was a legendary expert judge of horses.

18. This is the name of a mythological beast and a Chinese constellation, both associated with summer and the south.

19. This is both a mythological beast and a Chinese constellation, both associated with springtime and the east.

20. Feilian 飛廉 is the wind god.

# CHAPTER EIGHT

# "Summoning the Soul"
# 招魂
# "Zhao hun"

In ancient China when someone died, the family of the deceased would invite a shaman to call back the departed soul. The ritual consisted of climbing to the roof carrying outer garments the deceased used to wear, facing north, and calling out his or her name three times. The shaman would then climb down from the rooftop and lay the clothes on the corpse. The ritual was known as the Return (復 Fu), for people believed that it was possible to make the soul return to the body and bring the dead back to life. Accordingly, the Return was always performed before the funeral. At least, that is how the great Song scholar Zhu Xi describes it, based on his knowledge of the ancient ritual texts. He adds, however, that in Chu the same ritual could be performed for a living person.

The Song-dynasty poet Fan Chengda 范成大 (960–1279) describes the following version of the soul-summoning ritual for the living that was still popular in his day. When members of a family were on their way back from a long journey, they would stop thirty *li* from home, and the family would send a shaman out to welcome them with a basket. The travelers would then remove their undergarments and give them to the shaman, who would put them in the basket. Carrying that, he would lead them back home. It was believed that the shaman was thereby collecting their wandering souls. It appears that the purpose of performing the soul-summoning ceremony for the living was to comfort or reassure.[1]

There was disagreement about who wrote "Summoning the Soul" even as far back as the Han dynasty. Sima Qian was sure it was by Qu Yuan, whereas Liu Xiang and Wang Yi claimed it was by Song Yu 宋玉, supposedly a disciple of Qu Yuan. The question is still debated today, but modern scholars are equally concerned about the identity of the deceased in the poem—or whether in fact the soul addressed is that of a living person. Some think that the deceased was King Huai, who died in exile. Others prefer King Xiang. Still others say that it was Qu Yuan. There are even two Qing-dynasty scholars who think that it is Qu Yuan calling back his own soul as a means to console (no pun intended) himself.

The poem itself, however, tells us that its main speaker is Shaman Yang, a female shaman, and the way of life she describes to attract the soul back is extremely luxurious, if not extravagant, making it hard to avoid concluding that the deceased is an aristocrat, if not a king. Whether the poem was intended for use in an actual ritual summoning of the soul is an open question.

**Summoning the Soul**

In my youth I was pure and honest.
I clothed myself in a righteousness whose fragrance did not fade,
And I was secure in this great virtue.
But when the vulgar dragged me through their filth,
My sovereign had no way to see this great virtue,
And long were the troubles and bitter pain I endured . . .[2]

The Lord of the Skies told Shaman Yang:[3]
There is someone in the world below
Whom I wish to help.
His dark and bright souls[4] have abandoned his body and scattered.
Find them with divining slips and bring them back.

Shaman Yang answered:
This is the responsibility of the Minister of Dreams.[5]
Your order is difficult for me to follow.
If you insist that I divine and bring his souls back . . .

[The lord interrupted her:[6]]
I fear that if we wait longer, his body shall have withered away
And returning his souls will be of no use to him.

So Shaman Yang descended into the world and called out:
Come home, bright soul!
You have left your body.
Why wander the four directions,
Leaving your place of enjoyment,
To encounter unlucky things?

Come home, come home!
In the east you will find no haven.
Giants are there, a thousand fathoms tall,
Who seek only souls to snare.
Ten suns rise together there
Making metal flow and boulders melt.
They are used to that there,
But you will surely fall apart.
Come home, come home,
You will find no haven there.

Come home, come home!
In the south you will find no haven.
They scarify foreheads there, and blacken teeth,
And sacrifice human flesh
And use the bones to make a sauce.
Vipers swarm there,
And giant foxes run a thousand miles,
And poison snakes have nine heads there
And move about at uncanny speed.
And the more people they eat the more they want.
Come home, come home!
That is no place to linger long.

Come home, bright soul!
These are the dangers of the west:

Sands flow there, a thousand miles,
And then whirl down into the Thundering Abyss,
Where everything is helplessly ground to dust.
And even if you manage to escape going in,
Outside is but broad, barren expanse,
Where red ants as big as elephants roam,
And black wasps the size of wine jugs fly.
The five grains do not grow there.
And for food, only firewood and straw.
Don't touch the soil there, for it rots the flesh.
Don't look for water, for you'll find there none.
You will wander with no shelter there,
In a vastness that never ends.
Come home, come home!
For I fear you'll suffer injury there.

Bright soul, come home!
In the north you will find no haven.
Ice piles there, mountainously high.
And snow flies a thousand miles.
Come home, come home!
You will not last long there.

Bright soul, come home!
Do not ascend to the sky.
Nine gates are there, with tiger and leopard guards
That tear at the flesh with their teeth.
People have nine heads there
And strength to uproot nine thousand trees.
Jackals and wolves have vertical eyes there
And go about in packs.
They hang people for fun there,
And throw them into deep chasms.
And only after reporting to the Sky Lord,
Do they let you close your eyes.
Come home, come home!
You go there at your own risk, I fear.

Come home, bright soul!
Do not go down to the deep, dark city of the dead.
The Earl of the Earth is there with his nine tails,
And his horns are sharp as pikes.
And hump backed and bloody clawed,
He'll come charging after you,
With his three eyes in his tiger's head,
And his upper body shaped like an ox,
And his taste for human flesh.
Come home, bright soul!
You're heading for disaster, I fear.

Come home, bright soul!
Enter the adorned gates.
A skilled shaman calls to you,
Walking backwards leading the way in,
Carrying a hamper from Qin,
Wrapped in the soft cloth of Zheng,
By its Qi-made cords.[7]
All the tools for bringing you back are here.
And we wail and shout without cease.
Come home, bright soul,
Back to your old abode.

Heaven and Earth and the Four Directions
Are full of harm and evil.
Imagine your residence—
Quiet, tranquil, safe,

With its high chambers,
And deep courtyards,
Its tiers of balustraded galleries,
Level on level of terraces and clustered belvederes,
Looking down from high hills,
Latticework doors with their linked swastikas,
Painted in red.
And the warm rooms for winter, deep within the mansion,

And the outer rooms cool in summer.
A stream turning and curving through the valley,
Water whispering as it flows.
Bright breezes eddy in the basil,
And scuffle in the thoroughwort patches.
And from the outer halls into the private chambers,
The ceilings and floor mats are all cinnabar red.
Kingfisher feather dusters to clean the rooms of polished tile
Hang from jasper hooks.
Bedspreads of halcyon feathers studded with pearls
Shimmer a hybrid light.
Colorful wall hangings of fine silk
Surround bed-curtains of drifting gauze,
With their red ties, motley stays, embroidered bands, and silk ropes
Weighted with half rings of jade.

And what is there to see in the bedroom?
More treasures and wonders:
By the light of candles of thoroughwort paste,
A roomful of beautiful faces,
In two rows of eight, to keep you company through the night—
A different one every night.
Fine women from princely houses,
With agile wits above the common run,
With full heads of luxurious hair, each in her own style.
Women such as these crowd your palace,
In complexion and form all of equal beauty,
Each yielding to the next till all have been with you.
Yet behind each soft face there is strong attachment—
How every one of them longs for you!
They of the lovely faces and adorned forms
Crowd your bedchamber.
Those with the moth's eyebrows, adepts of the glance,
Whose eyes send you their galloping light.
The fine faces, radiant complexions,
And secret sidelong glances,

Under the great decorated tents of your pleasure palaces,
Wait on your leisure.
Curtains sewn with halcyon colors
Adorn the high-ceilinged room.
The walls are painted red,
The rafters embedded with black jade.
Look up and see the carved rafters,
Painted with dragons and serpents,
Under which you will sit leaning on a balustrade,
Looking out on a winding pool.
The lotuses are starting to open
Among the water-chestnut leaves,
And purple-stemmed floating heart
Make the waves flow in patterns.
Guards in eye-catching leopard-skin tunics
Patrol the banks and slopes.
And when the closed sleeping wagon arrives,
Foot soldiers and cavalry attend it in orderly rows.
Thoroughwort bushes front the gate,
Jasper bushes form circling hedges.
Come home, bright soul!
Why wander far away?

Once you're home your whole family will honor you
With a feast of many dishes—
Rice, millet, the early- and late-ripening wheat,
Mixed with yellow millet,
The very bitter, the salty, and tart,
The hot, and the sweet flavors will all be used.
Tendons of fat cows
Cooked till tender and fragrant,
Mixed with vinegar and bitter herbs,
Served with Wu-style sweet-and-sour stews,
And boiled soft-shell crab and roast lamb,
With sugarcane sauces.
Swan cooked in vinegar and wild-duck casserole,

Panfried goose and gray crane,
Dried chicken and terrapin stew,
All strong flavors that never cloy.

Deep-fried honey balls and sweet cakes
Coated with malt,
Fine wines mixed with honey
Fill the winged wine cups.
Filtered wines drunk chilled,
Fine wines clear and cool.
When the sumptuous feast is laid out,
There will be fine wines.
Come home to your old abode
We will honor you with a feast—and why not?

Even before all the delicacies have come out,
Female musicians arrange themselves in rows.
Then strike the bells with force, in rhythm with the drums.
They have composed new songs:
"Cross the River" and "Pick the Water Chestnuts."
But they open the show by singing in chorus "Raise the Lotus."
And once the beauties are drunk,
Their faces flush red,
And turn on you the alluring glint of half-closed eyes,
Like sparkling ripples on water.
They are dressed in light embroidered silk,
Luxurious but not overly so.
Long hair glossily hangs to their shoulders,
Sensuously hanging.
Sixteen women dressed alike
Rise to dance to the music of Zheng,
Their overlong sleeves fly up and cross like staves in a fight,
Then fall together on cue,
While the *yu* pipes and *se* strings wail,
And the drums thunder,
And the palace shakes,
As the chorus sings, "Rousing Chu,"

And the Wu songs and the Cai airs,
And the Great Lü Mode.
Women and men sitting side by side—
Now comes the orgy of no distinctions—
Clothes, sashes, and hat strings fall,
Mixing on the floor in colorful chaos.
Bewitching women of pleasure from Zheng and Wei
Are here to perform,
But the topknotted dancers of "Rousing Chu"
They cannot outdo.


Jade throwing rods and ivory tiles
For the *liubo*[8] game come out.
People pair off and make their first moves
Forcing each other's pieces into tight corners.
When each gets the "Owl" they are tied
Until one cries "Five Whites."
The strategic pincering plays move slowly
Consuming the light of day.


Musicians strike the bells till the bell frames sway,
And play the strings of the catalpa-wood *se*.
Here the wine of revelry constantly flows.
Submerge yourself in it day and night,
By the light of the candles of thoroughwort paste,
In their intricate candlesticks of openwork bronze.


And some search their hearts to express their thoughts
In words as fragrant as thoroughwort,
Each as best he can.
Sympathetic hearts chanting their poems,
Fine the wine drunk and pleasures enjoyed
To delight our departed ancestor.
Come home, bright soul!
Back to your old abode.

## Envoi

Spring opens, a new year enters.
We journey swiftly south.
Green duckweed spreads over slow water,
Angelica grows on the banks.
We pass over Lu River,
A long thicket to our left,
And from the pond,
Near the rice paddies,
We see vast flat marshland beyond.

And a thousand black-horsed quadrigas
File through the wilderness.
Flaming torches[9] bobbing over bushes,
Black smoke filling the air.

Men on foot arrive where the speeding chariots
Rush to be first to draw the quarry out,
And, stopping the helter-skelter horse play,
They lead the chariots around to the right.

Men hurried with the King to Dream Marsh[10] to test their skills,
But when the king's arrow flies, the black rhino falls.[11]

Red light giving way to night,
We can't hold back the hour.
Marsh thoroughwort covers the path,
A flood is on the road.
Over clear, deep Yangtze waters
Maple trees grow,
And the eye sees a thousand miles,
And springtime wounds the heart.

Take pity on the southland.
Come home, bright soul!

# NOTES

1. See Fu Xiren 傅錫壬, *Chuci duben* 楚辭讀本 (Taipei: Sanmin shuju, 1974), 168.

2. This stanza seems to have little to do with what follows. It may be that it was added to give the impression that the poem was by Qu Yuan.

3. Shaman Yang (巫陽 Wu Yang) is one of the female shamans mentioned in the *Shanhaijing*, "Hainei xijing"; see Yuan Ke 袁珂, *Shanhaijing jiaozhu* 山海經校注 (Shanghai: Shanghai guji chubanshe, 1985), 226.

4. The ancient Chinese believed that there are two souls—*hun* 魂, the yang or bright soul, and *po* 魄, yin or dark soul. The former animated the mental faculties and rose to the sky after death; the latter animated the physical faculties and stayed near the body (or sank into the ground) after death. The division was not one of good versus evil, but *po* tended to be somewhat dangerous.

5. Dreams were thought to be the result of wandering souls. The same officer was charged with interpreting dreams and finding the souls of the dead.

6. I added this line to make the meaning clear.

7. Most scholars assume that these lines describe the hamper containing the clothes of the deceased, which the shaman is using to attract the soul.

8. *Liubo* 六博, which means "six rods," is an ancient board game. The game was played by two people, each provided with six pieces and six throwing rods. The throwing rods were thrown like dice to determine how each of the six pieces was moved on the board on which was drawn a TLV pattern, which often appears on bronze mirrors as well. No one is entirely sure what the rules of the game were. The "Owl" probably meant a win, and "Five Whites" probably refers to throwing-rod results.

9. Flaming torches set fire to the bushes to smoke the quarry out.

10. Dream Marsh (夢 Meng) is generally identified as Yunmeng Daze 雲夢大澤 (Great Cloud Dream Marsh).

11. Here, with Wang Siyuan 王四原, I read 殫 *dan* for 憚 *dan*. See Wang Siyuan, *Chuci jiaoshi* 楚辭校釋 (Beijing: Renmin jiaoyu chubanshe, 1990), 143.

# CHAPTER NINE

# "The Great Summoning"

# 大招

# "Da zhao"

The Han scholar Wang Yi was not sure whether this poem was by Qu Yuan or by a shadowy figure named Jing Cuo, who was supposed to have been one of Qu Yuan's poetic successors. Few modern scholars attribute the poem to Qu Yuan. Like "Summoning the Soul" it appears to be a text that was used in the ritual recalling of the soul of someone who has recently died, in the belief that the corpse could be restored to life. The object of the recall here is most likely a ruler of some sort, probably a king. The state of Chu is mentioned in a few passages, but mostly as outsiders or people living after the fall of Chu would mention it. The official titles that appear in it, and the implied rankings, are not for the most part those of Warring States Chu; they belong to the Qin and Han dynasties. The same may be said of some of the administrative geography the poem outlines. Whether or not it is a Qin or Han pastiche, it is valuable for its descriptions of certain aspects of ancient Chinese aristocratic culture, especially food and feminine beauty.

### The Great Summoning

Green spring takes its turn again,
Sun shines bright,
Spring vigor surges,

Life wrangles forward,
But you rise high in the dark realm and drift.[1]
Don't flee, bright spirit,
Come home with your shadow twin,
Don't wander far.
Bright spirit! Come home!
Don't go east. Don't go west. Don't go south. Don't go north.


In the east there is a great sea,
Its undertow irresistible and swift,
Yet horned and hornless dragons flow there in pairs,
Leisurely rising and diving, in and out of the waves,
And fog and rain never end,
and the air is a gray-white paste.
Don't go east, bright spirit—
You'll find yourself alone in Daybreak Valley.[2]


Bright soul, don't go south!
The south is a thousand miles on fire,
Wriggling with pit vipers.
The dense mountain forests are perilous places,
Where tigers and panthers lurk,
And the ox-bodied hog-voiced fish,[3] the sand spitter,
And the poisonous python rear their heads.
Bright soul, don't go south—
The monsters there will maul you.


Bright soul, don't go west!
In the west where the Flowing Sands
Are as vast as the ocean,
There is a swine-headed vertical-eyed demon,
With shaggy hair down to his knees
And long claws and sawlike teeth,
Madly giggling.
Bright soul, don't go west—
There is much there to hurt you.

Bright soul, don't go north!
The cold mountains are in the north.
There the candle dragon[4] glows red.
Do not try to cross the Dai rivers[5]—
They are deeper than anyone knows.
And the air is always snowy white,
And everything is frozen tight.
Bright spirit, don't go there—
Such perils are rife
All the way to the North Pole.

Bright spirit, come home!
Here life is slow and quiet.
Come, feel at ease in Chu of the Chaste Trees,[6]
Safe and secure.
Do as you wish here,
With heart untroubled.
Live out your days in constant delight.
Your life will be long here.
Bright spirit, come home
To joy beyond words.

The five common grains[7] are piled six fathoms high,
But we serve you the best wild rice
And pots of cooked food as far as the eye can see,
Seasoned to the savory heights—
Fat[8] gray crane, pigeon, and swan,
Flavored with jackal broth.
Come home, bright soul—
Try whatever you wish.

Fresh terrapin and frog
Flavored with Chu vinegar sauce.
Piglet pork balls, minced bitter dog meat[9]
With finely sliced *myōga* ginger,
And Wu-style tarragon pickles,
Neither too strong nor too bland.

Come home, bright spirit—
Choose whatever you like.

Roast crow, wild duck steamed
And stewed quail,
Fried crucian carp and magpie soup,
Instantly restoring.
Come home, bright soul—
Be first to taste these delicacies.

The four fine wines are all ready—
Smooth wines, never astringent,
Clear with strong fragrance—drink them chilled
(for peace and quiet, don't let your servants drink them).
With white yeast we rebrew the sweet wine of Wu
To make the clear Chu liquor.
Come home, bright soul—
Have no fear.

The music of Dai, Qin, Zheng, and Wei[10]—
The singing *yu* pipes perform
Fu Xi's "Jia bian,"
And the "Lao shang" of Chu.
The chorus sings "Yang a" a cappella,
And between the stanzas flutes of Zhao play interludes.
Come home, bright soul—
Tune the strings of your Hollow Mulberry *se*.[11]

Sixteen women in two rows of eight
Dance to the singing.
Hammers strike heavy bells, and lithophones respond,
In the frenzied crescendo,
As the four main singers vie
Singing intricate variations to the limit of their voices.
Come home, bright spirit—
Listen as they sing their entire repertoire.

She of the scarlet lips and pearly teeth is here,
Beautiful and well bred.
Though variously talented, she prefers doing little—
Elegance is her expertise.
Delicately framed, yet shapely,
Attuned to what gives you delight.
Come home, bright spirit—
She will bring you peace and comfort.

She of the artful glance and winning smile is here,
Her arching eyebrows fine and long,
A face of surpassing refinement,
A tender blushing face.
Come home, bright soul—
She will bring you quiet and tranquility.

The tall, cultured one is here—
Radiantly beautiful,
Round cheeked with flat-lying ears.
Her eyebrows are compass-drawn arcs,
Her heart adoring, her manner soothing,
Her dazzling loveliness for you alone,
And she is as small waisted and long necked
As a Xianbei woman.[12]
Come home, bright soul—
She will banish your cares and resentments.

She who displays her heart's harmony and wit
In everything she does is here,
Face powdered white, eyebrows kohled black,
Hair dressed with a fragrant pomade,
Her long sleeve brushing his face as she dances
Is apt to cause the guest to linger.
Come home, bright spirit—
She'll keep the party alive all night.

And she of the straight-line blue-black eyebrows is here.
Her beautiful eyes cast cunning glances,

Her dimpled cheeks and marvelous teeth,
The better to smile.
Fine boned but shapely,
A lithe felicity in her limbs.
Come home, bright spirit—
All such women are yours.

Here is your mansion broad and high
From its imposing cinnabar-painted halls
To its small porches on south-facing rooms
That stay dry when rain runs off the broad-eaved belvederes above.
And in the roofed passageways to the encircling pavilions
You have space enough to train your hunting dogs or hawks.
And whether you ride in a leaping chariot or go on foot,
You will find springtime game in the royal parks.
Hubs of red jade and yoke bars studded with gold
Proclaim the magnificence of your vehicle
Where wild angelica, thoroughwort, and cinnamon trees grow dense
      on the paths.
Come home, bright spirit—
Enjoy yourself as much as you wish.

Peacocks fill your gardens,
Or are those simurghs and phoenixes in your care?
Your mornings will flock with jungle fowl and great geese,
Intermingled with adjutant storks and gray cranes,
And swans taking turns gliding over the water
Through a great expanse of emerald geese.
Come home, bright spirit—
Watch your phoenixes soar.

Lustrous, cheerful faces
Full of vitality—
People who always treat their bodies with care,
Ensuring healthy, long lives.
Such are your kinsmen, crowding your courtyard,
Prosperous with titles and emoluments.

Come home, bright spirit—
Your household is secure.

Setting forth on a thousand miles of crisscrossing roads,
With their retinues like clouds,
Are your high-ranking officers,
With their godlike intelligence,
Investigating early deaths, asking after the sick,
And bringing relief to orphans and widows.
Come home, bright spirit—
Share your bounty justly with both first and last.

A thousand paths run through your towns and fields,
Your subjects are prosperous and many,
Beauty envelopes all walks of life,
Everything glows with the dew of your virtue,
For first you awed and then you civilized.
Now goodness and felicity illumine your domains.
Come home, bright spirit—
Be your rewards and punishments just.

Your fame is like the sun.
It sheds light as far as the four seas.
Your virtue's reputation is as high as the sky.
Your myriad subjects enjoy order and peace
In the north as far as Youling,
In the south as far as Jiaozhi,
In the west as far as Yangchang,[13]
In the east as far as the sea.
Come home, bright spirit—
Elevate the worthy to lofty positions.

Govern in ways that attract the principled,
Exclude the violent and cruel,
Place your court in the most capable hands,
Ferret out and banish the dross,
Grant powers to the upright and skilled,

And your realm will approach the order under the reign of Yu.[14]
Grant the honest and talented the power
To broadcast the flowing dew of your benevolence.
Come home, bright spirit—
For the sake of state and family.

Glorious your martial prowess,
Your celestial virtue, bright.
The Three Dukes[15] in reverent dignity
walk up and down your audience hall.
The feudal lords have all arrived,
The Nine Ministers[16] stand in order.
The white bull's-eye is positioned,[17]
The bearskin target is hung,
Bow in one hand, arrows at his side,
Bowing lord yields precedence to bowing lord.
Come home, bright spirit,
Honor the way of the Three Kings.[18]

## NOTES

1. Tang Bingzheng 湯炳正, Li Daming 李大明, Li Cheng 李誠, and Xiong Liangzhi 熊良知, *Chuci jinzhu* 楚辭今注 (Shanghai: Shanghai guji chubanshe, 1997), 244.
2. Daybreak Valley is 暘谷 Yanggu or 湯谷 Tanggu (Hot Water Valley), where the sun bathes in the morning before it rises.
3. Ox-bodied hog-voiced fish is the 鮙鱅 *yuyong*. The sand spitter is the 短狐 *duanhu* or 蜮 *yu*, a small water monster that can spit sand with such force and accuracy it can kill even a human.
4. Here I read 逴龍 *chuolong* as 燭龍 *zhulong* on the advice of Hong Xingzu 洪興祖, *Chuci buzhu* 楚辭補注 (Beijing: Zhonghua shuju, 1986), 218. The candle dragon lives in the north and brings light to places where the sun does not shine, such as the world of the dead
5. This refers to all the northern rivers. Dai 代 was the name of an ancient northern kingdom. The name came to refer to the north in general.
6. Chu of the Chaste Trees (荊楚 Jing Chu) is one of the names of Chu, referring to its original capital close to Jing Shan, or Chaste Tree Mountain, in Hubei. The chaste tree (*Vitex agnus-castus*) produces a lilaclike flower that attracts butterflies.

7. The five common "grains" are rice, millet, wheat, soybeans, and sesame seeds. Wild rice (菰粱 *guliang*), in this case *Zizania latifolia*, was an upper-class delicacy.

8. Reading 内 *nei* as 肭 *na*, an alternative reading cited by Hong Xingzu.

9. Bitter dog meat (苦狗 *ku gou*) is either dried dog meat or dog meat flavored with gall bladder.

10. Dai, Qin 秦, Zheng 鄭, and Wei 衞, along with Zhao 昭, are the names of ancient states. The music of Zheng was condemned by Confucius as lascivious.

11. *Se* is the name of an instrument with twenty-five strings, similar to a koto.

12. The Xianbei 鮮卑 were a powerful nomadic people who inhabited northeastern China. During the Han dynasty they often harassed the Chinese border regions. During the period of the Northern and Southern dynasties (420–589), they established a number of dynasties in northern China. Wang Yi's explanation of these lines is odd. He takes the name of the Xianbei as referring to the belt buckles they were famous for and which may have given them their name. Yet the passage clearly refers to a Chu woman who has the looks of the Xianbei women, whose belt buckles may have accentuated their narrow waists. It appears that Wang Yi and many later commentators could not imagine that Chu men could have found Xianbei women attractive; see Tang et al., *Chuci jinzhu*, 251.

13. Youling 幽陵 may refer to the northern Hebei–Liaoning area. Jiaozhi 交阯 may refer to the border region between what was considered the deep south (Hunan and Jianxi) and foreign regions to the south of that (Guangdong and Guangxi). Yangchang 羊腸 (Sheep's Gut) is the name of a mountain northwest of Taiyuan in Shanxi. These locations appear to mark the limits of Han-dynasty borders rather than Warring States Chu borders.

14. Yu 禹 was the legendary founder of the Xia dynasty.

15. The Three Dukes (三公 San Gong) were the three highest officers after the head of state in ancient China.

16. The Nine Ministers (九卿 Jiu Qing) ranked just below the Three Dukes.

17. According to the "Xiangshe li" 鄉射禮 chapter of the *Yili* 儀禮, "For the Son of Heaven, a white bull's-eye is positioned in the middle of a target made of bear-skin. For the feudal lords, a red bull's-eye was positioned on an elk-skin target. For the high officers, tigers and panthers were drawn on a cloth target. For the knights, deer and pigs were drawn on a cloth target. All the pictures had red bull's-eyes." Ceremonial archery contests were an important showcase for ritual propriety (and therefore an opportunity to read character) among the powerful in ancient China.

18. The Three Kings (三王 San Wang) were the founders of the Yu 禹, Tang 湯, and Wen 文, the founders of the Xia, Shang, and Zhou, respectively.

# CHAPTER TEN

# "Regretting the Vows"

# 惜誓

# "Xi shi"

"Regretting the Vows" appears to have been added to the *Chuci* sometime between the Liu Xiang edition and the Wang Yi edition of the anthology. This does not necessarily mean that it was composed during that time. In fact, Wang Yi cannot name its author, merely telling us that "some people" thought that it was composed by Jia Yi. The fact that some parts of the poem are similar or the same as sections of Jia Yi's "Lament for Qu Yuan" seems to be the basis of that attribution. The Song scholars Hong Xingzu and Zhu Xi, in view not only of the style but also of the circumstances the poet apparently was lamenting, supported attributing the poem to Jia Yi. Scholars today are still divided on the issue.

Whoever the author was, the poem is unmistakably a product of Han times. It is one of the few places in the *Chuci* where the word *xian* 仙, meaning "transcendent" or "immortal," occurs. While this word occurs earlier, the *xian* is not an important figure in pre-Han literature. By the Han the *xian* represents one of the alternatives to worldly success: the quest for immortality. The thought system that supported this aspiration is traditionally called Daoism, but it should be distinguished from the philosophy represented in the *Laozi* and the *Zhuangzi*. In those texts immortality is not a worthy object of desire, as it was thought to be in disaccord with the Dao. In the *Zhuangzi* those who seek to live forever through exercises, diets, and potions are sometimes even ridiculed. In Han Daoism, however, such regimes were not only respected but also believed to have in fact transformed a substantial number of human beings into *xian*. The *xian* were thought to live in remote places like mountains, islands, and even heaven and to have many powers, including healing and flight. Two of the most famous mythical *xian*, Red Pine (赤松 Chi Song) and Wangzi Qiao 王子喬 (also known as 王僑 Wang Qiao), are mentioned in the poem. A fascinating feature of this poem is that the persona prefers continued life as a mortal to becoming an immortal so that he can better serve his lord.

The persona, however, also warns that there are other honest ministers who are leaving the king's court, repelled by its corruption.

I agree with Hawkes, Wang Siyuan, and others that this poem is made up of not altogether well-joined fragments, some apparently from other poems. I have indicated with ellipses where I think the major breaks in continuity occur.

**Regretting the Vows**

Deploring how I grow older by the year and weaker by the day,
    realizing how many harvests have come and gone never to return,
I float high, climbing toward blue skies,
    passing through the mountains, daily farther,
observing the winding river ways wriggling below.
    Then, with clothes dripping after skimming the four seas,
I ascend to the polestar to rest,
    and breathe in the air of midnight to satisfy my hunger.

The Vermilion Bird[1] flies ahead, on command, to scout for me,
    as I drive Great Unity's[2] ivory chariot,
with the Azure Dragon[3] undulating in the left harness,
    and the White Tiger[4] galloping in the right.

And I raise the sun and moon for canopies
    over the jade women[5] who ride in my rear wagons,
And with them I gallop through dark space,
    Then to rest in the Kunlun Mounds,

Where we exhaust the limits of pleasure. Still not satisfied,
    I want to wander in playful company with the clear-sighted spirits,
So I cross the Cinnabar River,[6] and pursue at full gallop . . .

And on my right the ancient customs of Bactria [7] . . .

On its first ascent the golden swan sees the wriggling network
    of mountains and rivers . . .
On its next ascent it observes the right angles of the earth and the
    curve of the sky,
and looks down on the teaming populations of the central states,
    As it yields to the play of the whirlwinds . . .

Then we alight in the wilds of the Plain of Youth.[8]
    Red Pine and Wang Qiao, two masters, join me,
Each bringing his many-stringed *se*, which they tune to each other, and
    Perform the "Qing shang"[9] at my request.
At peace and content,
    I wheel through the air absorbing its many energies,
Mindful, nevertheless, that I'd rather return to my old home
    Than live a transcendent's endless life . . .

When the golden swan comes to nest out of season,
    The owls flock to stop her.
When the spirit dragon seeks lodging in a waterless land,
    Ants and mole crickets make him their prey.
If that's what befalls golden swans and spirit dragons,
    How much worse for the virtuous in chaotic times?
Life passes gnomon slow, daily I grow weaker.
    As time turns, surely and unceasing,
The common run never stops following
    the crooked who gather to straighten the already straight,
and form secret cliques
    to advance each other illicitly,
while others withdraw from life,
    to hide deep in safety.
Bitter it is to be weighed in the scales of the careless,

to be mixed in a pail with the worthless, to be leveled by the same
   screed,
   and balanced against the same counterweight.

Some adapt to what is required, changing shape as needed,
   And others speak honestly, daring to contradict.
It hurts me that you can't distinguish the faithful from the frauds,
   you who twine your rope with both silk and straw.

This benighted age is the work of the vulgar.
They confuse black and white, beautiful and ugly.
   They reject turtles from the deep pools and high-mountain jade,
while they conspire to raise the price of pebbles.

Mei Bo[10] for his many remonstrations found himself pickled in brine.
While Lai Ge[11] obeying his lord's every whim won sway in the king-
   dom.
   Sad to see the humane maintaining their integrity
Only to be savaged by the small.
   After Bi Gan[12] offered his loyal critique, they split his heart open,
So Ji Zi[13] let his hair hang down and feigned insanity.

Water dammed off from its source stops flowing,
A tree cut off from its roots stops growing.
   It is not to preserve myself that I fret over the coming disaster
I simply regret that as a wounded man I'll be helpless to save my lord.

**Envoi**

It is too late!

Did you not see the *luan* birds[14] and phoenixes circling high over our
   heads,
   who then went to perch in the great unplowed wilds,
who will wander the four directions and never nest,
   save where they see the virtuous thrive?

Sages of godly virtue escape dirty worlds and hide—
　　for isn't a unicorn bridled and tethered
little different from a dog or a goat?

## NOTES

1. Vermilion Bird (赤鳥 Chi Niao) is a Chinese constellation associated with summer and the south.
2. The Great Unity (太一 Taiyi), worshipped in the *Nine Songs*, is a personification of the Dao.
3. Azure Dragon (蒼龍 Cang Niao) is the Chinese constellation associated with east and spring.
4. White Tiger (白虎 Bai Hu) is the collective name of the seven-member western group of the twenty-eight Chinese constellations.
5. Jade women (玉女 *yu nü*) are female *xian*, or immortals.
6. The Cinnabar River (丹水 Dan Shui) flows from the Kunlun Mountains.
7. Bactria (Daxia 大夏) is not a place mentioned in Chinese sources before the Han dynasty.
8. The Plain of Youth (少原 Shao Yuan) is one of the realms of the *xian*, or immortals.
9. "Qing shang" 清商 is an ancient mode associated with autumn and melancholy.
10. Mei Bo 梅白 was dismembered and soaked in brine for criticizing the cruelties of Djou, the last king of the Shang dynasty. Djou also fed Mei Bo's pickled flesh to his vassals.
11. Lai Ge 來革 was a courtier who flattered his way into the favor of the cruel last Shang king.
12. Bi Gan 比干 was the uncle of King Djou and was thought to be a sage. His cruel nephew had heard that the heart of a sage was different from that of most people, so he had Bi Gan's heart cut out to see if it was true.
13. Ji Zi 箕子, or Viscount Ji, was a Shang-dynasty prince who opposed the cruelties of Djou but escaped torture and execution at his hands by pretending to be insane. He escaped to North Korea after the Zhou overthrew the Shang and is believed to be buried in Pyongyang.
14. *Luan* 鸞 birds are fabulous birds in the "phoenix" category.

# CHAPTER ELEVEN

# "Mourning Qu Yuan"　弔屈原
## "Diao Qu Yuan"
## and
## "The Owl Rhapsody"　服賦　"Fu fu"

### *Jia Yi*

Jia Yi 賈誼 (200–168 B.C.E.) was an important writer, thinker, and political figure of the early Former Han dynasty. His scholarly accomplishments, even as a youth, were so impressive that Wu Gong, the governor of his home city of Luoyang, recommended him to Emperor Wen (r. 180–157 B.C.E.), who appointed him erudite (博士 *boshi*). At that time this rank designated an official with teaching and advisory responsibilities who was a specialist in at least one classic. Jia Yi's performance in that position was such that he rose rapidly to the rank of *dazhong dafu* 大中大夫, in which capacity he advocated governmental reforms. His success and his proposals attracted the envy and ire of the entrenched bureaucracy, who exerted pressure on the emperor to rein in the young upstart. The emperor eventually yielded and sent Jia Yi into exile to serve as grand tutor to the Prince of Changsha, near the city of the same name in modern Hunan. There he wrote both "Mourning Qu Yuan" and "The Owl Rhapsody."

Finding himself in Changsha, the main site of Qu Yuan's exile and suicide, he was moved by the similarity of their plights to write "Mourning Qu Yuan." The poem occupies a special position in *Chuci* studies because it contains the earliest known reference to Qu Yuan in a datable poem. It may also mark the beginning of the Han *Chuci* craze that increased in ardor later in the dynasty.

"The Owl Rhapsody" is a philosophical poem based in classical Daoism—that is, the Daoism of the *Laozi* and *Zhuangzi*, which advocates the calm acceptance of death based on the recognition of its inevitability in the larger process (or Dao) of the universe. That is, at least, part of the message Jia Yi imagines spoken by an owl, a bird of ill omen in China, after it flies into his room. Similarities between this poem and "The Raven" by Edgar Allan Poe naturally come to mind.

After about four years, the emperor summoned Jia Yi back to the palace to serve as grand tutor to his youngest son, Prince Huai of Liang (178–169 B.C.E.). Unfortunately the prince died after being thrown from his horse while still under his tutelage. Jia Yi, feeling somehow responsible, died in a state of depression shortly thereafter.

Jia Yi's work was not part of the Wang Yi edition of the *Chuci*, but Zhu Xi included these two poems in his Song-dynasty edition to replace some of the Han poems in Wang Yi's edition that he found mediocre.

**Mourning Qu Yuan**

Through the great kindness of His Majesty
I bring my blameworthy incompetence[1] to serve in Changsha,

Where I hear the story of Qu Yuan,
Who drowned himself in the Miluo River,
And as I come to reside near the flow of the Xiang,
I reverently mourn that gentleman,
Who in the grip of a generation that knew no limits,
Lost his life.

Alas, the pity!

To have the ill luck to live in such an era,
When the phoenix took cover,
While the buzzards soared—
When esteem and glory went to the worthless,

And slander and flattery assured success,
When worthies and sages were dragged by the feet,
And the upright were turned on their heads,

A time when Sui and Yi were called corrupt,
and Zhi and Qiao pure,
And the Moye[2] sword was reckoned dull,
and blades of lead thought sharp.

I sigh, speechless.
For it wasn't his fault that
They cast away the dynastic cauldrons of Zhou,
And valued worn-out clay jars,
That they yoked tired oxen to their chariots,
Or harnessed lame mules,
While the thoroughbred, ears drooping,
Pulled the salt carts,[3]
And the caps of royal officers
were cut to line their shoes.

How long could that have lasted?

Alas, how bitter for him
To suffer such wrongs alone.

**Envoi**

"It is all over now," he said,[4]
"No one in the kingdom values me."
Alone in your melancholy, to whom could you speak?
Rising on air the phoenix heads for a higher realm,
Ensuring its safety by keeping its distance.
The spirit dragon enters the deepest pool,
Its treasure, itself, submerged and out of sight.
If it shuns the crocodile and otter to live in hiding,
Why would it mingle with shrimp and leeches?
The divine virtue of the sage that you so value

protects itself by keeping far from the filthy world.
If a horse that can gallop a thousand miles is tethered and hobbled,
How does it differ from a dog or a goat?
You suffered similar wrong by tarrying in the chaos—
That indeed was your mistake.
You could have traveled the Nine Regions to find another ruler—
Why did you cling so to such a city?
The phoenix and simurgh soar a thousand fathoms high,
And land only where they see virtue's glory,
But seeing slight virtue's dangerous signs,
They beat their wings faster and depart.
Would a fathom-long puddle of stagnant water
Have room for a fish large enough to swallow a boat?
Surely even a sturgeon or whale, with its choice of any river or lake,
Will be bullied by mole crickets and ants in such a place.

## The Owl Rhapsody

In the *chanye*[5] year,
    the fourth month, summertime was just beginning,
On the *gengzi* day toward evening,
    into my room flew an owl.

Standing at the corner of my sitting mat,
    at ease and fearless,
Strange beast landing in my house
    I thought must be some sort of sign.

Rolling out the divination scroll
    I read it was an omen:
"Wild bird enters room,
    the master of the house will soon depart."

I respectfully inquired of the bird,
    "If I am going,
Where? If to a good place, tell me.
    If it's not, I want to know.

What disaster's in the offing? Sooner? Later?
    How long have I?"
    Sighed the owl with head uplifted, beat its wings,
And spoke no word.
    But let me tell you what it wished to say:

"Everything is in a constant state of change,
    moving in a circular flow,
        always pushing forward only to return,
from energy to form, from form to energy,
    like the cicada molting
mysterious, infinite,
    beyond the border of words.

"Misfortune depends on good fortune.
    Good fortune hides in misfortune.
Joy and grief crowd through the same gate.
    Calamity and felicity rule the same realm.

"The kingdom of Wu was great and strong,
    but, under King Fuchai, defeated.
The kingdom of Yue once fled to Mount Guiji,
    But, under King Goujian, it triumphed.[6]

"Li Si[7] wandered into success
    but died by the five cruelest penalties.[8]
Fu Yue once worked on a chain gang
    but rose to be Wu Ding's[9] prime minister.
Are not good fortune and bad
    But two strands entwining to make one rope?

"Fate cannot be fathomed.
    Who knows how you will end?
The swifter the water, the harder the sailing.
    The swifter the arrow, the farther it strikes.
There is no action that is not reaction,
    a resonance, a turning in turn,

clouds rising, rain falling,
  bound to each other by numberless threads.

"A great potter at his wheel
  turning out countless creations,
Heaven is unpredictable.
  You cannot foresee its Way.
Life, whether long or short, is predestined.
  How can you know when your time is at hand?

"Now Heaven and Earth are the furnace;
  creation and change, the smiths,
yin and yang, the charcoal,
  and the myriad creatures the bronze ware.
The joining, separating, destruction, and production
  what meaning or purpose gives shape to it all?

"One of countless changes and transformations
  without beginning or end,
you are an accident.
  What of you is worth clinging to?
You will change into something else.
  What about that makes you afraid?
Those of little wisdom think themselves precious,
  scorning the idea that they might become other.

"But the enlightened ones
  have broader vision.
To the next phase, whatever it brings, they nod yes.

"The greedy will sacrifice themselves for wealth.
  The ardent will sacrifice themselves for fame.
The ambitious will die for power.
  But most people simply want to live.
And, seduced by our desires,
  we sometimes rush east and sometimes west.
But the great do not so much as bend.
  To them the infinite forms of change are one.

"The stupid are bound to the ordinary.
They cannot escape it, they are like prisoners,
    while the perfected move beyond mere things
to come face-to-face with the Dao.

    "Most people wallow
in their pile of myriad likes and dislikes.
    Those who live in the true are tranquil,
finding peace only in the Dao.
    They abandon mind and transcend body.
Going beyond, they lose themselves
    in the boundless void.
Riding high on the Dao,
    going wherever it flows,
stopping only at the islets,
    they give themselves over entirely to destiny,
Seeing the self not as something to own.
    They live as though floating,
die as though pausing to rest.
    Theirs is the calm of water that fills an abyss,
and there they drift like unmoored boats.

    "Don't think yourself special merely for being alive.
Nurture yourself on emptiness and float.
    One of such virtue is unencumbered,
understands destiny and has no worry.

    "An owl is a trifle, a twig, a mustard seed.[10]
Why trouble your mind over something like me?"


NOTES

1. This an attempt to translate the florid self-deprecation, appropriate for an officer of the court addressing the emperor, that begins the poem and which would best not be translated literally.
2. Sui is Bian Sui 卞隨, who was so insulted when Tang, the founder of the Shang dynasty, offered to abdicate to him that he drowned himself by jumping into a

river. Yi is Bo Yi 伯夷, who refused to serve the Zhou after it overthrew the Shang and refused to eat the grain grown under its rule, eventually dying of starvation. Robber Zhi 盜跖 was a legendary bandit from Lu during the Spring and Autumn period. Zhuang Qiao 莊蹻 was a bandit from Chu during the Warring States period. Moye 莫邪 is one of two mythical swords, the other being Ganjiang 干將 (also the name of the sword smith), the former being the "female" and the latter being the "male."

3. The image of Ji 驥, a legendary wonder horse harnessed to a salt cart and stock metaphor for the virtuous and talented minister, occurs in the *Zhanguo ce*, in SBCK, 5:44a. See J. I. Crump, trans., *Chan-kuo Ts'e*, 2nd ed. (San Francisco: Chinese Materials Center, 1980), 49.

4. "Envoi" translates 訊 *xun*, which is the equivalent of the 亂 *luan* in early *Chuci* poems.

5. *Chanye* or *chanyan* is an astronomical term for one of the years in the Chinese twelve-year cycle. Some scholars think that in this case it was the sixth year of Emperor Wen's reign (174 B.C.E.), others think it was the seventh (173 B.C.E.). The beginning of summer (*mengxia*) is usually the fourth month of the lunar calendar. The *gengzi* day was the twenty-third or twenty-eighth day in the fourth month.

6. In the middle of the fifth century B.C.E., King Fuchai of Wu conquered the state of Yue. King Goujian, its king, fled to Mount Guiji, only to return and conquer Wu. He then became hegemon, a kind of strongman who maintained peace by keeping the other states in line.

7. Li Si 李斯, who was the famous minister of the First Emperor of Qin, was originally from Chu. He got into political trouble under the Second Emperor of Qin and was executed.

8. The five penalties were part of the penal code of Qin. They were tattooing the face, cutting off the nose, castration, amputation of the feet, and death. Li Si was in fact cut in half at the waist.

9. Legend has it that Wu Ding, the king of the Shang dynasty, had a dream about meeting a worthy minister. One day while out traveling, he noticed Fu Yue, a convict laborer, because he had the face of the man in his dream. He then took him back to the palace and made him his minister. Convict laborers were bound together like modern-day chain gangs, but more likely with rope rather than chains.

10. There are two schools of thought concerning this sentence. Some say that "a trifle, a twig, a mustard seed" is the displaced object of "why trouble your mind over (literally, 'have misgivings about')." Others take the phrase as the predicate of the suppressed subject "I," referring to the owl. I base my translation on the latter interpretation.

# CHAPTER TWELVE

# "I Lament It Was Not My Destiny"

## 哀時命

## "Ai shiming"

Zhuang Ji 莊忌 was a Han poet famous for his *fu*. He was first patronized by Liu Pi, Prince of Wu (r. 195–154 B.C.E.), who was a generous patron of the arts but who at the time was plotting the famous rebellion of the seven princes against Emperor Jing (188–141 B.C.E.), who, before he became emperor, had gotten away with murdering the prince's son. Zhuang Ji and a number of other literary men, including Zou Yang 諏陽 (ca. 206–129 B.C.E.) and Mei Sheng 枚乘 (d. 140 B.C.E.), decided that remaining at the court of the Prince of Wu would be dangerous and left to go serve in the court of Liu Wu, Prince of Liang (r. 166–144 B.C.E.), another great patron of the arts, who counted among his protégés Sima Xiangru (ca. 179–117 B.C.E.), one of the greatest of the *fu* poets. The Prince of Liang, however, was plotting to murder an imperial minister who had conspired with the emperor to block his ascent to crown prince. Zou Yang protested. Mei Sheng and Zhuang Ji did not. The Prince of Liang's plot was eventually exposed and he fell into disgrace; they remained at his court nevertheless.

Despite the praise his work received during his lifetime (he was known as 夫子 *fuzi*, "the master"), of the twenty-four *fu* ascribed to Zhuang Ji, only "Ai Shiming" survives. Zhu Xi believed that it was written at the court of the Prince of Liang, but it could very well have been written at the court of the Prince of Wu. In either case it would probably have been taken as a critique of the reigning emperor, spoken on behalf of the aggrieved prince. Given the political climate, it could not have been read as a mere exercise in writing in the *Chuci* style.

The poem contains many of the elements of the poems that make up the *Nine Cantos*. The persona is very Qu Yuan–like, and the language borrows heavily from the Qu Yuan corpus. The difference is that it is by a known author and mentions Qu Yuan as one of the exemplars of the past. Otherwise such a poem could easily have been attributed to Qu Yuan.

**I Lament It Was Not My Destiny**

I lament it was not my destiny to live in the time of the ancients.
Why was I born in the wrong era?
I cannot bring back those who have gone before me,
And those to come I can't arrange to meet.

With no other way to tell my heart's sorrow,
I'll inscribe it in the lines of a poem.

Sleepless all night, eyes wide open,
Heart full of secret worries, I have come to this.
I dare not speak my melancholy, for who
In the crowd would help me save the future?
Sadness harries my face and wearies my bones,
Old age, gnomon slow, overtakes me
Where I live in sad, obscure poverty,
Aspiration thwarted, frustrated,
By blocked roads I cannot pass,
And a broad river with no bridges.

I wish I could go to Kunlun's[1] Hovering Gardens
To gather flower of jade[2] on Zhong Peak,[3]
And pick the long branches of the *yao*-stone tree,[4]
And see Langfeng and Bantong Peaks.[5]
But there is no sailing the rushing waters of the Ruo,[6]
I cannot walk the midway ending road,

Nor have I fins to ride the waves that go there,
Or wings to soar high.

So I withdraw into self-pity and mute yearning,
Walking back and forth, idle and alone,
Sad and confused, constantly brooding,
A wronged man with heart indignant,
In secret anguish, in pain upon pain.

Here I languish immobilized,
Hungrier by the day, with little to eat and grain supply cut off.
No one with me, I stand embracing my shadow,
A heart yearning for home beyond,
And no companion in drear emptiness,
Who will join me to savor what fragrance is left?
As the white sun descends to enter the sea,
I grieve that my life will not be long.
My chariot creaks, my horse is a nag,
I am crippled and cannot leave.

Out of place in this generation's muddy waters,
Which is better for me—advance or retreat?
My cap towers so high it cuts through the clouds,
My richly wrought sword drags for miles at my side,
And my flowing robe is so wide
That my left sleeve catches on the Handhold Mulberry,[7]
And my right sleeve brushes against Imperfect Mountain.[8]
I find small range in this six-sided world,[9]

I carve the ax handle as did Fuxi,[10]
Calibrate compass and try square the same as Yao and Shun.
I wish to honor integrity and emulate the lofty,
But cannot look up to Yu of Xia and Tang of Shang.[11]

Although I've seen troubles, my principles endure.
Never would I harm the straight for the sake of the crooked.
A generation of factions is on the rise,

All leveled off with the same screed board,
Huddling shoulder to shoulder,
While the good keep their distance and hide,
For someone is making quail cages in which to keep phoenixes,
Where, even if they gather in their wings, they will not fit.

If the Spirit August will not wake up and take notice,
How will I state my case to prove my utmost loyalty?
If the vulgar in their envy block the worthy from view,
Who will even know how the worthy behave?
If I let my anger out to say the things inside my heart,
How do I know it will bring me good or ill?
Jade tablets are mixed in with clay rice steamers,
Long Lian and Meng Zou[12] live in the same palace.
Since the whole world takes this as normal,
I am sure to suffer misery till the end of my days.

Tossing and turning alone in the dark I cannot sleep,
Lonely anguish fills my breast,
My souls flit about unsettled,
Indignation struggles in my heart,
My thoughts are gloomy, remorseful, uneasy,
The road is rock strewn and dark.
Alone I keep to this cramped corner,
Ever in pain and constantly sighing,
I grieve the night long and cannot sleep.
My temper seethes like a choppy sea,
I hold the engraving knife but do not use it.
I take up compass and try square without a thing to measure.
Let Qi and Ji[13] run only the length of a courtyard,
And they'll never be able to run broad plains.
Shut a gibbon in a tiny cage with lattice windows,
But expect no agility when it's time to perform.
If you try to chariot up a mountain with a team of lame tortoises,
I know for sure you will never reach the top.
If you fire Guan Zhong[14] and Yan Ying[15] and give office to a servant
    boy,

The steelyard[16] of sovereignty will falsely weigh.
You mix arrow bamboo[17] with hemp straw,
You load your crossbow with tumbleweed to shoot through leather
     armor.
I am bent over and staggering under the burden of your folly,
I want to straighten up and walk but cannot.

Just outside, nets are set to trap me,
And tethered arrows aim to drag me out of the sky.
Sidling in with rounded shoulders I still do not fit.
If I pull my belly in further I won't be able to breathe.
Wu Guang[18] threw himself into deep water.
He did not take to the world's dirt—
No ladle with broken handle will long be used.

I am willing to withdraw and live in poverty,
Making a home by digging a cave into the side of a cliff,
Washing my clothes on the banks of a river,
Soaked with morning mist and dew,
Clouds gathering to serve as my roof,
With a crowd of rainbows at dawn,
And flooding downpours at night.

Despair all over the homeless waste
Thwarts a distant view in the deserted wilds.
Down here sinking my fishhook in a valley stream,
I look to those who achieved transcendence "up there."
I would befriend Red Pine,
Be the companion of Wang Qiao,[19]
Have Xiao Yang[20] as my guide.
With white tigers guarding me fore and aft,
Through clouds and mists I would enter the blue,
Calmly riding a white deer,[21]
Eyes straight ahead, my soul at home in solitude,
Speeding onward and beyond never returning,
Daily onward to dwell in high distance,
With a delirious mind, but a wounded heart.

Soaring through blue clouds, a *luan* phoenix
Is out of range of tethered arrows.
Hidden at the base of a whirlpool the dragon
Will never find itself caught in a net.
He knows it is better to play in the crystal waves,
Than lust for fatal bait.
I would rather hide far away, out of calamity's reach.
Whose attacks and insults could be aimed my way then?
Zixu[22] died but got his revenge,
Qu Yuan drowned in the Miluo River.
Such men never change even when torn limb from limb,
And what could change the truly loyal and trustworthy?
My will beats within an upright heart,
I walk a straight line with no deviation,
I work the scales with no dishonest thought,
Weighing truly the light and the heavy.
I cleanse the chaos of filth,
I clear away layers of dirt to restore the pristine state.
My form is clean, what I'm made of is pure,
Immaculate, gleaming to the core,
But my contemporaries, fed up with me, reject my service,
So I'll go far away and hide for now.
I'll hide away, erase my every trace,
Keeping quiet with nary a murmur,
Alone in worry, anger, and trouble,
To whom could I go to vent my rage, to open my heart?
The darkening hour, the day almost over,
Brings melancholy sighing but no good name.
Bo Yi[23] died on Shouyang Mountain,
Dying in the end, obscure and unsung.
A Taigong[24] without King Wen
Would have gone to his death unfulfilled.
I want to reveal the white jade and ivory in my bosom, the jasper hang-
    ing from my waist,
But no one has eyes to appraise them.
I was born it seems just to pass between heaven and earth.
I will disappear leaving no mark.

An evil influence assails my body,
Sprouting sickly discomforts.
I wish but to see once more the bright days of sunny spring,
For I fear my time is running out.

## NOTES

1. Kunlun 崑崙 here refers to the mythological mountain, not the real mountain range. During the Han dynasty it was thought to be the home of the Queen Mother of the West (西王母 Xi Wangmu). One of its peaks is called Hovering Gardens (懸圃 Xuanpu), because of the gardens that, according to some sources, float over it.
2. Flower of jade (玉英 yuying) is jade of such purity that it has magical powers.
3. Zhong Peak (鍾山 Zhong Shan) is northwest of Kunlun.
4. Yao-stone tree (瑤木 yaomu) would seem to be a tree that is made of the yao stone, which is a white stone similar to jade.
5. Langfeng 閬風 is the northern peak of Kunlun, where immortals reside. Bantong 板桐 is another peak in the Kunlun range.
6. The Ruo River (弱水 Ruo Shui) is a legendary river in the extreme west near Kunlun. Ruo means "weak" and is a designation of rivers that are too weak (i.e., shallow) to hold up a boat.
7. Handhold Mulberry is the fusang (扶桑 or 榑桑) tree. It grows where the sun rises in the east and serves as a handhold when it emerges from its bath.
8. Imperfect Mountain is Buzhou Shan 不周山, a legendary mountain and one of the supports holding up the sky. Gonggong dashed against it during his battle with Zhuan Xu and damaged it, thus causing the sky to tilt. It is northwest of Kunlun.
9. "Six sided" refers to the six directions, east, west, north, south, up, and down.
10. Fuxi is written 伏羲 or 伏戲. He is one of the mythical god-lords, first of the Three Augusts (三皇 Sanhuang), and inventor of such things as hunting, fishing, and the domestication of animals.
11. In the Chinese text, the first Yu and Tang refer to You Yu 有虞 and Tao Tang 陶唐, Shun and Yao, respectively, though Yao is chronologically first. The second Yu and Tang are Yu, founder of the Xia dynasty (夏禹), and Tang, founder of the Shang dynasty (商湯), respectively. This use of both pairs of Yu and Tang is a play on words based on Chinese characters that are different but sound more or less the same. The first Yu and Tang abdicated in favor of men whom they saw as meriting kingship. The second Yu and Tang created and perpetuated hereditary monarchy, which some later thinkers considered the beginning of the end of good government.

12. Long Lian 隴廉 and Meng Zou 孟娵 are the type of female ugliness and the ideal of female beauty, respectively. This pair seems to occur nowhere other than in this poem.

13. Qi 騏 and Ji 驥 are the wonder horses that can run a thousand *li* a day, stock symbols of talented, virtuous ministers.

14. Guan Zhong 管仲 (d. 645 B.C.E.) was the prime minister of Duke Huan of Qi during the Spring and Autumn period. His reforms helped strengthen Qi and led to Duke Huan's becoming hegemon.

15. Yan Ying 晏嬰 (d. 510 B.C.E.) was a celebrated prime minister of the state of Qi during the Spring and Autumn period.

16. Steelyard (權衡 *quanheng*) is the Chinese hand-held scale, a metaphor for just rule.

17. Arrow bamboo (箭竹 *jianzhu*) is the modern Chinese designation of 菎蕗 *kunlu* (*Sinarundinaria nitida*), sometimes known in English as fountain bamboo or umbrella bamboo.

18. Wu Guang 務光, like Bian Sui 卞隨, was so insulted when Tang, the founder of the Shang dynasty, offered him the throne that he threw himself into a river and drowned.

19. Red Pine (赤松 Chi Song) and Wang Qiao 王僑 are two of the most famous Daoist immortals (*xian*).

20. Xiao Yang 梟楊 is a mountain spirit that has an oversized human form, a black face, fur, and backward feet. When it sees a human, it laughs.

21. A white deer is the preferred mount of immortals.

22. Zixu is Wu Zixu 伍子胥 (d. 485 B.C.E.), a defector from Chu who served as military adviser to King Fuchai of Wu. King Fuchai ordered him to commit suicide when he opposed the king's plan to form an alliance with the state of Yue. His body was stuffed in a leather sack and floated on the Yangtze River. Legend has it that he became the god of Yangtze tidal floods.

23. When the Zhou dynasty overthrew the cruel last king of the Shang, Bo Yi, out of loyalty, retreated to Shouyang Mountain and there ate ferns rather than eat crops grown under Zhou rule and starved to death.

24. Taigong 太公 is Taigong Wang 太公望, also known as Jiang Ziya 姜子牙 (fl. ca. 1100 B.C.E.), a legendary sage who served King Wen of the Zhou dynasty as a military strategist.

# CHAPTER THIRTEEN

# "Calling the Hermit Back"

# 招隱士

# "Zhao yinshi"

## *Attributed to Huainan Xiaoshan*

Although this poem is attributed to Huainan Xiaoshan (second century B.C.E.), the name, which translates as "low mountains south of the River Huai," is probably not that of a person. Most scholars follow the Later Han commentator Wang Yi in taking it as the collective name of a group of literary men in the service of the Prince of Huainan (179–122 B.C.E.). It will be remembered that he was ordered by his nephew Emperor Wu to compose a commentary on the "Li sao," of which fragments are preserved in Sima Qian's *Shiji* (Records of the grand historian) and Hong Xingzu's edition of the *Chuci*. The court of the Prince of Huainan rivaled that of Emperor Wu in brilliance, especially in the literary arts, for the prince had gathered together the best minds from all over the empire. The most famous of these were known as the Eight Dukes. There were also two groups of scholars known as the High Mountains and the Low Mountains, who, under the prince's direction, cooperated with the Eight Dukes in compiling the philosophical miscellany known as the *Huainanzi*. Someone from the Low Mountain group probably composed "Calling the Hermit Back."

While there is little doubt about what the poem says, there is much disagreement as to what it means. Wang Yi, as usual, claimed that the hermit in the poem stands for Qu Yuan. Others say that the prince had it composed to attract the talented but disgruntled unemployed to his court. Still others say that the dangerous mountain wilderness described in the poem is a metaphor for the imperial court, and that the poem is warning the prince, who was visiting the capital, that the emperor was plotting against him. Liu An, in fact, was eventually accused of plotting a coup. He committed suicide to avoid arrest.

### Calling the Hermit Back

In the depths of the mountains,
 the cinnamon tree grows densely.
Its writhing branches
 wander and interlace
in high mountain mists
 that crowd the boulders looming
over the steep drop to wave upon wave
 of the river in the valley.
When gibbons in packs yell,
 and tigers and leopards roar,
climb the branches of the cinnamon tree
 and stay there awhile,
as you roam, my prince, not coming home,
 and the spring grass grows lushly.

But towards year's end you'll find no consolation
 in the summer cicada buzzing
on the endless paths winding
 the waists of the mountains,
as your heart aches flustered
 for having stayed too long,
and you climb in panic and terror
 through dense bush and deep woods,
trembling where tigers and leopards
 make their dens.
Gaunt peaks rise steeply,
 with strange rocks at all angles.
And in the forest thick with leaves and branches
 sagging over tangled shrubs

and green sedge growing in between
 and bog bulrush waving in the breeze,
the white deer and elk bucks
 leap or stand
with towering horns
 and glossy fur.
But when macaques and bears,
 longing for their species, keen,
climb the branches of the cinnamon tree
 and stay there awhile,
for tiger fights leopard
 and black bear roars at brown.
Even wild beasts quail
 when parted from their kind.
Return, my prince,
 for in the mountains
you cannot stay long.

# Appendix: Dating the Works in the *Chuci*

Aside from authorship, dating the works in the *Chuci* has long been a subject of controversy, especially in recent times. Most of the conclusions of traditional scholars were based on speculation about what part of the *Chuci* fit into what phase of Qu Yuan's life, and the main guide to that life was the *Shiji* biography. While traditional scholars see the *Chuci* as an outgrowth of the *Shijing*, Galal Walker sees in the *Chuci* a tradition quite distinct from the *Shijing*. Walker's concept of tradition overlaps with the concept of style. To write in a style is to consciously or unconsciously imitate work or works that already exist, and imitation involves repetition or sharing of distinct elements. There is very little that the *Chuci* shares with the *Shijing*. The works within the *Chuci* share with each other such elements as theme, imagery, prosody, and, most importantly, phraseology. Not just words and phrases, but whole sentences and rhyming lines recur, in some cases often, throughout the anthology. Walker's rigorous statistical analyses of both phraseology and phonology reveal that the early part of the *Chuci* tradition generated sentences and phrases that were borrowed into later works of the tradition, sometimes directly, sometimes indirectly—that is, through other works.[1] The earliest parts of the tradition also tend to rhyme according to the phonological standard observed in the text of the *Shijing*. Classifying these poems as early must come with the caveat that the received text of the *Shijing*, having been transcribed into characters (and possibly, therefore, a language) standardized during the Qin dynasty, probably reflects a stage of phonological evolution later than the probable date of the earliest *Shijing* poems.

The middle part of the *Chuci* tradition is marked by works that display characteristics, both stylistic and phonological, of Han provenance but are (mis)attributed to Qu Yuan or other Chu poets. It also includes works by known Han poets still strongly under the influence of the early tradition.

The later part of the *Chuci* tradition was produced by recognized Han-dynasty authors who consciously wrote in the Chu style drawing upon stylistic and thematic elements of both early and middle periods, but whose rhyming habits are characteristically Han.

Walker's work is pioneering, and, as he himself admits, may not be the final word on this topic (new reconstructions of Old Chinese phonology are being formulated even as I write), but I find it convincing enough to use as a starting point for determining the date and authorship of the anthology's contents.

With the exception of "Those Who Died for the Kingdom" (國殤 "Guoshang"), which was composed later, the *Nine Songs* (九歌 *Jiuge*) for Walker are the earliest works of the *Chuci* tradition. These beautiful and mysterious poems appear to have been originally hymns to accompany the performance of shamanic ritual. There is no trace of political complaint, allegorical or otherwise, in them. Walker places them at the head of the *Chuci* tradition, because their rhyming standard is the same as that of the *Shijing*, or at least of the final redactors of the *Shijing*, and their influence is visible, in terms of phraseology at least, throughout most of the anthology, especially "Leaving My Troubles" (離騷 "Li sao"). For this reason I have gone against traditional practice by placing them before the "Li sao," rather than the other way around; however, I will preserve intact Zhu Xi's order of the other works.

The "Li sao," the longest of the ancient Chinese poems and the centerpiece of the anthology, borrows sentences from the *Nine Songs*, as well as the world they describe, with its shamans, airborne spirits, and fragrant, wearable herbs. Its meter is also derived from the *Nine Songs*—it is simply the predominant *Nine Songs* verse line doubled. The basic "plot" of a number of the songs, where a spirit descends attracted by fragrances and then ascends suddenly to depart, is adapted to create the "Li sao" political allegory of which the surface narrative is about a spirit who, drawn by the fragrances of various medicinal herbs, descends upon what appears to be a shaman kingdom, and after much hesitation leaves in disappointment when the royal taste for fragrances changes in favor of malodorous weeds. What the poem is really about is a good king gone bad, his rejection of a virtuous minister and the consequent, imminent fall of his kingdom.

The next poem is "Mourning Ying" (哀郢 "Ai Ying"), the third piece in the *Nine Cantos* (九章 *Jiuzhang*). The title and the first part of the poem suggest that it was written to lament the fall of Ying, the Chu capital city, to the Qin army in the year 278. Wang Yi (d. 158 C.E.) thought it was written by Qu Yuan, but later scholars doubted that attribution because, according to Sima Qian's biography, Qu Yuan committed suicide before the fall of Ying. Walker finds evidence that argues that this piece was written shortly after the "Li sao." The meter and most of the rhyme pattern are the same. The narration and imagery, however, are very different. It is a realistic description of a journey into exile, first of refugees from a city that has been destroyed, and then, apparently, of an individual. The second part of the poem, oddly, concentrates not on why or how the city was destroyed but on the individual, who describes his plight as that of the loyal but rejected minister who has been sent into exile. It reminds one of the "Li sao," but the shamanistic and supernatural images are gone. I agree with Hawkes that the poem as we have it may be the result of the joining of two or more originally separate texts.

The next in line are what Walker calls the three early poems of the *Nine Cantos*, which is to say poems that were composed after "Mourning Ying." These are "Crossing the Yangtze" (涉江 "She jiang"), "Expressing My Longing" (抽思 "Chou si"), and "A Bosom Full of Sand" (懷沙 "Huai sha"). All these poems, like most of the rest of the poems in the series, are concerned with political frustration and exile and are mostly in the same meter as "Li sao," facts that were basis enough for Wang Yi to ascribe the whole set to the authorship of Qu Yuan. Evidence that they come after "Mourning Ying" is the fact that in addition to borrowing lines and phrases from the "Li sao" and the *Nine Songs*, they also borrow from "Mourning Ying."

"Summoning the Soul" (招魂 "Zhao hun") was probably composed around the same time that these *Nine Cantos* pieces were composed. It was one of the small number of poems Sima Qian attributed to Qu Yuan. Yet Liu Xiang (77–6 B.C.E.) and Wang Yi, the two later scholars responsible for compiling and editing the *Chuci*, thought it was by Song Yu.

"Summoning the Soul" represents a type of poem or song used to ritually call back the soul of someone who has just died in the hope of restoring life to the corpse. Its meter is that of the *Nine Songs*, with some admixture of "Li sao" meter. It also shares a few lines with the *Nine Songs*, but not with any other *Chuci* piece, even with the poem in the *Chuci* collection most similar to it, "The Great Summoning" (大招 "Da zhao"), another soul-recalling piece. On the basis of rhyme phonology, Walker placed "Summoning the Soul" in the early period, "The Great Call" in the late. In terms of sentence borrowing and sharing, they both stand outside the mainstream *Chuci* tradition.

Next come four other poems in the *Nine Cantos*: "Longing for the Beautiful One" (思美人 "Si meiren"), "I Deplore Pleading" (惜誦 "Xi song"), "I Grieve When the Whirlwind" (悲回風 "Bei huifeng"), and "I Look Back in Sadness" (惜往日 "Xi wang ri"). Walker observes that these are the first poems in the anthology that "do not borrow directly from the 'Nine Songs,'" the two main influences here being "Li sao" and "Mourning Ying," especially thematically. Here the tradition seems to divide into those poets who preferred the more supernatural imagery of the former and those who preferred the more realistic imagery of the latter. Nevertheless, phraseology from both occurs in all the poems, with the exception of "I Deplore Pleading," which has none from "Mourning Ying." Rhyming in these poems begins to display the influence of one or another Han-period dialect.

The only poem in the *Nine Cantos* that Walker does not classify is a poem that in being joyous rather than sad and short rather than long is very different from the rest— "Hymn to a Mandarin Orange Tree" (橘頌 "Ju song"). The brevity of the poem does not offer enough formal and phonological features for analysis and comparison. It, like "Summoning the Soul," stands outside the *Chuci* tradition.

The middle period of the *Chuci* tradition begins, in Walker's classification, with the *Nine Variations* (九辨 *Jiu bian*), a series that, unlike the previous poems, is generally attributed to Song Yu rather than Qu Yuan. These nine poems borrow more sentences from "Morning Ying" than any *Chuci* poem that follows. They also borrow from "Li sao," "Longing for the Beautiful One," and "I Grieve When the Whirlwind." "Li sao" meter appears here but so does every other meter occurring in the poetry previous to it, as well as a prosodic unit (two syllables plus carrier sound) from the *Shijing*. The text of the *Nine Variations* seems in some places to be made up of fragments from other sources. The themes of political frustration and exile predominate, but the series also contains interesting evocations of the autumn landscape of the south.

Next comes "I Lament It Was Not My Destiny" (哀時命 "Ai shiming"), which Walker's analysis places around the time of the composition of the *Nine Variations*. The two works share sentences, but Walker could not determine which was the "loaner" and which the "borrower." Here we see the influence of dialect on rhyme that began in the *Nine Cantos* becoming more obvious. "I Lament It Was Not My Destiny" is attributed to the Han poet Yan Ji 嚴忌, who was a native of Wu (modern Jiangsu province) and also served in the court of Pi, the Prince of Wu, during the middle of the second century B.C.E. He may well have written the poem there or at the court of Liu Wu, the Prince of Liang, where he served slightly later. That may account for the local-dialect-influenced rhyme phonology of the poem, which shares meter, imagery, and mood with the "Li sao," but none of the poetic heights.

Next comes "Regretting the Vows" (惜誓 "Xi shi"), which borrowed from the "Li sao" but mostly from "Seven Remonstrations" (七諫 "Qi jian," not included in my translation), ascribed traditionally to the Han poet Dongfang Shuo, which itself borrows heavily from the later tradition. Because some sentences in Jia Yi's "Mourning Qu Yuan" (弔屈原) are copied into "Regretting the Vows," some scholars ascribed it to Jia Yi; Wang Yi rejected this attribution but implied that he thought that an unknown poet had written the poem during the time of King Huai. This seems unlikely, for "Regretting the Vows," like "Wandering Far Away" (遠遊 "Yuan you"), features a spirit journey that has much more to do with Han Daoism than with the shaman fights of the early *Chuci* poems.

*Seven Remonstrations* (七諫 *Qi jian*) comes next. This set of seven poems was at one time attributed to the Han poet Dongfang Shuo 東方朔 (ca. 160–ca. 93 B.C.E.), which is unlikely. At any rate, it is now almost universally recognized as an anonymous work. The poems, which are written in the persona of Qu Yuan, seem to be an example of the use of the Chu mode to register complaint about Han political circumstances.

Exactly what those circumstances were is never made clear. Since Zhu Xi cut them from his edition of the *Chuci*, I do not include them in my translation.

"Wandering Far Away" seems to come after "Regretting the Vows," as one of the sentences from the former appears in the latter. It also borrows from "Li sao," the *Nine Songs*, "Crossing the Yangtze," "Lamenting It Was Not My Destiny," and the *Seven Remonstrations*. Wang Yi listed it as one of the works of Qu Yuan, and some scholars still do so today. Given its predecessors and the fact that twelve sentences from "Wandering Far Away" appear in "The Great Man Rhapsody" (大人賦 "Daren fu") by Sima Xiangru (179–117 B.C.E.), which was presented to Emperor Wu between 120 and 130 B.C.E., Walker concludes that the approximate date for the composition of "Wandering Far Away" would be about 125 B.C.E. This would support the theory, put forth by Hawkes, that "Wandering Far Away" was by an unknown poet and was a model for "The Great Man Rhapsody."[2] Some scholars think that both poems are by Sima Xiangru and that "Wandering Far Away" is a first draft of "The Great Man Rhapsody." Others think that "The Great Man Rhapsody." came first and someone else, borrowing from it, wrote "Wandering Far Away."

In any event, the year 125 B.C.E., which marks the approximate end of the middle period of the development of the *Chuci* tradition, the period after which it is dominated by Han poets, in Walker's reckoning, is the approximate date of the first performance of Chu poetry at the Han imperial court by someone deemed an expert in it, Zhu Maichen.

As noted, Walker believes, the "Ask the Sky" (天問 "Tian wen") and "The Great Summoning" were composed in the middle period. He thinks the same about "Calling the Hermit Back" (招隱士 "Zhao yinshi"), "The Fisherman" (漁夫 "Yufu"), and "The Diviner" (卜居 "Bu ju"). All these works stand outside the mainstream of the *Chuci* tradition, which is to say they seem uninfluenced by the foundational texts like the *Nine Songs*, "Li sao," and "Mourning Ying" or their imitators. There is little controversial in Walker's claim except for his dating of "Ask the Sky." Even Wang Yi was doubtful about the authorship of "The Great Summoning," though most scholars think it a Warring States–period work. "Calling the Hermit Back" was always recognized as a Han work produced at the court of the Prince of Huainan or by the prince himself. And most modern scholars no longer believe that the "The Diviner" and "The Fisherman" are the work of Qu Yuan. "Ask the Sky," however, is almost universally considered Qu Yuan's work.

Let us remember how Walker arrives at his conclusions. They are based on consideration of what sentences are borrowed from what other works and what words are allowed to rhyme with each other. "Ask the Sky" borrows no lines from the earlier *Chuci* tradition and no poems from the later tradition borrow lines from it, but the way it rhymes is characteristic of later poetry, which in this case means poetry written during the reign of Emperor Wu of the Han and slightly later.

Evidence that could be used to support Walker's conclusions comes from the research of John Major, the foremost American expert on the *Huainanzi* 淮南子, a compendium of essays on various subjects written at the court of the Prince of Huainan during the reign of Emperor Wu. Major noticed that when certain sections of "Ask the Sky" are juxtaposed with pertinent sections of the *Huainanzi*, the latter text seems often to offer "an expanded version of the Tian wen narrative." This is especially the case when one compares "Ask the Sky" cosmological sections (e.g., stanzas 1–9) with parts of the *Huainanzi* (e.g., chapters 3 and 4). In some of these expanded narratives, concrete answers are given to "Ask the Sky" questions. For example, where "Ask the Sky" asks,

> If each of the Nine Regions has its own sky,
>> How do the skies fit together,
> With their complex jagged edges,
>> And who knows how many junctures?

*Huainanzi* 3:4a answers, "Heaven has nine fields and 9,999 junctures." (Major astutely translates 隅 *yu* as "juncture." I follow him here by translating 隅隈 *yuwei* as "junctures" but try to give a sense of its double duty here by also translating it as "jagged edge.") The relationship between the two texts revealed by such juxtapositions could at the very least support the idea that the two texts emerged from the same intellectual milieu, if not at the same time.[3] On the other hand, given that the highly cultured princedom of Huainan was located in some of the former domains of Chu, "Ask the Sky" could have simply been an old text that ended up in the princely library and became the basis of scholarly discussion; its rhyming system may reflect regional patterns that were preserved in the south and subsequently taken north by aristocratic southerners who went to serve in the Han government. Those possibilities seem to leave the question of how to date "Ask the Sky" open.

Walker locates the late tradition in the last part of the anthology: "Nine Longings" (九懷 "Jiu huai") by Wang Bao (fl. 58 B.C.E.), "Nine Sighs" (九歎 "Jiu tan") by Liu Xiang, and "Nine Yearnings" (九思 "Jiu si") by Wang Yi. As mentioned, these sections, which were all written by known Han authors, along with "Qi jian," were excluded from Zhu Xi's Song-dynasty edition of the *Chuci* because he thought them examples of "moaning in the absence of pain." Most modern editions of the *Chuci* in China have more or less followed him in this, as have I. I also follow Zhu Xi in adding two pieces not included in Wang Yi's edition of the *Chuci*, "The Owl Rhapsody" (服賦) and "Mourning Qu Yuan," both fine pieces influenced by Chu poetics, by Jia Yi.

NOTES

1. My summary of Walker's conclusions is based on Galal Walker, "Toward a Formal History of the 'Chuci'" (Ph.D. diss., Cornell University, 1982), especially 425–53.

2. See David Hawkes, trans., *The Songs of the South: An Ancient Chinese Anthology of Poems by Qu Yuan and Other Poets* (Harmondsworth, U.K.: Penguin, 1985), 91–93.

3. John S. Major, "Some Questions Do Have Answers: 'Tian wen' and the *Huainanzi*," unpublished manuscript, cited by permission of the author.

# Selected Bibliography

WORKS IN CHINESE

Chen Mengjia 陳夢家. *Yinxu puci zongshu* 殷墟卜辭綜述. Beijing: Kexue chubanshe, 1956.

*Chu wenhua yanjiu hui* 楚文化研究會. *Chu wenhua yanjiu hui lunji* 楚文化研究會論集. Hubei: Jingchu shushe, 1987.

*Chunqiu Gongyang jingzhuan jiegu* 春秋經傳解. Zhonghua 1987 photocopy of the Song 1193 edition of the *Chunxi Fuzhou Gongshi ku kanben* 淳熙撫州公使刊本 text kept in the National Library, Beijing.

Dai Wang 戴望. *Guanzi jiaozheng* 管子校正. Vol. 5 of *Zhuzi jicheng* 諸子集成. Shanghai: Shanghai shudian, 1987.

Dong Chuping 董楚平. *Chuci yizhu* 楚辭譯注. Shanghai: Shanghai guji chubanshe, 1986.

*Ershier zi* 二十二子. Shanghai: Shanghai guji chubanshe, 1987.

Fu Xiren 傅錫壬. *Chuci duben* 楚辭讀本. Taipei: Sanmin, 1974.

Gu Jiegang 顧頡剛. *Shangshu tongjian* 尚書通檢. Beijing: Harvard-Yenching Institute, 1936; repr., Beijing: Shumu wenxian chubanshe, 1982.

———. *Shilin zashi: Peng Xian* 史林雜識。彭咸. Beijing: Zhonghua shuju, 1978.

Guo Maoqian 郭茂倩. *Juaner ji: Qu Yuan fu jin yi* 卷耳集。屈原賦今譯. Beijing: Renmin wenxue chubanshe, 1981.

———. *Yuefu shiji* 樂府詩集. Beijing: Zhonghua shuju, 1979.

*Guoyu* 國語. Shanghai 1987 reprint of Shangwu 1934 edition of the *Song Mingdao er nian* 宋明道二年 text of 1033.

*Hanshu* 漢書. Compiled by Ban Gu 班固. Beijing: Zhonghua shuju, 1962.

He Tianxing 何天行. *Chuci zuo yu Handai kao* 楚辭作於漢代考. Shanghai: Zhonghua shuju, 1948.

Hong Xingzu 洪興祖. *Chuci buzhu* 楚辭補注. Beijing: Zhonghua shuju, 1986.

Hu Nianyi 胡念貽. *Chuci xuanzhu ji kaozheng* 楚辭選注及考證. Changsha: Yueli chubanshe, 1984.

Hu Shi 胡適. "Du Chuci" 讀楚辭. In *Hu Shi wencun di er ji* 胡適文存第二集, 91–97. Taipei: Yuandong tushu gongsi, 1953.

Hu Wenying 胡文英. *Qusao zhi zhang* 屈騷指掌. Beijing: Beijing guji chubanshe, 1979.

Huang Zhongmo 黃中模. *Qu Yuan wenti lunzheng shi gao* 屈原問題史稿. Beijing: Shi-yue wenyi chubanshe, 1987.

Jiang Ji 蔣驥. *Shandaige zhu Chuci* 山帶閣註楚辭. Shanghai: Shanghai guji chubanshe, 1985.

Jiang Liangfu 姜亮夫. *Chongding Qu Yuan fu jiaozhu* 重訂屈原賦校註. Tianjin: Tianjin guji chubanshe, 1987.

——. *Chuci shumu wu zhong* 楚辭書目五種. Beijing: Zhonghua shuju, 1961.

——. *Chuci tonggu* 楚辭通故. 4 vols. Shandong: Qi Lu shushe, 1985.

——. *Chuci xue lunwen ji* 楚辭學論集. Shanghai: Shanghai guji chubanshe, 1984.

——. *Qu Yuan fu jin yi* 屈原賦今譯. Beijing: Beijing chubanshe, 1987.

Jiang Tianshu 蔣天樞. *Chuci lunwen ji* 楚辭論文集. Shaanxi: Shaanxi renmin chubanshe, 1982.

Jin Kaicheng 金開誠, Dong Hongli 董洪利, and Gao Luming 高路明. *Qu Yuan ji jiaozhu* 屈原集校注. 2 vols. Beijing: Zhonghua shuju, 1996.

Lin Geng 林庚. *Tian wen lunjian* 天問論箋. Beijing: Renmin chubanshe, 1983.

Liu Yongji 劉永濟. *Qu fu yin zhu xiangjie; Qu fu shici* 屈賦音注詳解；屈賦釋詞. Shanghai: Shanghai guji chubanshe, 1983.

Ma Maoyuan 馬茂元, ed. *Chuci yanjiu lunwen xuan* 楚辭研究論文選. Wuhan: Hubei renmin chubanshe, 1985.

——. *Chuci yaoji jieti* 楚辭要籍解題. Wuhan: Hubei renmin chubanshe, 1984.

——. *Chuci zhushi* 楚辭註釋. Wuhan: Hubei renmin chubanshe, 1985.

——. *Chuci ziliao haiwai bian* 楚辭資料海外編. Wuhan: Hubei renmin chubanshe, 1986.

*Mengzi zhengyi* 孟子正義. Vol. 1 of *Zhuzi jicheng* 諸子集成. Shanghai: Shanghai shudian, 1987.

*Mozi jiangu* 墨子閒詁. Vol. 4 of *Zhuzi jicheng* 諸子集成. Shanghai: Shanghai shudian, 1987.

Pan Fujun 潘富俊. *Chuci zhiwu tujian* 楚辭植物圖鑒. Shanghai: Shanghai shudian, 2003.

Pi Xirui 皮錫瑞. *Jingxue tonglun*. 經學通論. Beijing: Zhonghua shuju, 1982.

Qinghua daxue chutu wenxian yanjiu yu baohu zhongxin 清華大學出土文獻研究與保

護中心, ed. Chief editor, Li Xueqin 李學勤. *Qinghua daxue can Zhanguo zhujian (yi)* 清華大學藏戰國竹簡 (壹). Shanghai: Zhongxi shuju. 2010.

———. *Qinghua daxue can Zhanguo zhujian (er)* 清華大學藏戰國竹簡 (貳). Shanghai: Zhongxi shuju. 2010.

———. *Qinghua daxue can Zhanguo zhujian (san)* 清華大學藏戰國竹簡 (叁). Shanghai: Zhongxi shuju. 2010.

Ruan Yuan 阮元. *Shisanjing zhushu* 十三經注疏. Beijing: Zhonghua shuju, 1987.

Shi Quan 石泉. *Gudai Jingchu dili xin tan* 古代地理新探. Wuhan: Wuhan daxue chubanshe, 1988.

Sima Qian 司馬遷. *Shiji* 史記. Beijing: Zhonghua shuju, 1992.

Su Xuelin 蘇雪林. *Tian wen zheng jian* 天問正簡. Taipei: Wenjin, 1992.

Tang Bingzheng 湯炳正. *Qu fu xin tan* 屈賦新探. Shandong: Qi Lu shushe, 1984.

Tang Bingzheng 湯炳正, Li Daming 李大明, Li Cheng 李誠, and Xiong Liangzhi 熊良知. *Chuci jinzhu* 楚辭今注. Shanghai: Shanghai guji chubanshe, 1997. ———. *Chuci leigao* 楚辭類稿. Chengdu: Bashu chubanshe, 1988.

Tang Lan 唐蘭. *Gu wenzixue daolun* 古文字學導論. Jinan: Qi Lu shushe, 1981.

Tang Zhangping 湯漳平 and Lu Yongping 陸永品. *Chuci lunxi* 楚辭論析. Taiyuan: Shanxi jiaoyu chubanshe, 1990.

Wang Fuzhi 王夫之. *Chuci tong shi* 楚辭通釋. Preface dated autumn 1685. Shanghai: Zhonghua shuju, 1965.

Wang Guanghao 王光鎬. *Chu wenhua yuanliu xin zheng* 楚文化源流新証. Wuhan: Wuhan daxue chubanshe, 1988.

Wang Guowei 王國維. *Yin buci zhong suo jian xian gong xian wang kao* 殷卜辭中所見先公先王考. Shanghai: Cangsheng mingzhi daxue, 1916.

Wen Yiduo 聞一多. *Li sao jiegu* 離騷解詁. Shanghai: Shanghai guji chubanshe, 1985.

Weng Shihua 翁世華. *Chuci kaojiao* 楚辭考校. Taipei: Wenshizhe chubanshe, 1987.

Xiao Bing 蕭兵. *Chuci de wenhua poyi* 楚辭的文化破譯. Wuhan: Hubei renmin chubanshe, 1997.

———. *Chuci yu shenhua* 楚辭與神話. Nanjing: Jiangsu guji chubanshe, 1987.

Xu Chaohua 徐朝華, ed. *Erya jinzhu* 爾雅今注. Tianjin: Nankai daxue chubanshe, 1987.

Xu Shen 許慎. *Shuowen jiezi zhu* 說文解字注. Annotated by Duan Yucai 段玉裁. Shanghai: Shanghai guji chubanshe, 1986.

*Xunzi jijie* 荀子集解. Vol. 2 of *Zhuzi jicheng* 諸子集成. Shanghai: Shanghai shudian, 1987.

Yi Chonglian 易重廉. *Zhongguo Chuci xue shi* 中國楚辭學史. Changsha: Hunan chubanshe, 1991.

You Guo'en 游國恩. *Li sao zuanyi* 離騷纂義. Beijing: Zhonghua shudian, 1982.

———. *Tian wen zuanyi* 天問纂義. Taipei: Hongye wenhua, 1993.

Yuan Ke 袁珂. *Shanhaijing jiaoyi* 山海經校譯. Shanghai: Shanghai guji chubanshe, 1985.

——. *Zhongguo shenhua chuanshuo cidian*. 中國神話傳說詞典. Shanghai: Shanghai cishu, 1985.

Zhang Zhengming 張正名. *Chu shi luncong* 楚辭論叢. Wuhan: Hubei renmin chubanshe, 1984.

——. *Chu wenhua shi* 楚文化史. Shanghai: Shanghai renmin chubanshe, 1987.

Zhou Xunchu 周勛初. *Jiuge xin kao* 九歌新考. Shanghai: Shanghai guji chubanshe, 1986.

Zhu Junsheng 朱駿聲. *Shuowen tongxun ding sheng* 說文通訓定聲. Wuhan: Wuhan shi guji shudian, 1983.

Zhu Xi 朱熹. *Chuci jizhu* 楚辭集注. Edited by Jiang Lifu 蔣立甫. Shanghai: Shanghai guji chubanshe, 2001.

*Zhuzi jicheng* 諸子集成. Shanghai: Shanghai shudian, 1987.

## WORKS IN WESTERN LANGUAGES

Allan, Sarah. *Buried Ideas: Legends of Abdication and Ideal Government in Early Chinese Bamboo-Slip Manuscripts*. Albany: SUNY Press, 2015.

——. "Drought, Human Sacrifice and the Mandate of Heaven in a Lost Text from the *Shang shu*." *Bulletin of the School of Oriental and African Studies* 47 (1984): 523–39.

——. *The Heir and the Sage: Dynastic Legend in Early China*. Rev. ed. Albany: SUNY Press, 2015.

——. *The Shape of the Turtle: Myth, Art, and Cosmos in Early China*. Albany: SUNY Press, 1991.

——. *The Way of Water and Sprouts of Virtue*. Albany: SUNY Press, 1997.

——. "'When Red Pigeons Gathered on Tang's House': A Warring States Period Tale of Shamanic Possession and Building Construction Set at the Turn of the Xia and Shang Dynasties." *Journal of the Royal Asiatic Society* 25, no. 3 (July 2015): 419–38.

Allan, Sarah, and Crispin Williams, eds. *The Guodian "Laozi": Proceedings of the International Conference, Dartmouth College, May 1998*. Early China Special Monograph Series 5. Berkeley: Society for the Study of Early China and Institute of East Asian Studies, University of California, 2000.

Ames, Roger. *The Art of Rulership: A Study in Ancient Chinese Political Thought*. Honolulu: University of Hawai`i Press, 1983.

Barnard, Noel. *The Ch'u Silk Manuscript*. Canberra: Australian National University, 1973.

Bielenstein, Hans. *The Bureaucracy of Han Times*. Cambridge: Cambridge University Press, 1980.

Birrell, Anne. *Chinese Mythology: An Introduction.* Baltimore: Johns Hopkins University Press, 1993.

Blakeley, Barry B. "Chu Society and State: Image versus Reality." In Cook and Major, *Defining Chu,* 51–66.

———. "The Geography of Chu." In Cook and Major, *Defining Chu,* 9–20.

Bodde, Derk. *Festivals in Classical China: New Year and Other Annual Observances During the Han Dynasty.* Princeton, N.J.: Princeton University Press, 1975.

Branner, David Prager. "Common Chinese and Early Chinese Morphology." *Journal of the American Oriental Society* 122, no. 4 (2002): 706–21.

———. "On Early Chinese Morphology and Its Intellectual History." *Journal of the Royal Asiatic Society* 13, no. 1 (2003): 45–76.

Brooks, E. Bruce. "The State of the Field in Pre-Han Text Studies." *Sino-Platonic Papers* 46 (July 1994): 1–66.

Chan, Ping-leung. "*Ch'u Tz'u* and Shamanism in Ancient China." Ph.D. diss., Ohio State University, 1972.

Chang, K. C. *Art, Myth, and Ritual: The Path to Political Authority in Ancient China.* Cambridge, Mass.: Harvard University Press, 1983.

Chen Shih-hsiang. "The Genesis of Poetic Time: The Greatness of Qu Yuan, Studied with a New Critical Approach." *Tsing Hua Journal of Chinese Studies,* n.s., 10, no. 1 (June 1973): 1–44. Published posthumously.

Cheng, Anne. *Étude sur le confucianisme Han: L'élaboration d'une tradition exégétique sur les classiques.* Paris: Collège de France, Institut des Hautes Études Chinoises, 1985.

Childs-Johnson, Elizabeth. "Dragons, Masks, Axes and Blades from Four Newly-Documented Jade-Producing Cultures of Ancient China." *Orientations* 19, no. 4 (April 1988): 30–41.

———. *Enduring Art of Jade Age China: Chinese Jades of the Late Neolithic through Han Periods.* 2 vols. New York: Throckmorton Fine Art, 2001–2002.

———. "The Ghost Head Mask and Metamorphic Shang Imagery." *Early China* 20 (1995): 79–92.

———. "The Metamorphic Image: A Predominant Theme in the Ritual Art of Shang China." *Museum of Far Eastern Antiquities,* no. 70 (1998): 5–171.

———. "The Shang Bird: Intermediary to the Supernatural." *Orientations* 20, no. 11 (1989): 53–61.

Chow, Tse-tsung, "The Childbirth Myth and Ancient Chinese Medicine: A Study of Aspects of the *Wu* Tradition." In *Ancient China: Studies in Early Civilization,* edited by David T. Roy and Tsuen-hsuin Tsien, 43–89. Hong Kong: Chinese University Press, 1978.

Cook, Constance A. "Ancestor Worship during the Eastern Zhou." In *Early Chinese*

*Religion, Part 1: Shang through Han*, edited by John Lagerwey and Marc Kalinowski, 1:237–79. Leiden: Brill, 2009

——. *Death in Ancient China: The Tale of One Man's Journey*. China Studies 8. Leiden: Brill, 2006.

——. "Three High Gods of Chu." *Journal of Chinese Religions* 22, no. 1 (1994): 1–22.

Cook, Constance A., and John S. Major, eds. *Defining Chu: Image and Reality in Ancient China*. Honolulu: University of Hawai`i Press, 1999.

Cook, Scott. *The Bamboo Texts of Guodian: A Study and Complete Translation*. Ithaca, N.Y.: Cornell University Press, 2012.

DeWoskin, Kenneth J. *A Song for One or Two: Music and the Concept of Art in Early China*. Ann Arbor: Center for Chinese Studies, University of Michigan, 1982.

Diény, Jean-Pierre. *Aux origines de la poésie classique en Chine: Étude de la poésie lyrique à l'époque des Han*. Leiden: Brill, 1968.

Dubs, Homer H., trans. *The History of the Former Han Dynasty*. 3 vols. Baltimore: Waverly Press, 1938–1955.

Durrant, Stephen W. *The Cloudy Mirror: Tension and Conflict in the Writings of Sima Qian*. Albany: SUNY Press, 1995.

Ebrey, Patricia. "The Economic and Social History of Later Han." In Twitchett and Loewe, *Cambridge History of China*, 608–48.

Eco, Umberto. *Semiotics and the Philosophy of Language*. Bloomington: Indiana University Press, 1984.

Egan, Ronald. "Narratives in *Tso Chuan*." *Harvard Journal of Asiatic Studies* 37, no. 2 (1977): 323–52.

Eliade, Mircea. *Shamanism*. Princeton, N.J.: Princeton University Press, 1972.

Elman, Benjamin A. *From Philosophy to Philology: Intellectual and Social Aspects of Change in Late Imperial China*. Cambridge, Mass.: Council on East Asian Studies, Harvard University, 1990

Eno, Robert. *The Confucian Creation of Heaven*. Albany: SUNY Press, 1990.

Feuchtwang, Stephan. *The Imperial Metaphor: Popular Religion in China*. London: Routledge, 1992.

Field, Stephen. "Cosmos, Cosmograph, and the Inquiring Poet: New Answers to the 'Heaven Questions.'" *Early China* 17 (1992): 83–110.

Goldin, Paul Rakita. *The Culture of Sex in Ancient China*. Honolulu: University of Hawai`i Press, 2002.

——. *Rituals of the Way: The Philosophy of Xunzi*. Peru, Ill.: Carus, 1999.

Goody, Jack. *The Logic of Writing and the Organization of Society*. Cambridge: Cambridge University Press, 1986.

Graham, A. C., trans. *The Book of Lieh-tzu: A Classic of Tao*. New York: Columbia University Press, 1990.

Granet, Marcel. *Danses et légendes de la Chine ancienne.* 1926. Reprint, Paris: Presses Universitaires de France, 1994.

———. *Fêtes et chansons anciennes de la Chine.* 2nd ed. Paris: Leroux, 1929.

———. *La pensée chinoise.* 1934. Reprint, Paris: Albin Michel, 1968.

Hall, David L., and Roger T. Ames. *Anticipating China.* Albany: SUNY Press, 1995.

———. *Thinking Through Confucius.* Albany: SUNY Press, 1987.

Hansen, Chad. "Chinese Ideographs and Western Ideas." *Journal of Asian Studies* 52, no. 2 (May 1993): 373–99.

———. *Language and Logic in Ancient China.* Ann Arbor: University of Michigan Press, 1983.

———. *A Taoist Theory of Chinese Thought: A Philosophical Investigation.* Oxford: Oxford University Press, 1992.

Harper, Donald. "The Bellows Analogy in *Laozi* V and Warring States Macrobiotic Hygiene." *Early China* 20 (1995): 381–91.

———. "A Chinese Demonography of the Third Century B.C." *Harvard Journal of Asiatic Studies* 45, no. 2 (1985): 459–98.

———. "Wang Yen-shou's Nightmare Poem." *Harvard Journal of Asiatic Studies* 47, no. 1 (1987): 239–83.

———. "Warring States Natural Philosophy and Occult Thought." In *The Cambridge History of Ancient China: From the Origins of Civilization to 221 B.C.,* edited by Michael Loewe and Edward L. Shaughnessy, 813–84. Cambridge: Cambridge University Press, 1999.

———. "Warring States, Qin, and Han Manuscripts Related to Natural Philosophy and the Occult." In *New Sources of Early Chinese History: An Introduction to Reading Inscriptions and Manuscripts,* edited by Edward L. Shaughnessy, XXX–XXX. Berkeley: Society for the Study of Early China and the Institute of East Asian Studies, University of California, 1997.

Hawkes, David. "The Quest of the Goddess." In *Studies in Chinese Literary Genres,* edited by Cyril Birch, 42–68. Berkeley: University of California Press, 1974.

———, trans. *The Songs of the South: An Ancient Chinese Anthology of Poems by Qu Yuan and Other Poets.* Harmondsworth, U.K.: Penguin, 1985.

Henderson, John B. *Scripture, Canon, and Commentary: A Comparison of Confucian and Western Exegesis.* Princeton, N.J.: Princeton University Press, 1991.

Hsu, Cho-yun. *Ancient China in Transition: An Analysis of Social Mobility, 722–222 B.C.* Stanford, Calif.: Stanford University Press, 1965.

———. "The Changing Relationship between Local Society and the Central Political Power in Former Han: 206 B.C.–8 A.D." *Comparative Studies in Society and History* 7, no. 4 (July 1965): 358–70.

Huang Shengfa. *Qu Yuan et le Li sao: Text, étude et commentaires.* Beijing: Éditions en langues étrangères, 1985.

Hulsewe, A. F. P. *Remnants of Ch'in Law*. Leiden: Brill, 1985.

Jakobson, Roman. *Verbal Art, Verbal Sign, Verbal Time*. Minneapolis: University of Minnesota Press, 1985.

Jensen, Lionel M. "Wise Man of the Wilds: Fatherlessness, Fertility, and the Mythic Exemplar, Kongzi." *Early China* 20 (1995): 407–37.

Karlgren, Bernhard. "The Authenticity of Ancient Chinese Texts." *Bulletin of the Museum of Far Eastern Antiquities*, no. 1 (1929): 165–83.

——, trans. *The Book of Odes*. Stockholm: Museum of Far Eastern Antiquities, 1950.

——. "Compendium of Phonetics in Ancient and Archaic Chinese." *Bulletin of the Museum of Far Eastern Antiquities*, no. 26 (1954): 211–367.

——. "Early Chinese Mirror Inscriptions." *Bulletin of the Museum of Far Eastern Antiquities*, no. 6 (1934): 9–74.

——. "The Early History of the Chou Li and Tso Chuan Texts." *Bulletin of the Museum of Far Eastern Antiquities*, no. 3 (1931): 1–59.

——. *Glosses on "The Book of Odes."* Stockholm: Museum of Far Eastern Antiquities, 1964.

——. *Grammata Serica Recensa*. Stockholm: Museum of Far Eastern Antiquities, 1957.

——. "Legends and Cults in Ancient China." *Bulletin of the Museum of Far Eastern Antiquities*, no. 18 (1946): 199–365.

——. *Loan Characters in Pre-Han Texts*. Stockholm: Museum of Far Eastern Antiquities, 1967.

——. *On the Authenticity and Nature of the Tso Chuan*. Stockholm: Museum of Far Eastern Antiquities, 1926.

——. "Word Families in Chinese." *Bulletin of the Museum of Far Eastern Antiquities*, no. 5 (1934): 9–120.

Keightley, David N. "Akatsuka Kiyoshi and the Culture of Early China: A Study in Historical Method." *Harvard Journal of Asiatic Studies* 42, no. 1 (1982): 267–320.

——, ed. *The Origins of Chinese Civilization*. Berkeley: University of California Press, 1983.

——. *Sources of Shang History: The Oracle-Bone Inscriptions of Bronze Age China*. Berkeley: University of California Press, 1978.

Kern, Martin. "The Poetry of Han Historiography." *Early Medieval China* 10–11, no. 1 (2004): 23–65.

——, ed. *Text and Ritual in Early China*. Seattle: University of Washington Press, 2005.

——. "Western Han Aesthetics and the Genesis of the *Fu*." *Harvard Journal of Asiatic Studies* 63, no. 2 (2003): 383–437.

Kinney, Anne Behnke, ed. *Chinese Views of Childhood*. Honolulu: University of Hawai`i Press, 1995.

———. *Exemplary Women of Early China: The "Lienü zhuan" of Liu Xiang*. New York: Columbia University Press, 2014.

Knechtges, David R. "The Emperor and Literature: Emperor Wu of the Han." In *Imperial Rulership and Cultural Change in Traditional China*, edited by Frederick P. Brandauer and Chun-chieh Huang, 51–77. Seattle: University of Washington Press, 1994.

———. *The Han Rhapsody: A Study of the Fu of Yang Hsiung*. Cambridge: Cambridge University Press, 1976.

———. *Wen xuan; or, Selections of Refined Literature*, vol. 1. Princeton, N.J.: Princeton University Press, 1982.

———. *Wen xuan; or, Selections of Refined Literature*, vol. 3. Princeton, N.J.: Princeton University Press, 1996

———. *Wen xuan; or, Selections of Refined Literature*, vol. 2. Princeton, N.J.: Princeton University Press, 1987.

Knoblock, John. *Xunzi: A Translation and Study of the Complete Works*. 3 vols. Stanford, Calif.: Stanford University Press, 1988–1994.

Knoblock, John, and Jeffrey Riegel, trans. *The Annals of Lü Buwei: A Complete Translation and Study*. Stanford, Calif.: Stanford University Press, 2001.

Kramers, Robert. "The Development of the Confucian Schools." In Twitchett and Loewe, *Cambridge History of China*, 747–65.

Kroll, Paul W. "On 'Far Roaming.'" *Journal of the American Oriental Society* 116, no. 4 (October–December 1996): 653–69.

Le Blanc, Charles, and Rémi Mathieu, eds. *Mythe et philosophie à l'aube de la Chine impériale: Études sur le Huainan zi*. Montreal: Université de Montréal, 1992.

Lewis, Mark Edward. "The *Feng* and *Shan* Sacrifices of Emperor Wu of the Han." In *State and Court Ritual in China*, edited by Joseph P. McDermott, 50–80. Cambridge: Cambridge University Press, 1999.

———. *The Flood Myths of Early China*. Albany: SUNY Press, 2006.

———. *Sanctioned Violence in Early China*. Albany: SUNY Press, 1990.

———. *Writing and Authority in Early China*. Albany: SUNY Press, 1999.

Li Feng. *Landscape and Power in Early China: The Crisis and Fall of the Western Zhou, 1045–771 B.C.* Cambridge: Cambridge University Press, 2006.

Li Ling. "An Archaeological Study of Taiyi (Grand One) Worship." Translated by Donald Harper. *Early Medieval China* 2 (1995–1996): 1–39.

———. "Formulaic Structure of Chu Divinatory Bamboo Slips." Translated by William G. Boltz. *Early China* 15 (1990): 71–86.

Li, Wai-yee. "The Idea of Authority in the *Shiji* (*Records of the Historian*)." *Harvard Journal of Asiatic Studies* 54, no. 2 (1994): 345–405.

Li Xueqin. *Eastern Zhou and Qin Civilizations*. Translated by K. C. Chang. New Haven, Conn.: Yale University Press, 1985.

Loewe, Michael. *Chinese Ideas of Life and Death: Faith, Myth and Reason in the Han Period*. London: Allen and Unwin, 1982.

———. *Crisis and Conflict in Han China*. London: Allen and Unwin, 1974.

———. *Divination, Mythology and Monarchy in Han China*. University of Cambridge Oriental Publications 48. Cambridge: Cambridge University Press, 1995.

———, ed. *Early Chinese Texts: A Bibliographic Guide*. Berkeley: Society for the Study of Early China and the Institute of East Asian Studies, 1993.

———. *Ways to Paradise: The Chinese Quest for Immortality*. London: Allen and Unwin, 1979.

Maehle, Edward J. *Nature and Heaven in the Xunzi: A Study of the Tian Lun*. Albany: SUNY Press, 1993.

Major, John S. "Animals and Animal Metaphors in *Huainanzi*." *Asia Major*, 3rd ser., 21, no. 1 (2008): 133–51.

———. "Characteristics of Late Chu Religion." In Cook and Major, *Defining Chu*, 121–43.

———. "The Five Phases, Magic Squares, and Schematic Cosmography." In *Explorations in Early Chinese Cosmology*, edited by Henry Rosemont Jr., 133–66. Chico, Calif.: Scholars' Press, 1984.

———. *Heaven and Earth in Early Han Thought: Chapters Three, Four, and Five of the "Huainanzi."* Albany: SUNY Press, 1993.

Major, John S., Sarah A. Queen, Andrew Seth Meyer, and Harold D. Roth, trans. *The Huainanzi: A Guide to the Theory and Practice of Government in Early Han China*. New York: Columbia University Press, 2010.

Major, John S., and Jenny F. So. "Music in Late Bronze Age China." In *Music in the Age of Confucius*, edited by Jenny F. So, 13–33. Washington, D.C.: Freer Gallery of Art and Arthur M. Sackler Gallery, Smithsonian Institution; Seattle: University of Washington Press, 2000.

Marubbio, Mayvis. "Yi Yin, Pious Rebel: A Study of the Founding Minister of the Shang Dynasty in Early Chinese Texts." Ph.D. diss., University of Minnesota, 2000.

Maspero, Henri. *China in Antiquity*. Translated by Frank A. Kierman Jr. Amherst: University of Massachusetts Press, 1978.

———. "Légendes mythologiques dans le *Chou king*." *Journal Asiatique* 204 (1924): 1–100.

Mathieu, Rémi, trans. *Le Mu tianzi zhuan: Traduction annotée, étude critique*. Mémoires de l'Institut des Hautes Études Chinoises. Paris: Collège de France, 1978.

———. "Yu le Grand et le mythe du déluge dans la Chine ancienne." *T'oung Pao* 78 (1992): 162–90.

Mattos, Gilbert. *The Stone Drums of Ch'in*. Monumenta Serica Monograph Series 19. Nettetal, Ger.: Steyler, 1988.

McLeod, Katrina, and Robin Yates. "Forms of Ch'in Law." *Harvard Journal of Asiatic Studies* 41, no. 1 (1981): 111–63.

Needham, Joseph. *Science and Civilisation in China, Volume 4: Physics and Physical Technology, Part 1: Physics.* Cambridge: Cambridge University Press, 1962.

———. *Science and Civilisation in China, Volume 3: Mathematics and the Sciences of the Heavens and the Earth.* Cambridge: Cambridge University Press, 1970.

Nishijima Sadao. "The Economic and Social History of Former Han." In Twitchett and Loewe, *Cambridge History of China,* 545–607.

Nylan, Michael, trans. *The Canon of Supreme Mystery.* Albany: SUNY Press, 1993.

———. "The *Chin Wen/Ku Wen* Controversy in Han Times." *T'oung Pao,* 2nd ser., 80, fasc. 1/3 (1994): 83–145.

———. *The Five "Confucian" Classics.* New Haven, Conn.: Yale University Press, 2001.

———. "Golden Spindles and Axes: Elite Women in the Achaemenid and Han Empires." In *The Sage and the Second Sex,* edited by Li Chenyang, 199–222. La Salle, Ill.: Open Court, 2000.

———. "Han Classicists Writing in Dialogue About Their Own Tradition." *Philosophy East and West* 47, no. 2 (1997): 133–88.

———. "The *Ku Wen Documents* in Han Times." *T'oung Pao,* 2nd ser., 81, fasc. 1/3 (1995): 25–50.

———. *The Shifting Center: The Original "Great Plan" and Later Readings.* Monumenta Serica Monograph Series 24. Nettetal, Ger.: Steyler, 1992.

———. "Textual Authority in Pre-Han and Han." *Early China* 25 (2000): 205–58.

———. "Ying Shao's *Feng su t'ungyi*: An Exploration of Problems in Han Dynasty Political, Philosophical, and Social Unity." Ph.D. diss., Princeton University, 1982.

Owen, Stephen. *Readings in Chinese Literary Thought.* Cambridge, Mass.: Harvard University Press, 1992.

———. *Remembrances: The Experience of the Past in Classical Chinese Literature.* Cambridge, Mass.: Harvard University Press, 1986.

———. *Traditional Chinese Poetry and Poetics: Omen of the World.* Madison: University of Wisconsin Press, 1985.

Pankenier, David W. *Astrology and Cosmology in Early China: Conforming Earth to Heaven.* Cambridge: Cambridge University Press, 2014.

———. "The *Bamboo Annals* Revisited: Problems of Method in Using the Chronicle as a Source for the Chronology of Early Zhou." *Bulletin of the School of Oriental and African Studies* 55, no. 2 (1992): 272–97; no. 3 (1992): 498–510.

———. "The Cosmo-Political Background of Heaven's Mandate." *Early China* 20 (1995): 121–76.

———. "Reflections of the Lunar Aspect on Western Chou Chronology." *T'oung Pao* 78 (1992): 33–76.

Peerenboom, R. P. *Law and Morality in Ancient China: The Silk Manuscripts of Huang-Lao*. Albany: SUNY Press, 1993.

Petersen, Willard J. "Making Connections: 'Commentary on the Attached Verbalizations' of the *Book of Change*." *Harvard Journal of Asiatic Studies* 42, no. 1 (1982): 67–116.

Picken, Laurence E. R. "The Musical Implications of Line-Sharing in the *Book of Songs (Shih Ching)*." *Journal of the American Oriental Society* 89, no. 2 (1969): 408–10.

———. "The Shapes of the *Shi Jing* Song-Texts and Their Musical Implications." *Musica Asiatica* 1 (1977): 85–109.

Plaks, Andrew H. *Archetype and Allegory in the "Dream of the Red Chamber."* Princeton, N.J.: Princeton University Press, 1976.

Puett, Michael. *The Ambivalence of Creation: Debates Concerning Innovation and Artifice in Early China*. Stanford, Calif.: Stanford University Press, 2001.

———. "The Notion of *Shen* in the *Xici*." Conference on the *Xici zhuan*, University of Chicago, May 30–June 1, 1997.

———. *To Become a God: Cosmology, Sacrifice, and Self-Divinization in Early China*. Harvard-Yenching Institute Monograph Series 57. Cambridge, Mass.: Harvard University Asia Center, 2002.

Queen, Sarah A. *From Chronicle to Canon: The Hermeneutics of the "Spring and Autumn" According to Tung Chung-shu*. Cambridge: Cambridge University Press, 1996.

Raphals, Lisa A. "Gendered Virtue Reconsidered: Notes from the Warring States and Han." In *The Sage and the Second Sex*, edited by Li Chenyang, 223–47. La Salle, Ill.: Open Court, 2000.

———. *Sharing the Light: Representations of Women and Virtue in Early China*. Albany: SUNY Press, 1998.

Rawson, Jessica. "Statesmen or Barbarians? The Western Zhou as Seen Through Their Bronzes." *Proceedings of the British Academy* 75 (1989): 71–95.

Riegel, Jeffery K. "Kou-mang and Ju-shou." Special issue on Taoist studies II, *Cahiers d'Extrême-Asie* 5, no. 1 (1989–90): 55–83.

Roth, Harold D. "Psychology and Self-Cultivation in Early Taoistic Thought." *Harvard Journal of Asiatic Studies* 51, no. 2 (1991): 599–650.

Saussy, Haun. *The Problem of a Chinese Aesthetic*. Stanford, Calif.: Stanford University Press, 1993.

Schaab-Hanke, Dorothee. "The Power of an Alleged Tradition: A Prophecy Flattering Han Emperor Wu and Its Relation to the Sima Clan." *Bulletin of the Museum of Far Eastern Antiquities* 74 (2002): 243–90.

Schaberg, David. "Remonstrance in Eastern Zhou Historiography." *Early China* 22 (1997): 133–79.

Schafer, Edward H. *The Divine Woman: Dragon Ladies and Rain Maidens in Tang Literature*. Berkeley: University of California Press, 1973.

———. *Pacing the Void: Tang Approaches to the Stars*. Berkeley: University of California Press, 1977.

———. *The Vermilion Bird: Tang Images of the South*. Berkeley: University of California Press, 1967.

Schimmelpfennig, Michael. "'Die Schamanin in ihrer typisch südchinesischen Gestalt': Zur Rezeption der 'Neun Gesänge' aus den 'Liedern von Ch'u.'" In *Annäherung an das Fremde*, edited by Holger Preissler and H. Stein, 79–90. Stuttgart: Steiner, 1998.

———. "Die verborgene Kommentierung: Die *Ausführungen zum Lisao* (*Lisao zhuan*) als Grundlage der Auslegung des *Lisao* durch Wang Yi." *Oriens Extremus* 42 (2000/2001): 41–68.

———. "The Quest for a Classic: Wang Yi and the Exegetical Prehistory of His Commentary to the *Songs of Chu*." *Early China* 29 (2004): 111–62.

———. "Two Ages, One Agenda? Zhu Xi's Rules of Interpretation Versus Wang Yi's Exegesis of the *Songs of Chu*." In *Interpretation and Intellectual Change*, edited by Ching-i Tu, 149–59. New Brunswick, N.J.: Transaction Publishers, 2004

Schneider, Laurence A. *A Madman of Ch'u: The Chinese Myth of Loyalty and Dissent*. Berkeley: University of California Press, 1980.

Schwartz, Benjamin I. *The World of Thought in Ancient China*. Cambridge, Mass.: Harvard University Press, 1985.

Seidel, Anna. "Buying One's Way to Heaven: The Celestial Treasury in Chinese Religions." *History of Religions* 17, no. 3/4 (February–May 1978): 419–31.

Serruys, Paul L.-M. "Chinese Dialectology Based on Written Documents." *Monumenta Serica* 21 (1962): 320–44.

———. *The Chinese Dialects of Han Time According to Fang Yen*. University of California Publications in East Asiatic Philology 2. Berkeley: University of California Press, 1959.

———. "*Fang yen* IV.5 and 31: Knee Covers and Apron." *Bulletin of IHP* 39, no. 2 (1969): 245–66.

———. "Five Word Studies on *Fang Yen*." *Monumenta Serica* 19 (1960): 114–209; 21 (1962): 222–319; 26 (1967): 255–85.

———. "The Function and Meaning of *Yün* 云 in *Shih Ching*: Its Cognates and Variants." *Monumenta Serica* 29 (1970–1971): 264–337.

Shaughnessy, Edward L. "The Composition of the 'Zhouyi.'" Ph.D. diss., Stanford University, 1983.

———. "The Duke of Zhou's Retirement in the East and the Beginnings of the Ministerial-Monarch Debate in Chinese Political Philosophy." *Early China* 18 (1993): 41–72.

———. "A First Reading of the Mawangdui *Yijing* Manuscript." *Early China* 19 (1994): 47–73.

———. "The Role of Grand Protector Shi in the Consolidation of the Zhou Conquest." *Ars Orientalis* 19 (1989): 51–77.

———. *Sources of Western Zhou History: Inscribed Bronze Vessels.* Berkeley: University of California Press, 1991.

Sivin, Nathan. *Medicine, Philosophy and Religion in Ancient China: Researches and Reflections.* Variorum Collected Studies Series CS512. Aldershot, U.K.: Ashgate, 1995.

———. *Science in Ancient China: Researches and Reflections.* Variorum Collected Studies Series CS506. Aldershot, U.K.: Ashgate, 1995.

———. "State, Cosmos, and Body in the Last Three Centuries B.C." *Harvard Journal of Asiatic Studies* 55, no. 1 (1995): 5–37.

Smith, Kidder. "*Zhouyi* Interpretation from Accounts in the *Zuozhuan*." *Harvard Journal of Asiatic Studies* 49, no. 2 (1989): 421–63.

Smith, Morton. *Jesus the Magician.* Harper and Row, 1981.

Sukhu, Gopal. *The Shaman and the Heresiarch: A New Interpretation of the "Li Sao."* Albany: SUNY Press, 2012.

———. "Yao, Shun, and Prefiguration: The Origins and Ideology of the Han Imperial Genealogy." *Early China* 30 (2005–2006): 91–153

Svenbro, Jesper. *Phrasikleia: An Anthropology of Reading in Ancient Greece.* Translated by Janet Lloyd. Ithaca, N.Y.: Cornell University Press, 1993.

Swanson, Gerald. "The Concept of Change in the *Great Treatise*." In *Explorations in Early Chinese Cosmology*, edited by Henry Rosemont Jr., 67–93. Chico, Calif.: Scholars' Press, 1984.

Takeji Sadao. *A Concordance to the Chuci.* Tokushima: Tokushima Daigaku, 1964.

Thompson, P. M. *The Shen Tzu Fragments.* Oxford: Oxford University Press, 1979.

Todorov, Tzvetan. *Theories of the Symbol.* Translated by Catherine Porter. Ithaca, N.Y.: Cornell University Press, 1982.

Twitchett, Denis, and Michael Loewe, eds. *The Cambridge History of China, Volume 1: The Ch'in and Han Empires, 221 B.C.–A.D. 220.* Cambridge: Cambridge University Press, 1986.

van Ess, Hans. "The Meaning of Huang-Lao in *Shi ji* and *Han shu*." *Études chinoises* 12, no. 2 (1993): 161–77.

Van Zoeren, Steven. *Poetry and Personality: Reading, Exegesis, and Hermeneutics in Traditional China.* Stanford, Calif.: Stanford University Press, 1991.

von Falkenhausen, Lothar. "The Concept of *Wen* in the Ancient Chinese Ancestral Cult." *Chinese Literature: Essays, Articles, Reviews* 18 (December 1996): 1–22.

———. "Issues in Western Zhou Studies: A Review Article." *Early China* 18 (1993): 145–71.

———. "Sources of Taoism: Reflections on Archaeological Indicators of Religious Change in Eastern Zhou China." *Taoist Resources* 5, no. 2 (December 1994): 1–12.

———. *Suspended Music: Chime-Bells in the Culture of Bronze Age China*. Berkeley: University of California Press, 1993.

Wagner, Rudolf G. *The Craft of a Chinese Commentator: Wang Bi on the Laozi*. Albany: SUNY Press, 2000.

Waley, Arthur. *The Nine Songs: A Study of Shamanism in Ancient China*. London: Allen and Unwin, 1955.

Walker, Galal. "Toward a Formal History of the 'Chuci.'" Ph.D. diss., Cornell University, 1982.

Wallacker, Benjamin. "Liu An, Second King of Huai-nan." *Journal of the American Oriental Society* 92, no. 1 (January–March 1972): 36–51.

Wang, C. H. *The Bell and the Drum: "Shi Ching" as Formulaic Poetry in an Oral Tradition*. Berkeley: University of California Press, 1974.

———. *From Ritual to Allegory: Seven Essays in Early Chinese Poetry*. Hong Kong: Chinese University Press, 1988.

Wang, Hsiao-po, and Leo S. Chang. *The Philosophical Foundations of Han Fei's Political Theory*. Society of Asian and Comparative Philosophy Monographs, no. 7. Honolulu: University of Hawai`i Press, 1986.

Waters, Geoffrey R. *Three Elegies of Ch'u*. Madison: University of Wisconsin Press, 1985.

Watson, Burton, trans. *Basic Writings of Mo Tzu, Hsün Tzu, and Han Fei Tzu*. Translations from the Asian Classics. Records of Civilization: Sources and Studies, no. 74. New York: Columbia University Press, 1963.

———. *Early Chinese Literature*. New York: Columbia University Press, 1962.

Weld, Susan Roosevelt. "Chu Law in Action: Legal Documents from Tomb 2 at Baoshan." In Cook and Major, *Defining Chu*, 77–97.

———. "Covenant in Jin's Walled Cities: The Discoveries at Houma and Wenxian." Ph.D. diss., Harvard University, 1990.

Wilhelm, Richard, trans. *The I Ching or Book of Changes*. Rendered into English by Cary F. Baynes. 3rd ed. Bollingen Series 19. Princeton, N.J.: Princeton University Press, 1967.

Wu, Hung. *The Wu Liang Shrine: The Ideology of Early Chinese Pictorial Art*. Stanford, Calif.: Stanford University Press, 1989.

Yates, Robin. "The City Under Siege: Technology and Organization as Seen in the Reconstructed Text of the Military Chapters of Mo-tzu." Ph.D. diss., Harvard University, 1980.

———. "The Mohists on Warfare: Technology, Techniques, and Justification." *Journal of the American Academy of Religion*, thematic studies supplement 47, no. 3 (1980): 549–603.

——. "New Light on Ancient Chinese Military Texts: Notes on Their Nature and Evolution, and the Development of Military Specialization in Warring States China." *T'oung Pao*, 2nd ser., 74, livr. 4/5 (1988): 211–48.

——. "Some Notes on Ch'in Law." *Early China* 11–12 (1985–1987): 243–75.

——. "The Yin-Yang Texts from Yinqueshan: An Introduction and Partial Reconstruction, with Notes on Their Significance in Relation to Huang-Lao Daoism." *Early China* 19 (1994): 75–144.

Yu, Pauline. *The Reading of Imagery in the Chinese Poetic Tradition*. Princeton, N.J.: Princeton University Press, 1987.

# Index

Big Dipper, 16, 77n5
Black Warrior (Xuan Wu), 147, 150n29
Bo Chang, 73, 98n72
Bo Feng (Feng Zhu), 88n32
Bo Le, 120, 138n45, 165, 168n17
Bo Qiang (Yu Qiang), 78n10
Bo Yi, 101n82, 196, 201n2, 207, 209n23;
    in *Nine Cantos*, 129, 134, 140n67
"Bosom Full of Sand" ("Huai sha"; *Nine
    Cantos*), xxi, xxvi, xxviii, 103,
    117–21, 215
"Bu ju." *See* "Diviner, The"

"Calling the Hermit Back" ("Zhao
    yinshi"; Huainan Xiaoshan), 210–12;
    dating of, 218
*Cannabis sativa*, 23n24, 66, 83n25
Cao Zhi, xxxvi, 55n57
Chen Benli, 59n87
Cheng, King (Chu; Xiong Yun),
    102nn86–87
Cheng, King (Zhou), xii, 96n63, 100n77
*Cheng zhi* (Bringing things to
    completion), xvi
Chi Song. *See* Red Pine
China, People's Republic of (PRC),
    xxix–xxx, xil
Chonghua. *See* Shun
"Chou si" (Expressing My Longing;
    *Nine Cantos*), 114–17, 215
Chu, state of: in *Chuci*, 19, 34, 75, 110,
    127–28, 167n9, 180, 187n6; culture
    of, xii–xiii, 26; deities of, xiii–xiv,
    xvi, xxviii, 5, 16–17; diary from, xiv;
    and Han dynasty, xxvii–xxviii, 26;
    and human sacrifices, 17; legal
    system of, xiv, 104; poetry of,
    xxvi–xxvii; and Qin, xii, xix–xx, xxi;
    shamans in, xiv, 3, 4, 7, 12; and
    Zhou, xii, 26

*Chuci* (*Songs of Chu*): authorship of, xi,
    xiii–xiv, xxvi–xxxii, xxxvi, xxxix, xl,
    xliii, 216, 219; commentaries on,
    xviii, xxii, xxiv, xxvi, xxviii–xxix;
    dating of, xxviii, 213–20; influence
    of, xxix–xxx, xxxvii, xxxix, xl; as
    model, xxxi–xxxii; performances of,
    xxviii, 4, 218; and recently
    discovered texts, xiv–xvii, 5, 12, 62,
    80n13, 104, 124. *See also* Qu Yuan
*Chuci buzhu* (notes to *Chuci*; Hong
    Xingzu), xxviii
*Chuci zhangju* (Wang Yi), xviii
Chui, Craftsman, 119, 138n40
Confucianism, xiv, xxii, xxiii, 62;
    vs. shamanism, 4, 34
Confucius, xxx, 82n24, 136n21, 152,
    155n5, 167n5
Cook, Constance A., xvi
cosmology, xiv, xvi, 5, 30, 76n1, 219;
    correlative, xxii
"Crossing the Yangtze" ("She jiang";
    *Nine Cantos*), 107–10; dating of,
    215, 218
Cui Wenzi, 68, 89n36

"Da Siming" (Great Minister of Life
    Spans; *Nine Songs*), 1, 12–13
"Da zhao." *See* "Great Summoning"
Dan Zhu, 29, 48n6
*Daodejing* (*Laozi*), xiv, xvi, 189, 195
Daoism, xiv, 5; in *Chuci*, 62, 76n1, 118,
    142, 143, 152, 195; and dating, 217;
    and immortality, 189–90; and Li Bai,
    xxxvii; and Qu Yuan, xxvi; and
    *youxian* poetry, xxxiii, xxxiv–xxxv
"Daren fu." *See* "Great Man Rhapsody"
Daye (Hubei) site, 135n5
deities and spirits, xxv, xli; of Chu,
    xiii–xiv, xvi, xxxviii, 16–17; in

*fu* (rhapsody), xxvi–xxvii, xxix–xxxii, xxxvi, xl, xlii, 25, 152, 202. *See also particular titles*

"Fu fu." *See* "Owl Rhapsody"

"Fu on the Wind" ("Feng fu"; Song Yu), 156

Fu Xiren, 80n14

Fu Yue, xv, xliiin4, 144, 149n3, 198, 201n9

Fuchai, King (Wu), 136n23, 139n60, 198, 201n6, 209n22

Fufei (spirit of Luo River), xxxvii 42, 55n57, 56n59, 148, 151n35

Fuxi, 55n57, 92n44, 137n36, 151n35, 183, 204, 208n10

Gao Luming, 52n28, 77n3, 140n63

Gao Xin. *See* Di Ku

Gao Yao, 57n72, 105, 135n3

"Gaotang fu" (Rhapsody on Gaotang; Song Yu), xxxvi, xl, xlii, 156

Gaoyang. *See* Zhuan Xu

Gonggong (Kang Hui), 65, 77n6, 80n17, 82n23, 208n8

*Gongyang* commentary, xxiii

Gou Jian (king of Yue), 5, 198, 201n6

Goumang, 147, 150n21

"Great Man Rhapsody" ("Daren fu"; Sima Xiangru), xxx–xxxii, 142, 218

"Great Minister of Life Spans" ("Da Siming"; *Nine Songs*), 1, 12–13

"Great Summoning" ("Da zhao"), xxvi, 156, 180–88; dating of, 216, 218; food in, 180, 182–83, 188nn7–9

*Great Unity Gives Birth to Water* (*Taiyi sheng shui*), xiv, xvi, 5–6, 76n1

Guan Shu (Guan Shuxian), 100n77

Guan Zhong, 97n66, 205, 209n14

*Guanzi*, 59n91

Gugong Danfu (King Tai), 92n46, 99n73

Gun (Tao Wu; father of Yu), 29; in "Ask the Sky," 64–65, 68, 79n12, 80nn14–15, 82n22, 88n34; in "Leaving My Sorrow," 48n4, 50n25; in *Nine Cantos*, 106, 135n7

Guo Pu, xxxiii–xxxiv, xlii, 9; on "Ask the Sky," 79n12, 81n20, 83n26, 86n30, 92n44, 94n51

Guodian (Hubei) tomb, xiv–xv, xvi, 5, 124

"Guoshang" (Those Who Died for the Kingdom; *Nine Songs*), 2, 19–20, 214

*Guoyu*, xliiin4, 28–29, 30, 34, 82n24, 87n31

Han dynasty: and Chu, xxvii–xxviii, 26; *Chuci* in, xxii–xxiii, 27, 142, 152, 180, 189, 195; and dating, 217–18; deities of, 5, 12; dialects in, 216, 217, 219–20; and human sacrifices, 17; immortality in, 190; legal system of, 104; loyal dissent in, xxiii–xxiv; shamanism in, 3, 15, 34

*Han Feizi*, 21n7, 91n43

Han Zhong, 144, 149n4

Han Zhuo. *See* Zhuo

*Hanshu* (History of the Former Han dynasty; Ban Gu), xxvi, 78n10, 86n30, 138n50

Hawkes, David, xviii, xx, xxii, xxv; on "Ask the Sky," 61, 76n3, 78n9, 96n63; on dating, 215, 218; on "Leaving My Sorrow," 49n12, 53n38, 56n61, 57n69; on *Nine Cantos*, 108, 114, 121, 140n68, 140n71; on *Nine Songs*, 7; on "Regretting the Vows," 190; on "Wandering Far Away," 142

Jie (last Xia king): in "Ask the Sky," 69, 70, 91nn40–41, 92n47, 93n48, 95n58; in "Leaving My Sorrow," 31, 36, 40, 50n18, 53n32

Jie Zhitui (Jia Zi), 125, 134, 139n61

Jieyu (Madman of Chu), 109, 136n21, 167n5

Jin, state of, 135n6; shamans from, 3, 7, 12, 15

Jin Kaicheng, 77n3

Jing, Emperor (Han), 202

Jing Cuo, xxviii, 156, 180

"Jiu huai" (Nine Longings; Wang Bao), xxviii, 220

"Jiu si" (Nine Yearnings; Wang Yi), xxviii, 220

"Jiu tan" (Nine Sighs; Liu Xiang), xxviii, 50n23, 220

*Jiu zhang*. See *Nine Cantos*

*Jiubian*. See *Nine Variations*

*Jiuge*. See *Nine Songs*

"Ju song" (Hymn to a Mandarin Orange Tree; *Nine Cantos*), 103, 127–29, 216

Kang Hui. *See* Gonggong

Karlgren, Bernhard, 85n27

Kitchen God, 12

*Kongzi jiayu* (*Confucius Family Sayings*), 136n22

"Lady of the Xiang River" ("Xiang furen"; *Nine Songs*), 1, 8–12

Lai Ge, 192, 193n11

landscape poetry, xxxiii, xxxix, xli–xliii

Laozi, xxxv. See also *Daodejing*

"Leaving My Sorrow" ("Li sao"), xv–xxviii, 25–60; allegory in, xxiv–xxv, 25, 27–34; and "Ask the Sky," 52n29, 56n61, 61, 81n18, 99n75; dating of, xi, xviii, 214–18; deities in, 7, 26, 28–29; dialogue in, 25; and "Diviner," 155n3; food in, 32, 46, 49n14; on ideal ruler, xv; influence of, 25–26; and Li Bai, xxxvii, xxxviii–xxxix; and Liu An, xx, xxi, xxvi, xxvii, xxviii, 27, 210; loyal dissent in, xxiv, 27, 31; Lure Leaf in, 31, 36, 45, 50n19; metaphors in, xv–xvi; as model, xxxi–xxxii; and *Nine Cantos*, 103, 108, 111, 114, 121, 128, 130, 135n9, 136n11, 138n46, 138n52; and *Nine Songs*, 1, 30, 31, 50n19, 55n56, 214; and *Nine Variations*, 167n12, 216; plant imagery in, 28–29, 30–32, 34; and Qu Yuan, xxvii, 26–27, 28, 34, 103; shamans in, 28, 30, 32, 34, 50n24; Spirit Adorned in, 28, 31, 36, 38; story of, 28, 30–35; and "Wandering Far Away," 142, 143; and *youxian* poetry, xxxiv

legal systems, xiv, 104

Lei Kai, 73, 98n68

Leigong (Thunder God). *See* Feng Long

"Lesser Minister of Life Spans" ("Shao Siming"; *Nine Songs*), 1, 14–15, 31

Li, King (Zhou), xii, 97n65, 101n81

Li Bai, xxxiv–xxxv, xxxvii, 143

Li Cheng, 76n3, 187n1

Li Chenyu, 81n18

Li Daming, 76n3, 187n1

"Li Hun" (Serving the Spirits; *Nine Songs*), 21

Li Ji, 135n6

Li Lou (Lou Li), 119, 138n41

"Li sao." *See* "Leaving My Sorrow"

Li Si, 198, 201nn7–8

Li Xiang, 101n80

Li Zhouhan, 54n49

Liang, state of, 3

music, xiii, 4, 16, 22n8, 191; in "Great
    Summoning," 183, 188n10; in
    "Leaving My Sorrow," 55n58; in *Nine
    Cantos*, 103, 108, 114, 130; stolen, 40,
    47, 51n28, 67, 86nn29–31; in
    "Summoning the Soul," 176–77; in
    "Wandering Far Away," 148,
    151nn36–37, 151n39
mythology: in "Ask the Sky," 61, 76n1,
    84n27; in "Leaving My Sorrow,"
    28–30; in *Nine Songs*, 1–2, 4, 9, 15; in
    *Nine Variations*, 156. *See also* deities
    and spirits

*Nine Cantos* (*Jiu zhang*), 103–41; "Bosom
    Full of Sand," xxi, xxvi, xxviii, 103,
    117–21; "Crossing the Yangtze,"
    107–10; dating of, 215–17; "Expressing
    My Longing," 114–17; "Hymn to a
    Mandarin Orange Tree," 103, 127–29;
    "I Deplore Pleading," 103, 104–7; "I
    Grieve When the Whirlwind," 124,
    129–34; "I Look Back in Sadness,"
    124–27; and "Leaving My Sorrow,"
    103, 108, 111, 114, 121, 128, 130, 135n9,
    136n11, 138n46, 138n52; "Longing for
    the Beautiful One," 121–23;
    "Mourning Ying," xxvi, xxviii, 103,
    110–13, 124, 129–30
"Nine Longings" ("Jiu huai"; Wang
    Bao), xxviii, 220
Nine Regions (Jiu Zhou), 13, 23n23, 44,
    63, 65, 77n6
"Nine Sighs" ("Jiu tan"; Liu Xiang),
    xxviii, 50n23, 220
*Nine Songs* (*Jiuge*), xiv, xxvi, xxix, xxxi,
    1–24; "August of the East," 5–6;
    dating of, 214, 215, 216, 218; deities
    and spirits in, 1, 6–7, 12, 22n20; "Earl
    of the Yellow River," xxii, 4, 16–17;

"Great Minister of Life Spans," 1,
    12–13; and "I Lament It Was Not My
    Destiny," 203; influence of, xxxvii–
    xxxviii, xli, xlii; "Lady of the Xiang
    River," 1, 8–12; and "Leaving My
    Sorrow," 1, 30, 31, 50n19, 55n56, 214;
    "Lesser Minister of Life Spans," 1,
    14–15, 31; "Lord in the Clouds," 6–7;
    "Lord of the East," 15–16; "Mountain
    Spirit," 18–19; mythology in, 1–2, 4,
    9, 15; and *Nine Cantos*, 108, 121,
    136n20; numbering of, 1–2; and Qu
    Yuan, 2, 103; and "Regretting the
    Vows," 193n2; and "Ruler of the Xiang
    River," 1, 8–10; "Serving the Spirits,"
    2, 21; shamans in, 1–4, 7, 12; "Those
    Who Died for the Kingdom," 2,
    19–20; and "Wandering Far Away,"
    142; women in, 4, 8–13
*Nine Variations* (*Jiubian*), 156–68;
    dating of, 216–17; and "Leaving My
    Sorrow," 167n12, 216
Nine Variations and Nine Songs (stolen
    music), 40, 47, 51n28, 67, 86nn29–31
"Nine Yearnings" ("Jiu si"; Wang Yi),
    xxviii, 220
Ning Qi, 45, 58n75, 125, 139n59, 165,
    168n16
Nü Qi (Jiuzi Mu), 78n10, 90n39
Nü Wa, 69, 92n44, 137n36
Nü Xu, 32, 37, 50n24
Nü Ying, 8, 151n38

oracle bones, 93n50, 94n53, 100n78
"Owl Rhapsody" ("Fu fu"; Jia Yi), xxix,
    194, 195, 197–200, 220

Pankenier, David, 78n11
Peng and Xian: in "Leaving My Sorrow,"
    32–34, 37, 44, 47, 50n23, 60n94; in

Sanghu (Zi Sanghu, Zi Sang Bozi), 109, 136n22

"Serving the Spirits" ("Li Hun"; *Nine Songs*), 2, 21

"Seven Remonstrations" ("Qi jian"; Dongfang Shuo), xxviii, 217–18, 220

sexuality, xxxvi, xli; in "Leaving My Sorrow," 28, 30, 33; in *Nine Songs*, 4, 9, 12

shamans, xxv, xxxix, xlii; in "Ask the Sky," 68, 88n34; of Chu, xiv, 3, 4, 7, 12; and dating, 214, 215, 217; female, 3, 9, 12, 17, 28, 30, 32, 50n24, 169; in "Leaving My Sorrow," 28, 30, 32, 34, 50n24; in *Nine Cantos*, 135n4, 135n9; in *Nine Songs*, 1–4, 7, 12; in "Summoning the Soul," 169; terms for, 7, 15, 30, 57n71; in "Wandering Far Away," 143

"Shan Gui" (Mountain Spirit; *Nine Songs*), 18–19

Shang dynasty, xii, 29, 56n61; and "Ask the Sky," 72, 74, 94n55, 99n73

Shang Jiawei, 94n51

Shangguan Dafu, xviii, xx

Shanghai Museum texts, xvii, 62

Shangjia Wei (Hun Wei), 93n50, 94nn54–55

*Shangshu* (*Shujing*; *Documents*), 1, 50n25, 79n12, 85n28, 87n32, 91n42, 95nn58–59

*Shanhaijing* (Classic of mountains and seas): and "Ask the Sky," 79nn12–13, 80n16, 81n20, 82n21, 83nn25–26, 84n27, 86nn29–30, 87n32, 92n44, 93n50, 94nn51–52; and "Leaving My Sorrow," 51n28, 54n46, 54n49, 59n86, 60n94; and *Nine Songs*, 2, 9

Shao Hao, 48n10, 58n84, 134n3, 150n27

Shao Kang, 43, 53n31, 56n65, 69, 90n39

"Shao Siming" (Lesser Minister of Life Spans; *Nine Songs*), 1, 14–15, 31

Shao Tuo, 104

"She jiang" (Crossing the Yangtze; *Nine Cantos*), 107–10, 215, 218

Shen Baoxu, 162, 167n9

Shen Nong, 92n44, 137n36

Shen Yue, 90n39

Shensheng of Jin, 106, 135n6

Shentu Di, 134, 141n77

*Shiji* (Records of the grand historian; Sima Qian), xliiin5, 3, 8, 12, 17; on "Ask the Sky," 93n50, 95nn58–59, 96n63, 97n65, 99n74, 101nn80–81; biography of Qu Yuan in, xvii–xxii, xxv, xxvii, 28, 34, 103, 114, 117, 124; and dating, 213, 215; on "Fisherman," 152; on "Leaving My Sorrow," xxi; on Liu An, 210; on *Nine Cantos*, 136n23; on *Nine Variations*, 156

*Shijing* (*Book of Songs*), xi; and "Ask the Sky," 87n31, 98n70; and dating, 213–14, 217; and "Leaving My Sorrow," 56n61; and *Nine Variations*, 162, 163, 167n8

Shou Meng, 74, 100n79

Shu Dan. *See* Zhou, Duke of

Shu Qi, 101n82, 140n67

Shun (sage-king), xxiii, xxxviii; in "Ask the Sky," 69, 79n12, 91n42, 92n45; in "I Lament It Was Not My Destiny," 204, 208n11; in "Leaving My Sorrow," 31, 33, 36, 40, 42, 43, 50n18, 51n27, 56n65, 57n66; in *Nine Cantos*, 108, 113, 120, 135n3, 136n11, 137n34, 137n36, 138n48; in *Nine Songs*, 8, 9; in *Nine Variations*, 164, 165; in "Wandering Far Away," 151n39

*Shuowen jiezi*, 54n46, 56n62, 77n5

*Major Plays of Chikamatsu,* tr. Donald Keene 1961

*Four Major Plays of Chikamatsu,* tr. Donald Keene. Paperback ed. only. 1961; rev. ed. 1997

*Records of the Grand Historian of China, translated from the Shih chi of Ssu-ma Ch'ien,* tr. Burton Watson, 2 vols. 1961

*Instructions for Practical Living and Other Neo-Confucian Writings by Wang Yang-ming,* tr. Wing-tsit Chan 1963

*Hsün Tzu: Basic Writings,* tr. Burton Watson, paperback ed. only. 1963; rev. ed. 1996

*Chuang Tzu: Basic Writings,* tr. Burton Watson, paperback ed. only. 1964; rev. ed. 1996

*The Mahābhārata,* tr. Chakravarthi V. Narasimhan. Also in paperback ed. 1965; rev. ed. 1997

*The Manyōshū,* Nippon Gakujutsu Shinkōkai edition 1965

*Su Tung-p'o: Selections from a Sung Dynasty Poet,* tr. Burton Watson. Also in paperback ed. 1965

*Bhartrihari: Poems,* tr. Barbara Stoler Miller. Also in paperback ed. 1967

*Basic Writings of Mo Tzu, Hsün Tzu, and Han Fei Tzu,* tr. Burton Watson. Also in separate paperback eds. 1967

*The Awakening of Faith, Attributed to Aśvaghosha,* tr. Yoshito S. Hakeda. Also in paperback ed. 1967

*Reflections on Things at Hand: The Neo-Confucian Anthology,* comp. Chu Hsi and Lü Tsu-ch'ien, tr. Wing-tsit Chan 1967

*The Platform Sutra of the Sixth Patriarch,* tr. Philip B. Yampolsky. Also in paperback ed. 1967

*Essays in Idleness: The Tsurezuregusa of Kenkō,* tr. Donald Keene. Also in paperback ed. 1967

*The Pillow Book of Sei Shōnagon,* tr. Ivan Morris, 2 vols. 1967

*Two Plays of Ancient India: The Little Clay Cart and the Minister's Seal,* tr. J. A. B. van Buitenen 1968

*The Complete Works of Chuang Tzu,* tr. Burton Watson 1968

*The Romance of the Western Chamber (Hsi Hsiang chi),* tr. S. I. Hsiung. Also in paperback ed. 1968

*The Manyōshū,* Nippon Gakujutsu Shinkōkai edition. Paperback ed. only. 1969

*Records of the Historian: Chapters from the Shih chi of Ssu-ma Ch'ien,* tr. Burton Watson. Paperback ed. only. 1969

*Cold Mountain: 100 Poems by the T'ang Poet Han-shan,* tr. Burton Watson. Also in paperback ed. 1970

*Twenty Plays of the Nō Theatre*, ed. Donald Keene. Also in paperback ed. 1970

*Chūshingura: The Treasury of Loyal Retainers*, tr. Donald Keene. Also in paperback ed. 1971; rev. ed. 1997

*The Zen Master Hakuin: Selected Writings*, tr. Philip B. Yampolsky 1971

*Chinese Rhyme-Prose: Poems in the Fu Form from the Han and Six Dynasties Periods*, tr. Burton Watson. Also in paperback ed. 1971

*Kūkai: Major Works*, tr. Yoshito S. Hakeda. Also in paperback ed. 1972

*The Old Man Who Does as He Pleases: Selections from the Poetry and Prose of Lu Yu*, tr. Burton Watson 1973

*The Lion's Roar of Queen Śrīmālā*, tr. Alex and Hideko Wayman 1974

*Courtier and Commoner in Ancient China: Selections from the History of the Former Han by Pan Ku*, tr. Burton Watson. Also in paperback ed. 1974

*Japanese Literature in Chinese*, vol. 1: *Poetry and Prose in Chinese by Japanese Writers of the Early Period*, tr. Burton Watson 1975

*Japanese Literature in Chinese*, vol. 2: *Poetry and Prose in Chinese by Japanese Writers of the Later Period*, tr. Burton Watson 1976

*Love Song of the Dark Lord: Jayadeva's Gītagovinda*, tr. Barbara Stoler Miller. Also in paperback ed. Cloth ed. includes critical text of the Sanskrit. 1977; rev. ed. 1997

*Ryōkan: Zen Monk-Poet of Japan*, tr. Burton Watson 1977

*Calming the Mind and Discerning the Real: From the Lam rim chen mo of Tsoṇ-kha-pa*, tr. Alex Wayman 1978

*The Hermit and the Love-Thief: Sanskrit Poems of Bhartrihari and Bilhaṇa*, tr. Barbara Stoler Miller 1978

*The Lute: Kao Ming's P'i-p'a chi*, tr. Jean Mulligan. Also in paperback ed. 1980

*A Chronicle of Gods and Sovereigns: Jinnō Shōtōki of Kitabatake Chikafusa*, tr. H. Paul Varley 1980

*Among the Flowers: The Hua-chien chi*, tr. Lois Fusek 1982

*Grass Hill: Poems and Prose by the Japanese Monk Gensei*, tr. Burton Watson 1983

*Doctors, Diviners, and Magicians of Ancient China: Biographies of Fang-shih*, tr. Kenneth J. DeWoskin. Also in paperback ed. 1983

*Theater of Memory: The Plays of Kālidāsa*, ed. Barbara Stoler Miller. Also in paperback ed. 1984

*The Columbia Book of Chinese Poetry: From Early Times to the Thirteenth Century*, ed. and tr. Burton Watson. Also in paperback ed. 1984

*Poems of Love and War: From the Eight Anthologies and the Ten Long Poems of Classical Tamil*, tr. A. K. Ramanujan. Also in paperback ed. 1985

*The Bhagavad Gita: Krishna's Counsel in Time of War*, tr. Barbara Stoler Miller 1986

*The Columbia Book of Later Chinese Poetry*, ed. and tr. Jonathan Chaves. Also in paperback ed. 1986

*The Tso Chuan: Selections from China's Oldest Narrative History*, tr. Burton Watson 1989

*Waiting for the Wind: Thirty-six Poets of Japan's Late Medieval Age*, tr. Steven Carter 1989

*Selected Writings of Nichiren*, ed. Philip B. Yampolsky 1990

*Saigyō, Poems of a Mountain Home*, tr. Burton Watson 1990

*The Book of Lieh Tzu: A Classic of the Tao*, tr. A. C. Graham. Morningside ed. 1990

*The Tale of an Anklet: An Epic of South India—The Cilappatikāram of Iaṇḷkō Aikaḷ*, tr. R. Parthasarathy 1993

*Waiting for the Dawn: A Plan for the Prince*, tr. with introduction by Wm. Theodore de Bary 1993

*Yoshitsune and the Thousand Cherry Trees: A Masterpiece of the Eighteenth-Century Japanese Puppet Theater*, tr., annotated, and with introduction by Stanleigh H. Jones Jr. 1993

*The Lotus Sutra*, tr. Burton Watson. Also in paperback ed. 1993

*The Classic of Changes: A New Translation of the I Ching as Interpreted by Wang Bi*, tr Richard John Lynn 1994

*Beyond Spring: Tz'u Poems of the Sung Dynasty*, tr. Julie Landau 1994

*The Columbia Anthology of Traditional Chinese Literature*, ed. Victor H. Mair 1994

*Scenes for Mandarins: The Elite Theater of the Ming*, tr. Cyril Birch 1995

*Letters of Nichiren*, ed. Philip B. Yampolsky; tr. Burton Watson et al. 1996

*Unforgotten Dreams: Poems by the Zen Monk Shōtetsu*, tr. Steven D. Carter 1997

*The Vimalakirti Sutra*, tr. Burton Watson 1997

*Japanese and Chinese Poems to Sing: The* Wakan rōei shū, tr. J. Thomas Rimer and Jonathan Chaves 1997

*Breeze Through Bamboo: Kanshi of Ema Saikō*, tr. Hiroaki Sato 1998

*A Tower for the Summer Heat*, by Li Yu, tr. Patrick Hanan 1998

*Traditional Japanese Theater: An Anthology of Plays*, by Karen Brazell 1998

*The Original Analects: Sayings of Confucius and His Successors (0479–0249)*, by E. Bruce Brooks and A. Taeko Brooks 1998

*The Classic of the Way and Virtue: A New Translation of the Tao-te ching of Laozi as Interpreted by Wang Bi*, tr. Richard John Lynn 1999

*The Four Hundred Songs of War and Wisdom: An Anthology of Poems from Classical Tamil, The Puṛanāṇūru*, ed. and tr. George L. Hart and Hank Heifetz 1999

*Original Tao:* Inward Training (Nei-yeh) *and the Foundations of Taoist Mysticism*, by Harold D. Roth 1999

*Po Chü-i: Selected Poems*, tr. Burton Watson 2000

*Lao Tzu's* Tao Te Ching: *A Translation of the Startling New Documents Found at Guodian*, by Robert G. Henricks 2000

*The Shorter Columbia Anthology of Traditional Chinese Literature*, ed. Victor H. Mair 2000

*Mistress and Maid (Jiaohongji)*, by Meng Chengshun, tr. Cyril Birch 2001

*Chikamatsu: Five Late Plays*, tr. and ed. C. Andrew Gerstle 2001

*The Essential Lotus: Selections from the* Lotus Sutra, tr. Burton Watson 2002

*Early Modern Japanese Literature: An Anthology, 1600–1900*, ed. Haruo Shirane 2002; abridged 2008

*The Columbia Anthology of Traditional Korean Poetry*, ed. Peter H. Lee 2002

*The Sound of the Kiss, or The Story That Must Never Be Told: Pingali Suranna's Kalapurnodayamu*, tr. Vecheru Narayana Rao and David Shulman 2003

*The Selected Poems of Du Fu*, tr. Burton Watson 2003

*Far Beyond the Field: Haiku by Japanese Women*, tr. Makoto Ueda 2003

*Just Living: Poems and Prose by the Japanese Monk Tonna*, ed. and tr. Steven D. Carter 2003

*Han Feizi: Basic Writings*, tr. Burton Watson 2003

*Mozi: Basic Writings*, tr. Burton Watson 2003

*Xunzi: Basic Writings*, tr. Burton Watson 2003

*Zhuangzi: Basic Writings*, tr. Burton Watson 2003

*The Awakening of Faith, Attributed to Aśvaghosha*, tr. Yoshito S. Hakeda, introduction by Ryuichi Abe 2005

*The Tales of the Heike*, tr. Burton Watson, ed. Haruo Shirane 2006

*Tales of Moonlight and Rain*, by Ueda Akinari, tr. with introduction by Anthony H. Chambers 2007

*Traditional Japanese Literature: An Anthology, Beginnings to 1600*, ed. Haruo Shirane 2007

*The Philosophy of Qi*, by Kaibara Ekken, tr. Mary Evelyn Tucker 2007

*The Analects of Confucius*, tr. Burton Watson 2007

*The Art of War: Sun Zi's Military Methods*, tr. Victor Mair 2007

*One Hundred Poets, One Poem Each: A Translation of the* Ogura Hyakunin Isshu, tr Peter McMillan 2008

*Zeami: Performance Notes*, tr. Tom Hare 2008

*Zongmi on Chan*, tr. Jeffrey Lyle Broughton 2009

*Scripture of the Lotus Blossom of the Fine Dharma*, rev. ed., tr. Leon Hurvitz, preface and introduction by Stephen R. Teiser 2009

*Mencius*, tr. Irene Bloom, ed. with an introduction by Philip J. Ivanhoe 2009

*Clouds Thick, Whereabouts Unknown: Poems by Zen Monks of China*, Charles Egan 2010

*The Mozi: A Complete Translation*, tr. Ian Johnston 2010

*The Huainanzi: A Guide to the Theory and Practice of Government in Early Han China*, by Liu An, tr. and ed. John S. Major, Sarah A. Queen, Andrew Seth Meyer, and Harold D. Roth, with Michael Puett and Judson Murray 2010

*The Demon at Agi Bridge and Other Japanese Tales*, tr. Burton Watson, ed. with introduction by Haruo Shirane 2011

*Haiku Before Haiku: From the Renga Masters to Bashō*, tr. with introduction by Steven D. Carter 2011

*The Columbia Anthology of Chinese Folk and Popular Literature*, ed. Victor H. Mair and Mark Bender 2011

*Tamil Love Poetry: The Five Hundred Short Poems of the Aiṅkuṟunūṟu*, tr. and ed. Martha Ann Selby 2011

*The Teachings of Master Wuzhu: Zen and Religion of No-Religion*, by Wendi L. Adamek 2011

*The Essential Huainanzi*, by Liu An, tr. and ed. John S. Major, Sarah A. Queen, Andrew Seth Meyer, and Harold D. Roth 2012

*The Dao of the Military: Liu An's Art of War*, tr. Andrew Seth Meyer 2012

*Unearthing the Changes: Recently Discovered Manuscripts of the* Yi Jing (I Ching) *and Related Texts*, Edward L. Shaughnessy 2013

*Record of Miraculous Events in Japan: The* Nihon ryōiki, tr. Burton Watson 2013

*The Complete Works of Zhuangzi,* tr. Burton Watson 2013

*Lust, Commerce, and Corruption:* An Account of What I Have Seen and Heard, *by an Edo Samurai,* tr. and ed. Mark Teeuwen and Kate Wildman Nakai with Miyazaki Fumiko, Anne Walthall, and John Breen 2014; abridged 2017

*Exemplary Women of Early China:* The Lienü zhuan *of Liu Xiang,* tr. Anne Behnke Kinney 2014

*The Columbia Anthology of Yuan Drama,* ed. C. T. Hsia, Wai-yee Li, and George Kao 2014

*The Resurrected Skeleton: From Zhuangzi to Lu Xun,* by Wilt L. Idema 2014

*The* Sarashina Diary: *A Woman's Life in Eleventh-Century Japan,* by Sugawara no Takasue no Musume, tr. with introduction by Sonja Arntzen and Itō Moriyuki 2014

*The* Kojiki: *An Account of Ancient Matters,* by Ō no Yasumaro, tr. Gustav Heldt 2014

The Orphan of Zhao *and Other Yuan Plays: The Earliest Known Versions*, tr. and introduced by Stephen H. West and Wilt L. Idema 2014

*Luxuriant Gems of the* Spring and Autumn, attributed to Dong Zhongshu, ed. and tr. Sarah A. Queen and John S. Major 2016

*A Book to Burn and a Book to Keep (Hidden): Selected Writings,* by Li Zhi, ed. and tr. Rivi Handler-Spitz, Pauline Lee, and Haun Saussy 2016

*The* Shenzi Fragments: *A Philosophical Analysis and Translation*, Eirik Lang Harris 2016

*A Record of Daily Knowledge* and *Poems and Essays*: Selections, by Gu Yanwu, tr. and ed. Ian Johnston 2017

*The Book of Lord Shang: Apologetics of State Power in Early China,* by Shang Yang, ed. and tr. Yuri Pines